THE FIRST YEAR OF LIFE

A Psychoanalytic Study of Normal and Deviant Development of Object Relations

THE FIRST YEAR
OF LIFE

*A Psychoanalytic Study of Normal
and Deviant Development of
Object Relations*

RENÉ A. SPITZ

In Collaboration with
W. GODFREY COBLINER

INTERNATIONAL UNIVERSITIES PRESS, INC.

NEW YORK

Manufactured in the United States of America

TO MY CHILDREN

Preface

This detailed and painstaking description of the emotional interchange between mothers and their infants aims at a wider circle of readers than is usual with publications by psychoanalysts. The author's language, backed by striking illustrations, is direct and simple enough to be understood by mothers and workers in the field of infant care, even in the absence of previous psychological instruction. His mode of observation, documentary camera work and testing are accurate enough to appeal to academic workers. And his theoretical premises and conclusions are so strictly analytic that they cannot fail to attract the attention of all those analysts and child analysts who welcome a factual approach to what is still the darkest age of the human individual.

In the course of his book, Dr. Spitz touches on a number of subjects which are controversial in the psychoanalytic theory of our days, and he does not hesitate to take a determined stand on each issue. To trace the happenings in the first year of life, he advocates the use of direct observation and of the methods of experimental psychology, in contrast to those analytic authors who prefer to rely only on the reconstruction of developmental processes from the analysis of later stages. In fact, his earlier expositions on hospitalism and anaclitic depression have gone far toward establishing the value of observational methods, even in the eyes of many, otherwise reluctant, psychoanalysts.

When discussing the infantile personality in the preverbal period, Dr. Spitz opposes all those analytic authors who ascribe to the infant soon after birth a complex mental life in which fantasy content, conflicts between opposing drives, guilt feelings, tendencies of reparation, etc., play a part. Instead, he upholds the view, shared by many, of an initial undifferentiated state and of the slow and continuous unfolding of the functions, distinct drives, gradations of structure, i.e., of psychological processes emerging gradually from the physiological prototypes which underlie them.

He pursues the same theory of slow-motion development from primitive to more complex forms where the main theme of his book, the development of the first object relationship, is concerned. Here, again, he rejects the concept of an object relationship to the mother from birth, which is maintained by other analytic schools of thought.

Finally, when reviewing the disturbances in the early mother-child relationship, and their harmful consequences, Dr. Spitz goes further than most in ascribing specific psychotoxic disorders of the infant to specific emotional disorders of the mother—an intriguing suggestion which might prove less controversial if, in the case of the complex personalities of the mothers, assessment of their behavior were based not on observational methods but on analysis.

There have been frequent complaints from the reading public that books on child development, written by analysts, tend to be sketchy, unsystematic, and more explicit on pathology than on the normal processes of growth. Dr. Spitz's valuable study will go far toward refuting such charges and will fill a need of long standing.

Anna Freud, LL.D.

Contents

Foreword

In 1935, when I began my systematic investigations in the psychoanalytic psychology of infancy with the help of direct observations, I was a lonely figure. Ten years later others took interest in the subject—and since then, the number of those who are studying psychic processes in this and allied fields with similar and better methods has grown exponentially year by year. Accordingly, an avalanche of publications has appeared, both psychoanalytic and experimental psychological, to which even a textbook would be hard put to do justice. The selection of publications which are treated at somewhat greater length in this book is therefore an arbitrary one. They were chosen because I found them to be the most convenient to illustrate my thesis. The interdisciplinary nature of my approach introduced a further difficulty. When the first, brief version of this book was published in French in 1954, whole branches of science which now influence my thinking did not exist, or were in their beginnings. Communication theory is a good example. I therefore tender my apologies to all authors whom I may have slighted through omission. Such omission is not due either to malice or to ignorance, but rather to the limitations of my purpose. I do not have the gifts to write a textbook, nor do I think that the time to do so has already arrived.

Just as I found myself forced to expand the scope of this book, as a result of the extraordinary extension of knowledge in the intervening years, I similarly could no longer limit myself to the first year of life only. I shall overstep the boundaries of the period in many places, and take the reader here and there far into the second year of life.

Incomplete and inadequate though it is, this book proposes to introduce the reader to a variety of methods exploring the nonverbal stage of life from a psychoanalytic viewpoint. In this territory, which has been opened up only so recently, object relations provide us with the best orientation.

But when all is said and done, this study remains based on the propositions and concepts which Sigmund Freud set forth in the *Three Contributions to the Theory of Sex*. The second of these contributions contains in great lines the major part of what I have been able to observe in the course of many years of research on hundreds of infants. Freud's genius conceived a series of seminal ideas which several generations of his disciples now strive to confirm and to elaborate. It gives me a feeling of profound satisfaction that I had the opportunity to participate in this endeavor by applying the method of direct observation in the work of my teacher, Sigmund Freud.

R. A. S.

Denver, October, 1963

Acknowledgments

The first brief version of this book was published in French in 1954. It consisted mainly of a succinct report, a bird's-eye view of the results of my research, observations, and findings on many hundreds of infants. Today this research has been going on for nearly thirty years. An enterprise of such magnitude cannot be carried out or delineated by one single individual. I could not have conducted the observations, the experiments, the organization of data, collected through direct observation and motion pictures, and then statistically processed them, or coordinated this multidisciplinary approach, without the help of my numerous, able, and devoted associates. I wish to express my thanks to them here, though I realize the impossibility of assigning to each the share of his contribution.

But first I want to acknowledge my debt to the University of Colorado, its Department of Psychiatry, and especially to Dr. Herbert S. Gaskill, Chairman of this Department. His unwavering friendship and understanding, his liberality in securing help and the means for my work, the laboratory space for the mass of my films and records on which this book is based, provided me with the opportunity to continue and conclude the present work.

Over the last ten years my closest associate in this particular task has been W. Godfrey Cobliner, Ph.D. To him goes a full measure of my recognition and my gratitude. He contributed a concluding chapter, a scholarly monograph on Piaget and the Geneva school, on its relations to the psychoanalytic system of propositions on the one hand, to my own findings and conclusions on the other. But Dr. Cobliner's contribution to this book goes deeper and is more extensive. From the modest beginnings of the first, the French edition, to which he contributed a number of the bibliographical references, and sharpened some of the formulations in discussing them with me, he expanded both roles in the intervening ten years, acting as a patient, intelligent, yet severe critic of the successive editions of the original and of its translation into a variety of other languages. I wish to acknowledge gratefully his very real share in writing this book.

It is fitting at this place that the late Katherine M. Wolf, Ph.D., who assisted me during the first years of my work, should be remembered. Her untimely death is a loss to science, particularly psychology and psychoanalysis. Her assistance in conducting the observations and experiments, her intuitiveness and brilliance, were an ever-present stimulation to me during the eight years of our collaboration. My publications during these years carry the mark of her contributions.

My thanks go to the heads of the institutions who generously made my observations and my work there possible; to the parents who permitted me to follow and to film their children; to my associates and helpers who assisted me in observations and experiments; in the processing of data, the plotting and design of graphs, curves and profiles; in editing, correcting, proof reading, and typing manuscripts; in the taking, processing, editing, cutting, titling and cataloguing of my motion pictures. Their names, in chronological sequence are:

Annemarie von Leutzendorff
Josef Bohmer
Margarete Dengler, Ph.D.
Gilbert Haak
Rose Laub Coser, Ph.D.

Anneliese Riess, Ph.D.
Lilly Bernstein, Ph.D.
Angela Yaron
Alexandra Hendee
Eva Gruening
Paul R. Polak, M.D.
Robert N. Emde, M.D.
Sally Bondy
Elisabeth Root
Laura Powell

To Miss Henrietta Additon, whose understanding and deep humanity permitted me and my associates to conduct research with her wards freely through many years, I am deeply indebted.

But it is with a quite special feeling of gratitude that I turn to the last on my list of acknowledgments, to Mrs. Lottie Maury Newman. It is ultimately she who made it possible to terminate this task, through her friendship and encouragement during personally difficult periods, and the wisdom of her advice.

Part I

Definitions and Methodology

CHAPTER I

Theoretical Introduction

From the time ego psychology became a subject of psycho-analytic investigation, interest began to center on the libidinal object. Freud had introduced the concept of object choice much earlier, in 1905, in his *Three Essays on the Theory of Sexuality*. Indeed, this is probably the only time he discusses reciprocal relations between mother and child, between object and subject, in detail. Only rarely does he touch upon this topic again in the course of his subsequent work (see, however, Freud, 1931). Whenever he speaks of the libidinal object, it is primarily from the subject's point of view. He speaks of object cathexis, of object choice, of the discovery of the object, and exceptionally only of object relations.

In the following pages we shall study these reciprocal relations and try to apprehend what goes on between mother and child. Basing ourselves upon direct observations and experiments on infants, we shall present our findings and ideas on object relations—their beginnings, development, stages, and certain anomalies. We shall also attempt to throw some light on how these relations ensure survival and how they serve the unfolding of the psychic and somatic sectors of personality.

The major part of the first year of life is devoted to the effort to survive and to the forming and elaboration of the adaptive devices serving this aim. Again and again, Freud reminds us that the infant, during this period of his life, is

3

helpless and incapable of surviving by his own means. What the infant lacks, the mother compensates for and supplies. The mother provides for all his needs. The outcome is a complementary relation, a dyad. To the extent to which the infant's own potentialities are developed in the course of the first year of life, he will become independent of his surround. This process obviously takes place both in the somatic and in the psychological sectors of the infant's personality. We shall deal primarily with the latter in this study. We shall show how growth and development in the psychological sector are essentially dependent on the establishment and the progressive unfolding of ever more meaningful object relations, that is, social relations.

For the purpose of organizing my research, and that of interpreting my findings, I have used a number of psychoanalytic propositions. However, before discussing these propositions in detail, I wish to state my position vis-à-vis certain controversial assumptions on the neonate's psychological endowments current in some psychological and psychoanalytic circles. My own thinking is based on Freud's concept of the neonate as a psychologically undifferentiated organism, born with a congenital equipment and certain Anlagen. This organism still lacks consciousness, perception, sensation,[1] and all other psychological functions, be they conscious or unconscious. This opinion is shared by most scientists who have

---

[1] I am using the term perception (and also sensation) as defined in my article "Diacritic and Coenesthetic Organizations" (1945b). This is also the sense in which the terms are understood by and large in psychology, where perception is defined as an *awareness;* and sensation as an *element of consciousness* (see Warren, 1935; English and English, 1958). I follow Freud's opinion that at birth there is no consciousness; accordingly, there can be neither awareness nor conscious experience. I am not inclined to consider responses to stimuli per se "elements of consciousness." Obviously, since stimuli provoke responses from birth (and earlier), something is going on in the infant which produces responses to external stimuli. But this process is not of a psychological nature; therefore I think of these rather as processes of reception, at least until a rudimentary consciousness develops in the course of the weeks following birth.

studied the newborn with the help of observation and experiment. I have therefore refrained here from using any hypothesis positing the operation of intrapsychic processes in the infant at birth. Basically, I think of the neonate as a nondifferentiated totality in many respects. Various functions, structures, even the instinctual drives, will be differentiated progressively from this totality. This differentiation is initiated as the result of two distinct processes. With Hartmann, Kris, and Loewenstein (1946), we call one of these processes maturation, the other, development, and define them as follows:

Maturation: The unfolding of phylogenetically evolved and therefore inborn functions of the species, which emerge in the course of *embryonic development* or are carried forward after birth as Anlage and become manifest at later stages in life.

Development: The emergence of forms, of function, and of behavior which are the outcome of exchanges between the organism on the one hand, the inner and outer environment on the other. This is often referred to as "growth," a term we shall not use because it gives rise to confusion.

It also follows from this proposition concerning the neonate's state of nondifferentiation that at birth there exists no ego, at least not in the usual sense of the term. This was stated specifically by Freud in *The Ego and the Id* (Freud, 1923). Obviously, one can speak even less of the existence of an oedipus complex or that of a superego at birth. Similarly, symbolism and thinking in symbols are nonexistent, and symbolic (psychoanalytic) interpretations are inapplicable. Symbols are more or less contingent on the acquisition of language. Language, however, is nonexistent during the whole of the first year of life. Defense mechanisms also are absent, at least in the form in which the term is used in our literature. We can only detect traces of their prototypes in a more physiological than psychological form. Such physiological prototypes will serve, as it were, as a foundation on which the psyche will subsequently erect a structure of an entirely different nature (Freud, 1926a; Spitz, 1958, 1959, 1961).

PSYCHOANALYTIC PROPOSITIONS

The propositions which we shall enumerate below make no claim to completeness or even coherence. They have been chosen arbitrarily because of their usefulness in this book. Where the accepted definitions in psychoanalytic literature are ambiguous, I have quoted from Freud (and in some cases also from other psychoanalytic writers) to explicate the sense in which I am using the concepts. These quotations are taken from the original text, but left out parts of some sentences for brevity's sake. I also added the term "drives" in parenthesis where the *Standard Edition* insists on the misleading usage of the term "instinct."[2]

1. *The basic regulative principles of psychic functioning* postulated by Freud: (a) the Nirvana principle (constancy principle); (b) the pleasure principle (this is a modification of the former); (c) the reality principle.

---

[2] Throughout the *Standard Edition* the Editor uses the anglicized Latin term *instinct* wherever Freud used the German term *Trieb* in the original. The Editor states (*Standard Edition*, Vol. XIV, p. 111ff.) that the reasons for this choice will be discussed in the "General Introduction" to the forthcoming Volume I of the *Standard Edition*. Pending the opportunity to examine his argument, we shall continue to use the English word "instinctual drive" instead of the Latin "instinct" for the following reasons: (1) Freud, in his writings, primarily uses the term *Trieb;* he rarely uses the term *Instinkt.* (2) A widespread usage of the term "instinct" in biology, with a definition in terms different from the psychoanalytic one, is generally accepted in science. (3) An equally general usage of the term "instinct" with still another definition, basically different from, indeed practically the opposite of, that used in psychoanalysis, has been accepted in ethology. (4) Accordingly, as stressed by Waelder (1960), "the understanding of psychoanalysis in English-speaking countries has been seriously threatened by the lack of a word in the English language that corresponds to the German *Trieb;* the English word, instinct, that appears in most translations, carries implications which are alien to the idea of *Trieb.*"

2. *The descriptive division of the psyche* into conscious and unconscious (Freud, 1912).

3. *The topographical viewpoint:* This is the division of the psychic apparatus into the system *Ucs., Pcs., Cs.* (unconscious, preconscious, conscious) (Freud, 1915a).

4. *The dynamic viewpoint:* This holds that, in essence, mental processes derive from the interplay of forces, which are "originally in the nature of *instincts* [instinctual drives]: thus they have an organic origin. They are . . . represented mentally as images or ideas with an affective charge. . . . An empirical analysis leads to the formulation of two groups of instincts [instinctual drives]" (Freud, 1926c). In our presentation we shall refer to two drives, libido and aggression, with the meaning Freud gave them in his later publications (1920, 1923).

5. *The economic viewpoint:* "Endeavors to follow out the vicissitudes of amounts of excitation and to arrive at least at some *relative* estimate of their magnitude" (Freud, 1915a). "From the *economic* standpoint psycho-analysis supposes that the mental representatives of the instincts [instinctual drives] have a charge (*cathexis*) of definite quantities of energy" (Freud, 1926c). These cathexes are displaceable quanta of energy.

6. *The metapsychological approach:* In Freud's words: "When we have succeeded in describing a psychical process in its dynamic, topographical and economic aspects, we should speak of it as a *metapsychological* presentation" (1915a). Freud conceives of such a presentation as a three-dimensional view of a psychic phenomenon. He expresses this explicitly elsewhere (1925b) by speaking of the three viewpoints as the three coordinates of mental process.

7. *The structural viewpoint:* In this metapsychological triad, Freud later replaced the topographical viewpoint with the *structural* one, "on the basis of the analytic view of patho-

logical facts" (1925b). The structural viewpoint states that the mental apparatus is divided into *ego, id,* and *superego.*

8. *The genetic viewpoint:* Beginning with his earliest publications Freud postulated that psychic processes obey the laws of determinism. To the end he considered this one of the essential elements of psychoanalytic theory, mentioning it specifically as such in "A Short Account of Psycho-Analysis" (1924b). The genetic viewpoint holds that any psychological phenomenon, in addition to its contemporary and experiential aspects can be traced back through its ontogenesis to its psychological origin. In regard to the developmental vicissitudes this takes us back to birth. In regard to the maturational and congenital factors, it takes us back through ontogeny into embryology and phylogeny.

9. *Libido theory and erotogenic zones:* The application of the genetic viewpoint to sexual development led to the discovery of the key role of the erotogenic zones. "From the appropriate sensory excitation of these zones satisfaction arises" (Freud, 1905b). In the course of maturation the oral, the anal, and the genital zones are activated, marking the successive stages of libido development.

(a) At this point a definition of the instinctual drives appears indicated. This, however, is not an easy task. As late as 1924 Freud remarked: "the libido theory of psycho-analysis is by no means complete . . . its relation to a general theory of the instincts is not yet clear, for psycho-analysis is a young science, quite unfinished and in a stage of rapid development" (1924b). And he continues by defining libido as follows: "Libido means in psycho-analysis in the first instance the force (thought of as quantitatively variable and measurable) of the sexual instincts directed toward an object— 'sexual' in the extended sense required by analytic theory."

(b) Freud conceived of aggression as the other fundamental drive operating in the psyche. Less endowed with quality, it mainly indicates pressure as well as direction in relation to the object. This aggression serves to approach, to seize, to hold, to overpower, or to destroy the object—and by extension things. It is expressed or carried out "through the instrumentality of a special organ. This special organ would seem to be the muscular apparatus" (Freud, 1923).

(c) Erikson's proposition (1950a) of zonal modes expands this theory. The mode of each zone, its taking-in or its expelling function, enters into the determinants of the distinctive quality of the partial drive and of the given libidinal stage. This quality is then generalized to other zones, organs, and behavior, and acquires an adaptive function. I have stressed the specific sensory quality of voluntary and involuntary sphincter musculature and its role in the economy and dynamics of instinctual drives as a component part of major importance in every erotogenic zone found only in few other locations of the human body (Spitz, 1953a).

10. *The complemental series:* This is a hypothesis which Freud first adumbrated in the *Three Essays on the Theory of Sexuality* (1905b) and which he then applied to the definition of the etiology of neurosis (1916-1917). It posits that an *experiential* (psychological) factor interacts with a *congenital* one to produce the disturbance. In my opinion, this hypothesis applies to all phenomena of human (and animal) psychology; for all psychological phenomena surely are the outcome of the mutual influence and the interaction of innate factors with experiential events.

11. *The adaptive point of view:* This idea was studied and elaborated relatively recently by Hartmann (1939), Erikson (1950a), and Spitz (1957). Without using the term, Freud formulated the concept in "Instincts and Their Vicissitudes" (1915b). The best definition is that of Rapaport and Gill (1959): "The adaptive point of view demands that the psychoanalytic explanation of any psychological phenomenon include propositions concerning its relationship to the environ-

ment."[3] This is not the place for a detailed discussion of the assumptions which underlie the adaptive viewpoint. I shall later discuss those assumptions which apply to alloplastic and autoplastic processes (Freud, 1924a), to Erikson's (1950a) propositions, and to my own (Spitz, 1957) on the role and the functions of affects in the dyadic relationship.

CONGENITAL FACTORS

Every one of us is born an individual in his own right. Each one of us is different from every other individual, first because of what exists observably in him already at birth; and second by virtue of the potentialities laid down as Anlage in the germ cell. That with which the newborn is endowed and which makes him unique, I will call *congenital equipment*. This equipment is composed of three parts:

1. Inherited equipment, determined by genes, chromosomes, DNA, RNA, etc.
2. Intra-uterine influences operating during gestation.
3. Influences becoming operative in the course of delivery.

We shall give a simple example for each of these three components. Inherited equipment is comprised of such obvious elements as that we are born with two legs, with two eyes, but with only one mouth. At the same time less evident constituents, like the laws and the sequences of maturation, are also part of the inherited equipment. These laws and sequences involve not only the progressive unfolding of organs and functions but also the nonreversible sequence of phases through which organs and functions must progress. That applies to physiology as well as to psychology, for it is

[3] I wish to acknowledge my indebtedness to Rapaport and Gill (1959) for certain formulations contained in this chapter, particularly their emphasis on the different viewpoints in psychoanalysis. Their definite formulations (see also Gill, 1963) were published after completion of this manuscript and therefore could not be considered in detail.

no less true that the deciduous teeth precede permanent teeth than that the oral stage precedes the anal, and this in turn the phallic phase.

The intra-uterine influences can be exemplified by the relatively recent discovery that a rubella infection in a pregnant woman may have a damaging effect on the optic organs of the fetus (Swan, 1949).

Finally, regarding possible influences *during* delivery: We are, of course, familiar with gross physical injuries which may be inflicted on the infant during delivery. Other, less obvious injuries have come to our attention through a number of investigations, for instance, those of Windle (1950) who demonstrated the destructive influence of cerebral anoxia during the birth process, or those of Brazelton (1962) who studied the effect of maternal premedication on the infant's behavior.

Environmental Factors, Their Scope and Complexity

The subject of this investigation is the genesis of the earliest object relations, that is, the relations between mother and child. It might also be considered an investigation of social relations, were it not that the relation to be examined is fundamentally different from all those with which social psychology is usually concerned. One might well wonder why sociologists have ignored the fact that, in the mother-child relation, they had the opportunity to observe the inception and the evolution of social relations, so to say, *in statu nascendi*.

Among the peculiarities of this relation is that, before our very eyes, a state of social unrelatedness, a purely biological bond, is transformed, step by step, into what is eventually to become the first social relation of the individual. What we witness is a transition from the physiological to the psychological and social. In the biological state (*in utero*) the fetus's relations are purely *parasitical*. But in the course of the first year of life, the infant will pass through a stage of psychological *symbiosis* with the mother, from which he will graduate to the next stage, in which social, i.e., hierarchical, interrelations are developed.

An equally peculiar and perhaps unique aspect of the mother-child relation is that the psychic structure of the mother is fundamentally different from that of her child. The relation between such conspicuously unequal partners cannot be anything but asymmetric; accordingly, the contribution of each of them to the mutual relationship will be dissimilar. Aside from the somewhat comparable relation of a human being with a domesticated animal (a pet, for instance), such a high degree of disparity in two as closely associated and interdependent individuals is not found anywhere else in our social organization. I believe that the first sociologist who called attention to the possibilities of sociological investigation of the mother-child group (which he called a "dyad") is Georg Simmel (1908). He stresses that in this relation one could find the germ of all subsequent development of social relations of the higher order. Independently from Simmel and thirteen years earlier, Freud (1895) had already suggested this line of research.

In our investigation of object relations and their genesis I have made a sharp distinction between the clinical approach to the study of infants and that applied to adults. The reasons for the differences are twofold, structural on the one hand, environmental on the other. It is readily obvious that the child's rudimentary personality structure is very different indeed from the mature one of his mother. But we usually do not realize as readily that his environment is also quite different from that of the adult.

To begin with, the personality structure: the adult's personality is a clearly defined, hierarchically structured organization; this personality is manifested through specific individual attitudes, specific initiatives, which enter into a series of circular interactions with the surround. The opposite is true of the newborn. At birth, even though individual differences are clearly demonstrable, the infant lacks an organized personality comparable to that of the adult; no personal initiative, no interchange with the surround, except a physiological one, is present. That is to say, we have here an organism of a quite different nature, the infantile organism, which we will discuss further on.

The second difference between infant and adult, the difference in environment, is perhaps even more impressive, once we consider it objectively. The adult's surround is constituted of numerous and extremely diverse factors, of a variety of individuals, a variety of groups, a variety of inanimate things. These and many other factors in their multiplicity as well as their variable dynamic constellation, their variable dignity, duration, weight, significance, etc., form shifting fields of forces which impinge on and influence the organized personality of the adult while interacting with it.

For the newborn, the surround consists, so to say, of one single individual, of the mother or her substitute. Even this single individual is not perceived by the newborn as an entity distinct from himself. It is simply part of the totality of his needs and of their gratification. Obviously, this situation changes in the course of the first year of life. Nevertheless, during this whole period the normally raised infant and his surround form what we might call a "closed system" which consists of two components only, namely, the mother and the child. Therefore, a psychiatric exploration of infancy has to investigate the pattern of the dynamics and of the fabric of this closed system.

Let me stress already here, and I will come back to this statement later on, that the infant's universe nonetheless is imbedded in the total reality setting. It is enmeshed with the interrelated roles and relationships of the various persons who comprise the child's family, or, as the case may be, the institution in which this child is being raised. However, this universe and its forces are transmitted to the child by that individual who gratifies his needs, that is, by the mother or her substitute. This is why in the following pages the personality of the mother, on the one hand, and the personality of the infant on the other, their interactions, their influence on each other, will be explored in great detail.

THE LIBIDINAL OBJECT

Since this book is devoted to the genesis of object relations, a few words need to be said about the psychoanalytic concept of the libidinal object. In his study "Instincts and Their Vicissitudes" Freud (1915b) defined the libidinal object as follows:

> The object of an instinct[4] is the thing in regard to which or through which the instinct is able to achieve its aim. It is what is most variable about an instinct and is not originally connected with it, but becomes assigned to it only in consequence of being peculiarly fitted to make satisfaction possible. The object is not necessarily something extraneous: it may equally well be a part of the subject's own body. It may be changed any number of times in the course of the vicissitudes which the instinct undergoes during its existence; and highly important parts are played by this displacement of instinct. It may happen that the same object serves for the satisfaction of several instincts simultaneously . . . [p. 122f.].

According to this definition, the libidinal object can change in the course of life—to be more exact, it must change inevitably and frequently. These changes are predicated on the progressive maturation and differentiation of the instinctual

---

[4] And we read "instinctual drive" instead of instinct.

drives, on the dynamic interplay between them, on the structure of the partial drives, and on other factors, some of which, like the defense mechanisms of the ego, have been investigated, and others which as yet have hardly been explored in detail.

The fact that the libidinal object changes frequently (and sometimes rapidly) distinguishes it in principle from the concept of object in academic psychology. The object of academic psychology, which we shall call a "thing," remains constant, identical with itself, and can be described by a system of spatio-temporal coordinates.

The libidinal object is a concept of a quite different order. It cannot be described in spatial and temporal coordinates, for it does not remain constant or identical with itself. We should except from this statement the periods during which there is no major redistribution of the drive quanta with which the libidinal object is cathected. Therefore, the libidinal object is chiefly described in the conceptual terms of its genesis, that is, of its history. The spatio-temporal coordinates which define the object of academic psychology play a minor role in the case of the libidinal object. Instead the libidinal object is characterized by and can be described in terms of the structure and vicissitudes of instinctual drives and partial drives directed to it.[5]

Object relations are relations between a subject and an object. In our particular case, the newborn is the subject. As already mentioned, in the beginning the newborn is in a state of nondifferentiation; hitherto no psyche or psychic functioning could be demonstrated in neonates. In accordance with our definition, there is neither an object nor are there object relations in the world of the newborn. Both will develop progressively step by step in the course of the first year, in the latter part of which the libidinal object proper will be

[5] For a detailed exposition, see Appendix.

established. I have distinguished three stages in this development and have called them:

1. The preobjectal or objectless stage.
2. The stage of the precursor of the object.
3. The stage of the libidinal object proper.

Before discussing these developmental stages, I shall first present in Chapter II our methods of data gathering and data processing as well as relevant information on our subjects. The reader who is not interested in the details of data gathering and data processing may without loss of continuity omit this chapter.

CHAPTER II

The Method

*Ita, Domine, Deus meus, metior
et quid metior, nescio.*
—St. Augustine

As already stated, the psychoanalytic method as such is not applicable during the preverbal stage. For the investigation of our subjects we resorted therefore to direct observation and utilized the devices of experimental psychology. We applied the criteria of reliability and validity by using tests and observational methods standardized on a statistically significant number of infants; and we eliminated the possibility of sex bias by using male and female observers on alternate weeks. Throughout our study we used a longitudinal method,[1] observing the infants in our population through relatively prolonged periods, lasting maximally two to two and a half years. During the study, personality tests were administered at monthly intervals, numerous experiments carried out, and individual infants observed, on an average, for four hours per week. These observations were protocoled and entered into the case history of the subject. This research

1 For the purpose of a study of the first year of life, we have defined "longitudinal" as comprising a period sufficient to detect significant developmental changes in the subject. In the first year of life such studies require at least two and preferably three months.

17

design permitted us to combine the advantages of the longitudinal with those of the cross-sectional method. We spared no effort to include a sufficiently large number of infants to permit relevant and preferably statistically significant findings.

For the main part of our study, we did not limit ourselves to the so-called clinical approach, in which a few selected subjects are studied intensively; in some special cases, though, where the complexity of the problem made this appear desirable, we investigated individual subjects both extensively and in depth. Case studies of this nature will be mentioned specifically in this presentation. Instead of a general use of the clinical method, we chose an experimental approach, working with a large number of subjects and carrying out a variety of measurements.

In view of the nature of the problems under investigation, we established as one of the fundamental rules of our method that in every case the *unselected* total population of a given environment had to be observed. This procedure insured that a maximum of factors and conditions were held constant in the given environment. It permitted us to study the effect of a single variable at a time. The constancy of the setting insured optimal uniformity of conditions for all our experimental subjects in the given population.

We obtained our populations in a series of settings which differed from one another in such basic respects as cultural background, race of the subjects, socioeconomic condition of the parents, as well as other factors which we reported in our various previous publications.

CONSTRUCTION AND VALIDATION OF THE TESTS

By far the most important factors which determine object relations are the personality of the mother and that of the child. However, object relations are influenced also by a number of other factors, such as cultural influences, economical and geographic conditions, as well as historical tradition. This diversity made it imperative that we study object relations in various populations and environments, so that we could ascertain whether certain phenomena are universal in man, and to what extent their pattern and content undergo modification by environmental variables such as culture, social class, location, etc. For this purpose we had to obtain the norms of the given phenomena which we derived from the findings of previous studies carried out in typical "normal" environments of Western culture. For the purpose of measurement we selected the Bühler-Hetzer baby test, a standardized, extensively employed personality and developmental test which allowed interindividual as well as intraindividual comparisons; the standing of a given infant could be presented in forms of quotients or indices; finally, the device allows the measurements of different personality sectors in addition to an over-all assessment. The validity and the reliability of this test had been worked out previously both in Europe and in the United States (Herring, 1937; Hubbard, 1931; Reichenberg, 1937; Simonsen, 1947; Wolf, 1935).

The Bühler-Hetzer test, also known as the Viennese test, was designed, standardized, and validated by Charlotte Bühler and Hildegard Hetzer (1932) and their associates, the late Katherine M. Wolf and Liselotte Frankl (see Hetzer and Wolf, 1928). The preliminary steps consisted in 24-hour continuous observation of 69 infants at seven successive age levels during the first year of life, with the purpose of establishing an inventory of the average expectable behavior during this period. Tests constructed on the basis of this inventory were tried out and standardized on a sample of 20 subjects per age level. The intervals between the age levels during the first eight months of life were monthly ones. During the remaining four months of the first year, the intervals were bimonthly. Thus the test for the first year of life was standardized on a total of 220 subjects.

This standardization of the test on 20 subjects per age level was not arbitrary, as shown in my later infant observations. Certain behavior patterns emerge in the infant at certain age levels and not before. The dividing line between the absence and the generalized presence of such behavior patterns is mostly quite sharp. Thus it is rare to find the smiling *response* before the third month of life; but equally rare are the infants in whom it cannot be elicited during the third, fourth, and fifth month. Up to two months of age only 3 of our 145 subjects produced the smiling response. Between two and six months 142 of them produced it and 3 did not. We found that by the time 20 of our subjects produced a given behavior pattern, we could reliably expect the overwhelming majority of all our subjects at that age level to show it also. When the number of subjects observed for this behavior was increased beyond 20, those who did not produce the behavior came to represent a rapidly decreasing percentage of the total of our experimental population.

The Psychological Department of the University of Vienna applied the standardized test extensively for ten years, from 1928 to 1938. It was used systematically on all children who were committed to the *Kinderübernahmestelle der Stadt Wien* [Center of Dependent Children of the City of Vienna]. The number of children housed in this institution during the first year of life averaged 400 to 500 per year. In other words, the test was applied to roughly 5,000 infants over this decade, providing the staff with the opportunity to correct shortcomings in the tests.

It remained to be seen what this test contributes to psychiatric and clinical research. I therefore administered it systematically in the same setting, namely, in the *Kinderübernahmestelle der Stadt Wien,* to over 100 children committed there. I found the test to be a useful psychometric adjunct to our clinical evaluation. Its particular value lies in the fact that it indicates in numerical terms the standing of an individual baby, both over-all and in particular subsectors of the personality relative to the average standing of children coming from the same background.

For the purpose of establishing the validity of these tests in the Western hemisphere, we selected two populations in New York State. The first of these were children of white-collar intellectual workers, mostly professional, raised in their families. They were observed in their family setting and are shown in Table II (column: Private Families). A total of 18 of these were studied, mostly throughout the first year of life and later. These children were brought up by their own parents, under what I would consider optimal conditions, mostly in modest but comfortable apartments. The measurements made on these children generally agreed with the norms of the Bühler-Hetzer tests, though it should be mentioned that they were all somewhat advanced in the D.Q. above the averages established in Vienna.

The second population used for our gathering of normative data was obtained from a foster home agency, where children placed by the agency were seen for check-ups at 4-weekly intervals. Here we tested and observed 23 children during their visits. The background of these children was a mixed one, mostly from lower socioeconomic levels, as can be expected in such an agency in a large city. These children achieved consistently lower scores at all age levels within the first year of life than the first population, the children raised in private families. They tended to approximate the level of the average scores established in the well-baby clinic in Vienna, where I had started my work and where the test was developed. The progressive inaccessibility of the subjects prevented us from carrying out our planned research on these children. These findings suggested to me that the norms of the Bühler-Hetzer Baby Tests could serve for my own research as a practical guide and orientation device for the psychometric personality assessment of children from both middle and lower economic circles in the United States and the Western hemisphere.

The tests permit the monthly quantification of six sectors of the personality. They are the following:

1. Development and maturation of perception.
2. Development and maturation of body functions.
3. Development and maturation of interpersonal relations.
4. Development and maturation of memory and imitation.
5. Development and maturation of manipulation of things.
6. Intellectual development.

The quantitative evaluation of the tests provides a series of developmental quotients. From these a developmental profile for the given period is constructed—in other words, we get a cross-section of the infant's performance at a given stage of development, relative to the norm or average development.

PLACE AND LIMITATIONS OF THE TESTS IN OUR RESEARCH DESIGN

As stated above, our test results should not be considered as a yardstick either for evaluating or for diagnosing the individual infants and their development. When it came to judging the over-all personality of our subjects we relied primarily on prolonged clinical observation, and on the case history of the individual child. The tests, however, provided the following additional information:

1. As regards the individual child, the monthly test score informed us whether and how much his development had progressed, whether it had been arrested, or whether it had regressed. In other words, the score indicated the trend of development, its rate and direction.

2. It also indicated asymmetries in the rate and direction of development of various sectors of the personality of one and the same child.

3. The test further permitted intergroup and intragroup comparisons of a plurality of children. Such comparisons pointed out uniformities appearing in the profile charts of whole groups or subgroups of children.

4. The test further provided supportive evidence for our clinical findings.

5. Finally, the profile charts provided a graphic illustration for our descriptions.

On the other hand, the test did not provide, and could not provide, such clinical information as the presence or absence of emotions, and of what nature these were. It did not inform us on drive dynamics, on moods, or whether a child was outgoing or withdrawn, anxious or aggressive, alert or lethargic —in one word, it gave us neither clinical nor even behavioral information and told us very little about the child's object relations. Though the tests were unquestionably useful, the picture derived from them was, as Anna Freud remarked in one of her lectures, a flat one; it cannot stand on its own merits, it has to be made meaningful and come to life through the clinical picture.

Screen Analysis and Case Material

We endeavored to secure an objective and permanent record of our visual observations and impressions which would enable us to repeat, to compare, and to analyze in detail our observation of one and the same behavioral phenomenon. For this purpose we took motion picture records of the individual infant's behavior, using a procedure introduced by me in 1933 which I call "screen analysis." This consists in taking motion pictures at the rate of 24 frames per second, permitting us by means of routine projection to repeat our observations any time later as often as necessary and also to slow down the sequence of visual observation to 8 frames per second. Thus one obtains a three-times slower rhythm of the movements as well as of the facial expressions; in other terms, a three-times magnification of behavior.

Each child was filmed once when first seen, that is, as close to birth as possible and, in some cases, already during the expulsion stage of delivery. We also filmed any behavior of the infant which deviated from the average behavior of other children at the same developmental level, as well as all experiments performed with infants.

The case history of each child includes, besides the films, the records of clinical data, the protocols taken during observation, and a written report of the content of interviews with the child's parents as well as with the nursing personnel. In a large number of cases the file of the individual children included the mother's Rorschach and Szondi tests.

Table I illustrates the experimental procedure.

STUDY POPULATIONS

1. The distribution of our populations is shown in Table II. The children enumerated in the columns Private Families and Foster Home have already been mentioned; these groups served us in the beginning for the validation of the Bühler-Hetzer Test in the Western hemisphere.

2. One of our most important problems was to investigate some widely held assumptions on the nature of the neonate's "personality" at birth and immediately afterward, such as Otto Rank's (1924) statements on the birth trauma, or Wat-

TABLE I

EXPERIMENTAL PROCEDURE
OF INFANT OBSERVATION

Duration of Observation Per Child	4 Hours Per Week	200 Hours Per Year	These Observational Protocols Form Case History
Tests	Hetzer-Wolf Baby Tests at Monthly Intervals Developmental Quotients and Profiles		
Interviewer (Sex of) Bias	Weekly Alternation of Male with Female Observer		
Exploration of Environment	Interview with Parents and Nursing Personnel	Rorschach and Szondi Tests of Large Number of Mothers	
Film Records at 24 Frames Per Second for Later Screenanalysis Each Child Filmed:	When First Seen	When Showing Deviant Behavior	During Experiments

son's (1928) contention that the neonate's emotive behavior consists of love, fear, and rage, etc. We shall discuss these points in subsequent chapters.

We studied in detail a total of 35 deliveries in a semi-governmental, university-affiliated, small delivery hospital in the Western hemisphere, patronized by mothers of modest economical status. We selected this hospital because deliveries there were made by natural means without anesthetics (except in those infrequent cases where surgical intervention became necessary) under the supervision of excellent obstetricians assisted by trained nurses. Of these 35 deliveries, 29 were filmed within the first 5 minutes after birth; in 2 cases we started filming during the delivery itself. In principle, these neonates and their mothers were released to their homes after 10 days. However, I had the opportunity to follow 29 of

Table II
TOTAL INFANT POPULATION OBSERVED

Length of Observation	Nursery	Private Families	Foster Home	Foundling Home	Obstetrics Ward	Indian Village	Well-Baby Clinic	Total
More than 6 months	185	9	—	62	—	—	Several	256
At least 3 months	18	3	—	—	29	—	hundred	50
Less than 3 months	—	6	23	2	6	23	children observed	60
Died in First Year	—	—	—	27	—	—	for three	27
Total	203	18	23	91	35	23	weeks	393
Number of children filmed	138	14	10	25	29	3	27	246*

* This total represents 47,200 feet of 16 mm. film.

26

them for about 3 months after delivery, on occasion of their periodical visits to the hospital.

3. In view of the frequency of controversies regarding cultural, racial, and other influences on the human personality, we wished to test how far such differences exist, or might affect personality in the course of the first year of life. With this problem in mind, we endeavored to include in our populations infants from various cultures and races. We were able to study infants of white, Negro, and (American) Indian parentage. The latter were observed in an Indian village situated in Latin America, where we had the opportunity to examine babies during their first three months of life. The first observation was made when they were brought to church for their baptism; we saw them in the sacristy. Subsequently we managed to visit them again in their village home. These 23 infants were seen for less than three months; accordingly this part of the study is of cross-sectional nature. Their observed behavior did not differ from that of the children of the same age level observed in the other environments.

4. Finally, our design called for the investigation of large groups of infants under conditions where an optimal measure of constancy of the environment could be guaranteed. For this purpose we selected primarily two institutions. These institutions will be designated as Nursery and Foundling Home.

DESCRIPTION OF THE INSTITUTIONS

The two institutions were similar in certain important aspects. Both were situated outside the city, in large, spacious gardens. In both, hygienic conditions were carefully safeguarded. In both, the infants were segregated from the older babies at birth and kept in a special newborn's ward, to which visitors were admitted only after washing their hands and putting on freshly sterilized smocks. After two or three months, the infants were transferred to the ward of the older babies and placed in individual cubicles. These were completely glass-enclosed in the Nursery; glass-enclosed on three sides and open on the end in the Foundling Home. In the Nursery the children were transferred, after six months, to rooms containing four to five cots each; in the Foundling Home they remained in the cubicles until fifteen or eighteen months, or even longer. In the Foundling Home, about half of the ward was somewhat more dimly lighted than the other half, though both had plenty of light; in the Nursery all children had well-lighted cubicles. While the Nursery was the wealthier institution, the Foundling Home was also adequately provided for, except from one point of view, of which more later. In the Nursery the walls were painted in light neutral colors, giving a cheerful impression, whereas the Foundling Home, with its light green-grey painted walls and its cubicles, appeared cheerless. Whether this impression is due to my personal reaction or not, I cannot say.

In both institutions the food was well prepared, adequate, and varied according to the needs of the individual child at each age; the bottles and utensils were sterilized. In both institutions a large percentage of the younger children were breast-fed; but in the Nursery this percentage seemed to grow smaller, and formula was added, soon leading to weaning from the breast. In the Foundling Home the large majority of children were breast-fed until their third month. In both institutions, clothing and temperature were appropriate.

As for medical care, the Foundling Home was visited at least once a day by the head physician and the medical staff, who during their rounds inspected each child and his chart. A laryngologist and other specialists also made daily rounds. In the Nursery no daily rounds were made, but the institution's pediatrician saw the children when called.

On the whole, the Foundling Home showed a slight advantage over the Nursery in the selection of the children admitted. The Nursery was a penal institution to which delinquent girls, pregnant on admission, were committed. They delivered their children in a nearby maternity hospital. After the lying-in period, their children were cared for in the Nursery from birth to the end of the first year. In view of the fact that the mothers were mostly delinquent minors, to a certain extent socially maladjusted, sometimes feeble-minded, sometimes psychically defective, psychopathic or criminal, heredity and background represented a negative selection from the viewpoint of the children. In the Foundling Home this negative selection was nonexistent. The children represented a cross-section of dependent children in a large city; a part of them had a background not very different from that of the children in the Nursery, but a relevant number of the children came from socially well-adjusted, normal mothers, who were unable to support themselves and their children.

The basic difference between the Nursery and the Foundling Home centers around the care of the children. The Nursery, which houses from forty to sixty children at a time, was run by a head nurse and her assistants; their duties consisted in teaching the children's mothers simple and efficient hygiene and child care, and in supervising and advising them. Each child was fed, nursed, and cared for by his own mother. If for any reason a mother had to be separated from her child, she was replaced by the mother of another child or by a pregnant girl, who in this way acquired the experience necessary for the care of her own future baby. Each child in the Nursery thus had the full-time care of his own mother or at least of a substitute, chosen by the very able head nurse, who tried to find a substitute who liked the child.

The children in the Nursery always had at least one toy and most of the time several toys. Their visual radius included not only the pleasant landscape before the windows; in addition, the enclosures were kept sufficiently low for each child to be able to look through the glass panes into several cubicles. The older children watched these with avid interest, trying to participate in the activities outside of their cubicles, and also visibly fascinated by the bustling activities of mothers carrying their children in the corridor, tending, feeding, playing with their children in the cubicles, chatting with one another, their babies in their arms.

The Foundling Home was the kind of institution commonly used for dependent children about fifty years ago. It was endowed with inadequate funds but with an ample pleasantly situated building. The infants housed there belonged to two categories: the first were the children of married women who were unable to support their families for one reason or another and who paid a modest amount for the care of their children. The other category was made up of children of unwed mothers, who were admitted on condition that they would nurse their own child and one other during the first three months of their stay and help in preparing and distributing the food of the older babies.

As mentioned, the Foundling Home was run by a head nurse and five assistant nurses. After the third month, each child was removed to the single cubicle of the general ward, where he shared the ministrations of the five nurses. In purely mathematical terms, this would mean that each nurse cared for somewhat more than seven children. But it did not work this way in practice, because the nurses had to supervise the preparation of the food for the babies, organize and distribute it; they had to wash, clean, and diaper the babies. Inevitably, bottle propping was resorted to, and also inevitably at least one nurse was removed from circulation during feeding time or the weighing of the babies, etc. As a result, each child received at best one tenth of the time of a nurse, one tenth of the substitute for maternal care, one tenth of a mother. When I first came to the Foundling Home, there was hardly a toy in the whole place. Perhaps as a result of my activity and that of my associates, after a few months more and more toys began to appear, and when I left the Foundling Home nearly half the children had a toy.

Another noteworthy aspect of the treatment of children in the Foundling Home was that of visual radius. The Foundling Home was bleak and deserted except for the time when the nurses and their helpers from the ranks of the nursing mothers came in at feeding time to look after the children's needs. To this picture should be added a practice peculiar to the Foundling Home and many children's institutions and hospitals: to keep the children quiet, the nurses hung bedsheets or blankets over the foot and side railings of each cot, screening the infant effectively from the world and all other cubicles, placing him in solitary confinement, with only the ceiling visible. As a result the babies lay supine for many months, wearing a hollow into their mattresses, out of which they were unable to turn by the time when normal babies turn from the back to side, in their sixth or seventh month.

Part II

The Constitution of the Libidinal Object

CHAPTER III

The Objectless Stage

In Chapter I, I have defined the psychoanalytic concept of libidinal object and indicated that in the world of the neonate there is neither an object nor an object relation. I have called this first stage the preobjectal or objectless stage. This Chapter as well as the subsequent one are devoted to a discussion of this earliest stage. In them I shall focus on the infant's responsiveness, and present some speculations on the nature of the neonate's perception and its role in psychoanalytic theory.

The objectless stage coincides more or less with that of primary narcissism. Hartmann (1939) speaks of this stage as the undifferentiated phase.[1] I prefer to speak of this stage as that of *non*differentiation, because the newborn's perception, activity, functioning are insufficiently organized into units

[1] Hartmann's concept of the undifferentiated phase refers to a lack of differentiation between ego and id, conscious and unconscious of the newborn's personality. Within this undifferentiated personality, conscious and unconscious, and later ego and id, will separate from each other. Thus Hartmann's concept essentially serves data which we encounter in psychoanalytic practice and theory; it is a descriptive concept.

My concept of nondifferentiation includes Hartmann's postulates; it is the major term, for it takes in also description and nonpsychoanalytic, observable aspects, such as neuromuscular, physiological, behavioral aspects, for example, perception and action. In the stage of non-differentiation, there is no clear distinction between psyche and soma, between inside and outside, between drive and object, between "I" and "Non-I," and not even between different regions of the body.

35

except to a certain extent in areas which are indispensable for survival, like metabolism and nutritional intake, circulation, respiratory function and such.

At this stage the newborn cannot distinguish one "thing" from another; he cannot distinguish an (external) thing from his own body, and he does not experience the surround as separate from himself. Therefore, he also perceives the need-gratifying, food-providing breast, if at all, as part of himself.[2] Furthermore, the newborn *in* himself is not differentiated and organized either—even in such fundamental respects as the relation between discrete neural centers on the one hand and their muscular effector organs on the other; only very few privileged areas appear to be segregated into functional units (Tilney and Kubie, 1931).

A host of observations, ours among them, confirm that the perceptual apparatus of the newborn is shielded from the outside world by an extremely high stimulus barrier. This barrier protects the infant during the first weeks and months of life from perceiving environmental stimuli. Consequently, we feel justified in stating that during the first days certainly, and during the first month or so, in a decreasing measure, the outside world is practically nonexistent for the infant. During this period all perception goes through the interoceptive and proprioceptive systems; the infant's responses occur upon the perception of needs communicated by these systems. Stimuli coming from outside are perceived only when their level of intensity exceeds that of the threshold of the stimulus barrier. Then they break through the stimulus barrier, shattering the newborn's quiescence and he reacts violently with unpleasure. Unpleasure responses can be observed from birth.

However, I wish to stress categorically that I dissociate myself from the speculations of some authors who claim that the

---

[2] "An infant at the breast does not as yet distinguish his ego from the external world as the source of the sensations flowing in upon him" (Freud, 1930, p. 66f.).

unborn baby expresses unpleasure already *in utero*. We have no way of knowing what the behavior of the fetus "expresses." I find equally unacceptable speculations on the infant's sensory perception during delivery, or on psychic activity in the neonate, and mentation in the first weeks and months following birth. Such speculations are on a par with the assertion of authorities in bygone centuries about the so-called "birth-cry" of the neonate, supposed to express his despair at being confronted with our sorry world for the first time. All these naïve notions honor the imagination of their inventors but can be neither proved nor disproved. In Freud's incisive words: "Ignorance is ignorance; no right to believe anything is derived from it" (1927).

PRIMITIVE PROTOTYPES OF AFFECTIVE RESPONSES

I am not inclined either to go along with interpretations couched in more "scientific" language about the trauma of birth as the first manifestation of anxiety proper and as the ultimate determinant of man's individual fate (e.g., Rank, 1924). A whole psychological doctrine was based on the impact of this "trauma"; it was assigned a role out of all proportion and made the villain responsible for all later psychic disturbance.

Freud, with characteristic scientific caution, stresses that at birth there is no consciousness; that the so-called birth trauma leaves no memory; that "the danger of birth has as yet no psychical content" (Freud, 1926a).

In view of the periodic recurrence of this controversy, I decided to carry out a number of direct observations to obtain objective records of the infant's behavior at birth in its fullest detail. For this purpose I have attended and made careful records of 35 deliveries performed without anesthetics or sedatives. In 29 of these cases, the behavior of the neonate was filmed during expulsion or immediately after delivery.

We continued to observe the neonates during the following two weeks and filmed their behavior repeatedly during nursing and also their responses to a set of standardized stimuli.

These records show that the neonate's reaction to being born could hardly be called a traumatic one. In infants delivered normally—and this is the vast majority of all infants, for only fractions of 1 per cent are not born this way—the reaction is an extremely fleeting one, far from violent, lasting only a few seconds. Immediately after delivery the infant shows brief respiratory distress and the manifestations of negatively tinged excitation. If the infant is left alone, this subsides literally within *seconds* and gives way to complete quiescence. The so-called trauma of birth, of which misinterpreters of Freud have made so much, is conspicuous by its short duration and unimpressiveness. What can be observed is a brief state of excitation, which appears to have the quality of unpleasure (see Spitz, 1947a).[3] By contrast, the instillation of silver nitrate into the neonate's eyes (performed immediately after cutting the cord) provokes a much more vocal, prolonged unpleasure response, which may last up to half a minute.

These observations further showed that during the first hours and even days of life, only one manifestation of anything resembling emotion could be detected. This was a state of excitation, which appeared to have negative quality. This negative excitation ensued when the newborn was exposed to stimulation strong enough to overcome his high perceptive threshold (e.g., the slapping mentioned in the footnote above). Excitation of this quality is also experienced as unpleasurable at a later age. For simplicity's sake we will use this term unpleasure also to describe negative excitation in the infant.

---

[3] The various vocal manifestations of the infant at birth, such as they are, can be attributed in part to mechanical reasons, like the beginning of breathing; in an even smaller part, to actual unpleasure. In their vast majority, they are the result of the well-meaning efforts of obstetrician and midwife to accelerate the beginning of breathing by slapping lustily the infant's backside.

The counterpart of unpleasure manifestations in the neonate, however, are not manifestations of pleasure, which at this age cannot be observed. The counterpart of the unpleasure manifestation in the newborn is *quiescence*. Negative excitation in the newborn in response to excessive stimulation should be considered as a process of discharge as described by Freud (1895). As such it is a specifically physiological process; it exemplifies the rule of the Nirvana principle, according to which excitation is maintained at a constant level and any tension rising above this level has to be discharged without delay. From these beginnings psychological functioning will develop and consolidate in due course. Once established, psychological function will be governed by the rule of the pleasure-unpleasure principle for some time, until the pleasure principle will in turn be relieved, though never completely, by the regulative mechanisms of the reality principle.

It is of major interest to note that, in the beginning, the organism operates both physiologically and psychologically after the manner of a binary system, according to the principle of the "excluded third" (law of contradiction), one of "the so-called three laws of thought" (Baldwin, 1940). We have good reason to wonder whether the physiological beginnings on which subsequently psychic function and ultimately thought processes are founded do not have unsuspected, far-reaching, and enduring effects, and whether they do not also determine the eventual structure of the laws of logic.

Let us now examine the newborn's response from the viewpoint of perception and behavior.

PRIMITIVE COGNITIVE RESPONSES

One might well ask how the newborn perceives any of the stimuli coming from the outside which are necessary for his functioning. To answer this question, even tentatively, we have to say a few words about the nature of perception. For it is difficult to see how one can speak at all of perception in the newborn, whether we do so on the basis of what we know today from experimental physiology and experimental psychology—let alone in terms of Freud's concept of the mental apparatus. I cannot discuss here the vast field of perception and its intricacies from any of these viewpoints. Likewise, I cannot even begin to refer to the numerous recent experiments on perception (such as undertaken by George Klein, E. von Holst, W. Rosenblith, Selig Hecht, Riley Gardner, and many others), particularly since none of them were done with children, let alone with infants.

I find it useful to limit myself here, arbitrarily, to the discussion of the investigations of M. von Senden (1932) which are paralleled by the experimental findings on chimpanzees by Riesen (1947); both have opened vast, hitherto neglected, areas of perception.

Briefly, von Senden investigated 63 subjects born blind, and then operated for their congenital cataracts between the ages of three and forty-three. Von Senden reports that their reaction to the "blessing" conferred on them, namely, the gift of sight, was, to say the least, unexpected. None of them experienced their gain as a blessing. It turned out that though they had *vision*, they could not *see*. Literally, they had to learn how to see in a long, drawn-out, laborious, and painful process, causing them endless mental anguish. When we say "long, drawn-out process," we mean months and years; many of them never learned to see—some of them actually expressed the wish to be blind again.

What is the meaning of these findings? It became clear that these patients had managed to conduct their lives without the use of their eyesight. Their relation with the surround, both animate and inanimate, was established with the help of the nonvisual modalities available to them—touch, hearing, smell, and other, less familiar modalities. By using these nonvisual sensory modalities they had acquired a substantial code of meaningful sensory percepts, that is, meaningful signs and signals. These signs and signals had become interrelated and had produced an intricate web of memory traces from which these patients' "image" of the world was formed. With the help of this "image" they oriented themselves, performed thought processes, steered themselves through obstacles to their goals, communicated and related.

The sudden, massive influx of countless visual stimuli, which they could neither regulate nor control, could not be transformed into meaningful cues. On the contrary, the visual stimuli were completely meaningless; in fact, they disturbed the use of the existing meaningful code of signals which until then had constituted their world; or in the language of communication theory, these unintelligible visual stimuli were experienced as confusing, unbearable "noise."

The "perceptive" experience of the blind-born, to whom sight had been restored in adulthood or adolescence, can be applied, *mutatis mutandis,* to the newborn, or rather to the first six months of the infant's life. Of course, there is a fundamental difference between the two. The world image of the operated blind-born consists in an already coherent, organized system of signals, derived from every sensory modality except the visual one. After the cataract operation, a hailstorm of alien, never experienced, meaningless visual stimuli breaks into and disrupts this coherent system. An enormous task of reorganization, of mental processing faces the hapless blind-born. His mental and emotional capacities are unbearably overloaded, he feels disoriented and helpless.

By contrast the newborn has no world image at all, no stimuli from any sensory modality that he can recognize as signals; even by the time he is six months old, only very few such signals have been established and laid down as memory traces. Therefore, stimuli impinging on the infant's sensorium are as alien in the visual as in all the other sensory modalities. Any stimulus will first have to be transformed into meaningful experience; only then can it become a signal, to which other signals are added step by step to build up the coherent image of the child's world.

A diversity of conditions enables the newborn to perform this extraordinary feat:

1. One is the stimulus barrier which protects him from the great majority of the stimuli to which we are ordinarily exposed. This protection consists of several parts. First, the receptor stations at birth are not yet energized (Spitz, 1955b, 1957). Second, the larger part of the day is passed in sleep or in dozing (Bühler, 1928). Finally, the mental processing of incoming stimuli develops gradually over many months in direct relation to the infant's maturing capacity for voluntary action.

2. A second factor is implicit in the above: namely, as a result of this filtering, the process of endowing stimuli with meaning is also an extremely gradual one.

3. A third factor is the unique environment, a world in itself, with which the mother surrounds the infant and which the mother extends into many directions. To begin with, the mother actually protects the infant physically from being overloaded with stimuli of any kind. Much of our child-rearing practices, the crib, the cot, the warmth, the clothing, etc., serve to shield him from stimuli coming from the outside.

4. She assists the infant in dealing with stimuli coming from inside by affording him tension discharge. Feeding the infant when hungry, diapering him when wet, covering him when cold, etc., modifies these conditions and relieves unpleasurable tension.

5. By far the most important factor in enabling the child to build gradually a coherent ideational image of his world derives from the reciprocity between mother and child. It is that part of object relations which I have called the "dialogue" (Spitz, 1963b). The dialogue is the sequential action-reaction-action cycle within the framework of mother-child

relations. This very special form of interaction creates for the baby a unique world of his own, with its specific emotional climate. It is this action-reaction-action cycle that enables the baby to transform step by step meaningless stimuli into meaningful signals.

Our emphasis on the overriding importance of object relations for the emergence of affects and for organizing perception is in good agreement with von Senden's findings. His data show that perception has to be learned, coordinated, integrated, and synthetized through experiencing the unceasing and shifting tides, the quiet pools, the rapids of object relations.

Accordingly, we are disinclined to speak of perception in the infant as long as the stimuli which impinge on the sensorium and are processed centrally have not been made meaningful through the infant's experience. In this sense the newborn does not perceive; in this sense perception proper is predicated upon apperception. This does not imply that no memory traces are laid down while perception is being acquired.

Neurophysiological Givens Underlying Behavior

Still, even in this early period, the neonatal period, the infant shows quite a number of manifestations that have the semblance of responses and actions, some of them quite structured and complicated. They appear to be innate responses like the behavior patterns surrounding rooting. Rooting comprises the sequence of orienting movements which are followed by seizing the nipple and sucking, and which end up with swallowing, so that the whole series forms a well-defined coherent behavior complex. Indeed, one should include in this behavior complex the pressor movements of the hands and arms and of the legs—connected as they seem to be with the degree to which the stomach is filled. Other such patterns are less obvious and are still being explored.

How does the newborn "perceive" the stimuli which trigger these behavior patterns? Some of the perceptive pathways triggering them seem to be inbuilt, that is, innate, as demonstrated by the investigations of Tilney and Kubie (1931).

It is my opinion, however, that a large proportion of the pathways involved belong to a system of "sensing" basically different from the system of perception that operates at a later age and with which we are familiar. I have discussed the nature of these two systems and the differences between them elsewhere (Spitz, 1945b) and have called the one present at birth the *coenesthetic organization*. Here, sensing is extensive, primarily visceral, centered in the autonomic nervous system, and manifests itself in the form of emotions. Accordingly, I prefer to speak of this form of "perception," which differs so fundamentally from sensory perception, as *reception*.[4] It is an all-or-none phenomenon operating as a binary system.

In contrast to this stands the later development of what I have called *diacritic organization,* where perception takes place through peripheral sense organs and is localized, circumscribed, and intensive; its centers are in the cortex, its manifestations are cognitive processes, among them the conscious thought processes.

In discussing a number of aspects of the psychic organization on the coenesthetic level (1955b), we stressed that already at birth visceral sensitivity is connected with some of the peripheral sensory modalities, such as the skin surface. Furthermore, there appear to exist in the human child at birth certain zones and sensory organs which I consider transitional ones, mediating between peripheral sensory organs and visceral ones, between the inside and the outside. As one of these I have described the oral region, which extends on the one hand into the laryngopharynx, soft palate, tongue, and inside of cheeks, and on the other includes the lips, the chin, the

4 See Chapter I, footnote 1.

nose, and the outside of the cheek surface—in one word, the "snout" (see also Rangell, 1954). Here the transition actually is anatomically demonstrable in the successive changes in the covering of these organs, going from cutis to mucosa. Another such transitional organ is situated in the inner ear.

It is noteworthy that those transitional organs which mediate between inner reception and outer perception all have a major function in the survival-centered food-intake process; in Freud's terms, they have an anaclitic function. Thanks to this they actually become suitable to form the bridge between coenesthetic reception and diacritic perception.

At the same time we should remain aware of the fact that, however different from each other, the coenesthetic and the diacritic organizations are both contained in one and the same organism. In Chapter VII we shall show that, much as the coenesthetic organization has become muted in the consciousness of Western man, it continues to function covertly; what is more, it plays a momentous determining role in our feelings, our thinking, our actions—even though we try to keep it under wraps.

All this is familiar to the psychoanalytically sophisticated reader; after all, we are accustomed to think of the attributes of the coenesthetic organization in terms of the unconscious. But from the developmental viewpoint, its role in the total economy of the "system person" is compellingly evident for two reasons:

1. As already indicated, the diacritic organization has evolved from the coenesthetic one. Not only will it bear the traces of this origin, but the channels connecting the two organizations are never completely occluded—not even neurologically.

2. The coenesthetic organization continues to function throughout life, powerfully one might say, as the wellspring of life itself, even though our Western civilization has fitted a silencer on its manifestations. In emergencies, under stress,

the archaic forces sweep the silencer away, and break through with terrifying violence, for they are not under rational conscious control. Then we are confronted with the more or less random explosive discharge of primal emotions, with malignant psychosomatic disease, or with certain forms of psychotic outbreaks.

If we have touched in passing on the terrifying spectacle of naked emotion in the adult, this was to make the reader aware that the "normal" manifestations of affect in the newborn are not as trifling as we usually like to think of them. We perceive them as minor, because the infant is small and powerless. Therefore, these manifestations are neither as loud nor as spectacular as they would be in the adult. We have come to accept that this is the way an infant is, and that this is perfectly "normal."

True enough. But we should remember all the other implications of this "normalcy." We should remember that not only affects are chaotic and undifferentiated in the infant but also "perception"; that diacritic perception is absent; that the neonate cannot distinguish one thing from another, let alone single out the libidinal object; and that he responds primarily to interoceptive stimuli. Somewhere around the eighth day of life, a certain specificity of response appears; obviously a certain time must elapse after birth before learning can take place.

MODIFICATION OF BEHAVIOR THROUGH EXPERIENCE

It is around the end of the first week of life that the infant begins to respond to cues. The first traces of aim-directed behavior appear, that is, activity, presumably associated with psychic process, which seems to take place according to the mode of the conditioned reflex.

In the beginning, these cues stimulate deep sensitivity. The first such cue that triggers a response is a change of equilib-

rium. If, after the eighth day, one lifts a breast-fed child from
the crib and places it in one's arms in the nursing position
(that is, in a horizontal position), the infant turns his head in
the direction of the chest of the person, male or female, who
is lifting him (Bühler, 1928). By contrast, if the same infant
is lifted from his crib in a vertical position, the turning of the
head does not take place (see Fig. 1).[5]

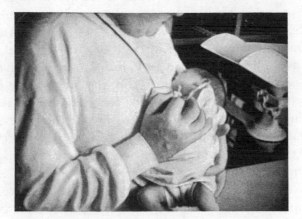

FIGURE 1

Reaction of the Newborn to Being Placed
in the Nursing Position.

The recognition of such cues and the response to them become increasingly specific in the course of the following eight
weeks. Volkelt (1929) and Ripin and Hetzer (1930) examined
in great detail the successive stages in the perception of these
cues in the course of the first two months of life. Their study
was followed by the studies of Rubinow and Frankl (1934),
who demonstrated in a series of experiments the steps which
eventually lead to the recognition of the food object as such.

5 Mead and McGregor (1951) report that the Balinese nurse their children
in the vertical position. One might suspect that the equilibrium response of
the Balinese infant would be the opposite of that of the Western infant.

Rubinow and Frankl showed that up to the beginning of the second month of life, the infant recognizes the cue of food only when he is hungry. Actually he does not recognize milk as such, nor the bottle, nor the rubber nipple, nor the breast, nor anything else. He "recognizes," if one can say so, the nipple when he receives it in his mouth, and in response to this stimulus he usually begins to suck. However, even this elementary form of perception has to be qualified. If the infant happens to be concerned with something else,[6] if, for instance, he is screaming because his need for food has not been immediately satisfied, he will not react to the nipple, even when it is inserted into his mouth, but will go on screaming. It will take prolonged oral stimulation to make him direct his attention again to the food for which he is screaming, and which had been available to him all the time. To recapitulate, we deal here with two behavioral sequences:

1. At this time the infant recognizes the cue of food *only when he is hungry*.

2. When he is screaming for food, he does *not* recognize the nipple in his mouth and goes right on screaming (see Fig. 2).

What have these two behavioral sequences in common? Although the two situations appear to be dissimilar, their underlying cause is the same. To enable the infant to perceive an external stimulus at this age level (between the second and sixth week of life) two factors must be present *jointly* and combine. The first is an external stimulus, the stimulus which the infant has come to associate with impending need gratification; the second stimulus is of proprioceptive origin, it is the infant's hunger condition, his need for food.

Placing the nipple into the child's mouth is the necessary

---

[6] See Escalona (1962) for an excellent discussion of the degree to which the infant's state affects his responsiveness and the need to take this essential factor into account in designing and interpreting experimental studies of infants.

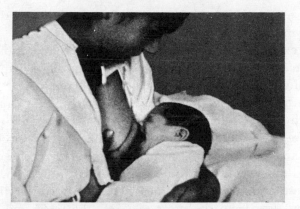

FIGURE 2

The Newborn Does Not Perceive the Nipple in His
Mouth When He is Hunger-Screaming.

but not the sufficient condition for his perceiving it. The
proof for this thesis is supplied by the second experiment;
here the infant's proprioceptive system is engaged by the experience of unpleasure; consequently the infant is unable to
perceive the need-gratifying stimulus within his mouth.

Conversely, at this age, the infant will perceive the stimulus
of the nipple in his mouth if the following conditions are fulfilled: (1) if the proprioceptive apparatus is not inactivated,
"flooded," by the massive unpleasure tension; and (2) if the
infant is hungry, which puts the apparatus into readiness for
external perception.

The second experiment—that of nonperception of the nipple in the mouth when the infant is screaming because of
hunger—illustrates the operation of the Nirvana principle;
as soon as unpleasure (tension) arises, it must be eliminated
through discharge (motor, vocal, etc.). As long as this continues, perception of the outside is not operating. In order
to perceive, unpleasure and discharge must cease; that is, the
self-perpetuating operation of the Nirvana principle must be
halted through external intervention. Only when this hap-

pens can perception of the outside be resumed and the need-gratifying stimulus be perceived.

An excellent example of this inexorable operation of the Nirvana principle was presented long ago in an experiment of Wolfgang Köhler (1925). A dog was offered a piece of meat, from which he was separated by a long, high wire fence, open at both ends. Under normal circumstances the dog was able to solve the problem without any difficulty, by circling the fence and grabbing the meat. However, when the dog was starved for several days, he could not tear himself away from the close proximity to the meat. He was in conflict between moving away from the meat to circle the fence and rushing back to get close to the meat—a conflict ending in exhaustion after desperate and futile attempts to climb the fence.

The infant's inability to perceive his surround lasts for a number of weeks. Toward the beginning of the second month an approaching human being begins to acquire a unique place among the "things" in the baby's surround. At this stage the infant begins to perceive the approaching adult visually. If you approach the hungry, crying baby at the hour of feeding, he will become quiet, open his mouth or make sucking movements. No other "thing" will produce such response at this age, except the intra-oral, tactile perception of food. However, the reaction only sets in at the hour of feeding, when the infant is hungry. In terms of perception, in his second month the infant reacts to the external stimulus only when it coincides with the baby's interoceptive perception of hunger. At this stage the perception of the surround is predicated upon tension generated by an ungratified drive.

Two or three weeks later, we note a further progress; when the infant perceives a human face, he follows its movements with concentrated attention (see Fig. 3). No other "thing" can elicit this behavior in the infant at this age level. Gesell and Ilg (1937) explain that this happens because the human face is offered to the infant in innumerable situations of expec-

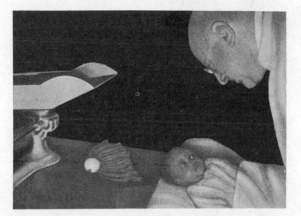

FIGURE 3

In the Second Month of Life the Infant Follows With
His Eyes the Adult's Moving Face.

tancy. Actually, during the first month of life, the human
appears in the visual field of the infant every time one of his
needs is gratified. Thus the human face becomes associated
with relief from unpleasure as well as with the experience of
pleasure.

In our own studies we could add an important element to
Gesell's assumption. We have observed that in the great majority of cases the breast-fed baby stares at the face of his
mother unswervingly throughout the act of nursing without
turning his eyes away until he falls asleep at the breast (see
Fig. 4); in bottle-fed babies this phenomenon is neither consistent nor reliable.

Obviously, nursing is not the only ministration of the
mother during which the baby can stare at her face. We are
rarely aware of the fact that, whatever we may do with the
infant, whether we lift him up, wash him, diaper him, etc.,
we always offer our face straight on for the baby's inspection,
fixating him with our eyes, moving our head, and mostly saying something. It follows that the face as such is the visual

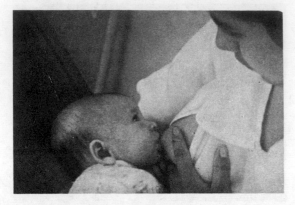

FIGURE 4

During Nursing the Breast-Fed Baby Stares
Unwaveringly at His Mother's Face.

stimulus offered most frequently to the infant during the first
months of life. In the course of the first six weeks of life a
mnemonic trace of the human face is laid down in the infantile memory as the first signal of the presence of the need-
gratifier; the infant will follow all the movements of this
signal with his eyes.

CHAPTER IV

The Cradle of Perception

> For the ego, perception plays
> the part which in the id falls
> to instinct.
>
> —FREUD (1923)

In Chapter III, I described an experimental approach to the problem of the genesis of perception. Using objective data, such as direct observation of behavior, experiments, and neurophysiological data, we traced, step by step, the infant's progress in the cognition and recognition of a percept. It became evident that need gratification (that is, the pleasure-unpleasure experiences) plays a major role in the recognition of this first percept.

The genetic approach is the guiding principle in the methodology of this study. We shall therefore retrace the steps to a period which, in my opinion, precedes the events presented in the previous chapter. This is the period during which the coenesthetic system reigns supreme in the infant's existence. It is the age of deepest nondifferentiation, in which affect and percept are still, so to say, one. However, here the experimental method cannot serve us adequately and we are forced to use a reconstructive approach, in the hope that future observers may find themselves encouraged systematically to explore the situation and the givens present at this very dawn of the human being. For if such data can be obtained, we will achieve a much better understanding of the role played by affects in perception at later ages. In general I do not much favor the application of the reconstructive, introspective method of interpretation to account for behavior of subjects lacking speech and therefore unable to supply data to confirm or disprove our conclusions. In the case of the preverbal child we have access to direct observation as well as to experiments. Neither of these will yield much information from the neonate, for his behavior is random, unstructured, and his responses are inconsistent.

Therefore, we have chosen a rather complex procedure. First we will put ourselves into the infant's subjective situation and we will try to conjecture how and what he perceives. We will then relate these assumptions to such observable givens as are available and to the data of neurophysiology. Second, we will examine our construct in the light of certain regressive phenomena in the adult, notably those which occasionally occur in falling asleep or waking up, in the dream, and in psychosis. Finally, observations like those made by von Senden (1932) on operated blind-born persons will contribute to our understanding of the very archaic perceptual experiences which we may assume to parallel those of the infant in his first weeks of life. Pending access to other objective data, I will regard the convergence of data obtained by these diverse approaches (if indeed such convergence can be demonstrated) as the equivalent of a validation of our reconstructively obtained propositions. Lest I be misunderstood, this procedure is in no way to be confused with that which E. Bibring (1947) called "retrojection"—a felicitous, if somewhat disparaging, term describing the attribution of adult fantasies and wishes to the infant.

Let us now begin with an attempt at reconstruction, and ask ourselves: how does the perceptual world of the infant look before differentiation has begun? If we think back to our own childhood, we get a first inkling: remember how wide every street looked—how big the house—how vast the garden? And when we see it twenty years later, how surprisingly all of them have shrunk. The shrinkage is the result of the increase in our own size. "Man is the measure of all things," said Protagoras.

Freud was well aware of these apperceptive distortions; in *The Interpretation of Dreams* (1900), he already mentioned that Swift illustrated this distortion in *Gulliver's Travels*. Later, Lewin (1953a) referred to the distortion in the perception of the newborn and specifically described its neurophysiological aspect when he spoke of the "diplopic, amblyopic baby, with its weak powers of accommodation and its confused depth and color perceptions" (Lewin, 1953a, p. 183).

THE WORK OF M. VON SENDEN ON PERCEPTUAL LEARNING AND SOME OTHER EXPERIMENTAL FINDINGS

> . . . and see ye indeed, but perceive not.
> —*Isaiah* 6, 9.

Of course, as of today, we do not know whether the newborn perceives anything. What he perceives—*if* indeed he perceives—must be inferred. We have one promising source for such inferences in the already quoted work of von Senden (1932); he investigated the beginning and the development of visual perception in individuals who had been born blind because of congenital cataract and whose cataract had then been removed at a later age.

The way these patients describe their first experience of visual perception is extremely informative. Case No. 65, an eighteen-year-old girl, "saw, but it did not mean anything but a lot of different kinds of brightness. *She was not even positive that these new strange sensations were coming through her eyes* until she proved it by closing the lids and finding that this stopped the sensations . . ." (my italics).

This description, which is typical of most of the comparable cases examined, appears to us to be an extremely suggestive document for the understanding of what the newborn may experience when he first sees the light of day—or rather when he first opens his eyes. Not only are *shapes* not seen—the very sensation itself was not recognized as originating in the eyes; indeed it could be attributed by the subject to any of the other sensory modalities. The statement of case No. 65 provides us with some very essential pieces of information:

1. Perception appears to begin as a totality, and the various perceptive modalities have to be segregated from each other in the course of development. Perhaps even maturation plays a role in this process.

2. Perception in the sense in which adults perceive is not present from the beginning; it must be acquired, it must be learned.

This assumption finds support in the following quotation about Patient No. 17, the eighteen-year-old son of a doctor, of whom the surgeon states: "On opening the eyes for the first time, on the third day after the operation, I asked the patient what he could see; he answered that he saw an extensive field of light, in which everything appeared dull, confused, and in motion. He could not distinguish objects."

Depth perception, localization, are also absent; of Patient No. 49, a fifteen-year old boy, the surgeon reports: "The newly operated patients do not localize their visual impressions. They do not relate them to any point, either to the eye, or to any surface, even a spherical one"; and the disorientation between the various sensory modalities could hardly be better described than by the statement of the same surgeon: "They see colours much as we smell an odor of paint or varnish, which enfolds or intrudes upon us, but without occupying any specific form of extension in a more exactly definable way."

The examples provided in von Senden's book again and

again direct our attention to the fact that man acquires visual perception by learning. The behavior of the operated patients, the content of the impressions reported by them are essentially similar, no matter what their age levels. One example for many: pieces of cardboard, different in shape and color, were displayed successively before the eyes of a recently operated seven-year-old boy. He was asked to distinguish them from each other. This exercise was repeated daily, with the following result: "So little had he gained in 13 days that he could not, without counting their corners, one by one, tell their shape. This he did with great facility, running his eye quickly around the outline, so that it was evident that he was still learning, just as a child learns to read."

This is in good agreement with direct infant observation. One of the items of the Bühler test consists in displaying a 5-inch, color-striped rubber ball before the infant and watching the movements of his eyes. By the fourth month of life, the infant will carefully circumscribe the contours of the ball with his eyes (Bühler and Hetzer, 1932).

In the first days after the operation, matters are not that simple: "There are in fact a number of examples, even on first exercise of vision, where in spite of the nystagmus the patients, on *simultaneous* confrontation with two or more figures, *incontestably report differences of shape,* even though they cannot state the shape of any of the figures presented" (my italics). Or take case No. 17, the eighteen-year-old son of a doctor, who on the fifth day after the operation "was now for the first time able . . . to perceive a difference, but *merely a difference,* in the surrounding objects" (my italics).

Some of the problems raised by these clinical accounts were recently studied experimentally by Fantz (1957, 1958a, 1958b). He carried out a series of observations and experiments on newly hatched chicks and on infants from one to fifteen weeks of life. His observations, in contradistinction to those of von Senden, are cross-sectional, as *ad hoc* experiments usually are. In essence his experiments are designed to validate or to invalidate the proposition that form perception in both animal and man is already present at birth, hence innate, and inherited. He was able to confirm this thesis in the case of chicks. From the first second of life, the chick is indeed able, innately, without learning, to perceive shape, three-dimensionality, and size. This capacity has obvious survival value; the chick being a precocial,[1] a nidifugous bird, it has to provide for its food right from the beginning and therefore must be endowed from birth with an innate, unlearned ability to perceive the food object.

Man, however, is primarily an altricial, nidicolous animal, born immature and helpless. He is not capable of locomotion or of any of the directed, volitional behavior indispensable for self-preservation. To ensure his survival visual discrimination is unnecessary. Man's survival at birth is predicated on devoted parental care, as it is in other nidicolous animals (e.g., kittens, puppies, etc.). Hence in the evolution of man there was no selective pressure for phylogenetic transmission of the capacity to discriminate visually already at birth. It is unlikely, therefore, that in man this capacity has ever been part and parcel of his innate hereditary equipment.

For this reason it is surprising to learn that Fantz, on testing thirty infants, aged one to fifteen weeks, at weekly intervals, found that, like newly hatched chicks, they had innate form perception. This would seem diametrically to contradict the observations found in von Senden's blind-born and later operated humans. However, closer examination of von Senden's material reveals that this contradiction is only apparent. The patients studied by von Senden were incapable of seeing

---

[1] *Altricial* (from the Latin *altrix*, nurse, also known as nidicolous) is the zoological term for the species whose young are born in an immature and helpless condition so that they require care and nursing for some time after the birth; *precocial* (from the Latin *praecox*, premature, also known as nidifugous) designates animals whose young at birth are covered with down and are able to run about.

forms, they did not see shapes, they could not distinguish size —but from the very first, they did visually distinguish *differences* and they could state that two objects were different from each other. It would seem, therefore, that the experiments of Fantz fail to prove that the baby at birth, or even in the first weeks of life, distinguishes forms or, for that matter, patterns; they merely show that he notes *differences*.

The discrepancy between the claims made by Fantz and my own (as well as von Senden's) findings is due to a difference in conceptual approach. What von Senden and I call "seeing" refers to an act of perception involving an apperceptive process, without which "seeing" (in the sense in which the adult perceives visually) cannot be achieved. This is quite different from what Fantz designates as "seeing." This statement is not arbitrary; it rests upon neuroanatomical and physiological givens, in that it is supported by the experimental work of von Holst (1950) in the visual sphere and that of Rosenblith (1961) in the auditory sphere. Owing to this apperceptive process man has, among others, the capacity to lay down mnemonic traces suitable to be reactivated as presentations, that is, as memories and as images; and also to activate such traces without the stimulus of a corresponding external perception. The above-quoted work of Fantz ignores apperception.

Again when Fantz claims that he has "disproved the widely-held notion that very young infants are *anatomically* incapable of seeing anything but blobs of light and dark" (italics mine) he is perfectly correct. *Anatomically* they are indeed capable of seeing more than just blobs. The eye is there, ready and willing; neuroanatomically and physiologically it does function. But this function does not extend to central processes, particularly to mentation. The *apperceptive* function is not yet available. It will be acquired through experiences provided in the course of affective exchanges with another person in the setting of object relations.

Von Senden's reports bear this out: throughout his case histories we find statements testifying that, in learning to see, the operated patients must be emotionally involved. It has to be realized, of course, that von Senden's conceptual framework is basically different from ours. He presents his findings as phenomena; he displays a strong bias against introspective psychology, as evidenced in his words: "The arguments of these two authors have inevitably seemed to me to smack too strongly of *introspective psychology,* so that I could not expect much profit from controversy with them" (italics mine). I believe that we may trust von Senden to have made every effort to remain objective at all cost. Yet he inferentially refers to emotions as "will to see," "courage and cheerfulness," and he states: ". . . his [the patient's] *will* must then be activated as strongly as possible in this direction. This direction will normally be much more readily retained by reshaping the *satisfaction of his daily needs"* (italics mine). Or in his conclusion: ". . . the patient's adaptation to his new surroundings often takes a highly dramatic form and leads to violent conflict." And then again: "For the patient needs this activity and emotional tensity."

Von Senden's work inspired an interesting series of studies by Riesen (1947) on the consequences of visual deprivation in man and chimpanzee.[2] Both in Riesen's and in Fantz's observations and experiments the role of emotion in perception is ignored. The reader will recall that we for our part consider emotion within the framework of object relations the most potent incentive for learning. It is obvious, for example, that in the cases cited by von Senden the capacity to see had to be slowly acquired through a learning process

[2] These fascinating experiments yielded many other highly relevant and interesting findings. It was shown, for instance, that apes deprived of vision for a number of weeks showed less interest in patterned objects than the babies of the same species at birth (Riesen, 1947). For a discussion of these findings in the framework of critical periods, see Spitz (1959).

in a setting of affective experience provided by object relations.

The various experiments and observations on the beginnings of perception, which I have discussed (including von Senden's and our own), refer to the conjunction of archaic mental processes with one sensory modality only, namely, vision. What about the other modalities? In von Senden's case material we have already noted that other sensory modalities were also involved. Indeed, in the first days after the operation the patients were unable to distinguish visual sensations from sensations originating in other sectors of the sensorium. But if this is so, where does perception as such really begin?

The Primal Cavity: Psychoanalytic Considerations

In the preceding pages we have posited that, at birth, the baby responds in effect only to sensations originating within his own body (that is, proprioceptive coenesthetic sensations); that he is protected from the intrusion of outside stimuli by the stimulus barrier. Von Senden's study shows that when stimuli impinge on the eye *before* it has learned to *see,* they are not meaningful. Moreover, the sensation is as generalized, extensive, and unlocalized as coenesthetic inner perceptions, and is actually not distinguished from them.

However, there is one perceptual zone which operates with great specificity from birth. In this zone sensory organs for stimuli coming from the outside meet with sensory receptors for stimuli coming from the inside. This zone is the mouth and the oral cavity. Already at birth, and even in the fetus, (Minkowski, 1922, 1924-1925, 1928; Hooker, 1939, 1942, 1943, 1952) a response to stimulation can be demonstrated in and around the mouth. Stimulation of the external part of the mouth region regularly elicits a specific behavior which consists in the rotation of the head toward the stimulus, followed by a snapping movement of the mouth. In the nursing infant this response eventuates in taking the nipple into the mouth. I have spoken of this behavior as the rooting reflex and discussed it in several of my publications; I have advanced the proposition that this behavior is predicated upon an innate releasing mechanism with survival value.

No reflex is fully reliable at birth. The rooting response, however, is less unreliable than the rest, second only to the clutch reflex, which consists in closing the hand on palmar stimulation. It is noteworthy that the rooting reflex in combination with sucking represents the only *directed* behavior of the infant at birth. This includes finger sucking and lends support to Hoffer's (1949, 1950) propositions on the hand-mouth relationship. Perhaps all the familiar reflexes (including rooting and clutching) are so unreliable at birth because they are provoked by stimuli coming from the outside, against which the stimulus barrier is still operating (see Chapter III). But when the nipple fills the mouth of the newborn, and milk flows through the pharynx, sensory receptors for the outside as well as receptors for the inside are stimulated simultaneously. This summative and compound stimulation appears to elicit a much more consistent and reliable response: the baby begins to suck and to swallow what he has sucked.

From the perceptual aspect, the oral cavity, including the pharynx, represents both outside and inside; it is equipped both as interoceptor and exteroceptor and operates accordingly. Because at birth the reflexes located within the oral cavity are the most specific and reliable of all; because these reflexes trigger the only directed, though not intentional, behavior in man, I have advanced the proposition that all perception begins in the oral cavity, which serves as the primeval bridge from inner reception to external perception.

These assumptions found a corroboration by way of convergence in certain propositions advanced and elaborated by Lewin (1946, 1948, 1950, 1953a, 1953b) and in those offered by Isakower (1938, 1954). Isakower (1938) studied the psychopathology of falling asleep. He concluded on the basis of his clinical observations in adults that the combination of the oral cavity with the hand probably represents the model for the earliest postnatal ego structure. He assumed, furthermore, that the sensations of the oral cavity are possibly merged with those of the external cutaneous covering. I consider that this threefold source of sensation and experience constitutes an ego nucleus in terms of the felicitous concept introduced by Glover (1930, 1932, 1933, 1943).

Lewin (1953a) quotes another author to the effect that "the original cavity might well be the inside of the mouth, as discovered and perceived by the suckling's finger" (p. 188). I agree with this formulation as far as it concerns sensation mediated by the inside of the mouth. I cannot share Lewin's view that the suckling's finger is capable of discovering or perceiving at this stage. As stated above, the only organ in the first weeks of life in which perception operates (and even here it is doubtful whether we are actually dealing with perception *as such* or whether this is reception, that is, a precursor of perception) is the oral cavity. The infant responds with a specific behavior sequence when something is introduced into the oral cavity, be it the nipple, the food, the finger. This ties in with Isakower's clinical observations on the sensations experienced by adults undergoing a regression of the ego while falling asleep. It is very convincing to assume that the gritty, sandy sensations (experienced while falling asleep) represent archaic memory traces of a primeval beginning of perception. They are analogous to the uncertain diffuseness and inappropriate quality of visual sensations described by von Senden's operated blind-born. The earliest external sensations perceived in the tactile field can be expected to be as incorrect as the sensations of von Senden's operated blind-born in the visual field. It is as convincing to find Isakower's subjects describing oral sensations as "gritty or sandy" as it is to hear von Senden's operated subjects describe visual sensations as "comparable to the smell of varnish."[3]

Our contention is that the oral cavity with its equipment of tongue, lips, cheeks, and nasopharynx is the first surface in life to be used for tactile perception and exploration. It is well suited for this purpose, for in it are represented the sense of touch, of taste, of temperature, of smell, of pain, and even of deep sensitivity, as the latter will be involved in the act of swallowing. It should be stressed that all perception which

[3] I believe that some propositions contained in my article, "The Derailment of Dialogue" (1964), may convey some understanding of these sensations. For instance, we might speculate whether the "gritty sensation in the mouth" (Isakower, 1938), the seeing of colors "much as we smell an odor of varnish" (von Senden, 1932) may not represent the perception of an overload of stimulation in two different sensory modalities, the tactile and the visual. The gritty sensation, the odor of varnish, carry with them a certain implication of the unpleasant. This fact is evident in its extreme form in Patient No. 17 who, four days after the operation, cannot keep his eyes open on account of his intolerance to light.

Individuals sensitive to sound will readily recognize the unpleasant sensations (of a nonmusical nature) which accompany an excessive volume of musical sound, such as that of a large choir in a closed space. Simultaneously with the music, they hear something like clattering pebbles, or the hissing sound of retreating waves on the beach. The phenomenon belongs to the category called "recruitment" in neurology. I suspect also that the photomata in migraine, the luminous serrated line which persons suffering from this affliction experience during the attack, belong to the same order of phenomena. Can these photomata be conceived as a response to an overload of sensory stimulation? Is it possible that the sensory process appears as a visual presentation without ideational or representational content, like the sound of clattering pebbles and the feel of grittiness in the mouth in the previous two examples? In all three cases, the tactile, the auditory, the visual example, the sensation is nonrepresentational; the actual sensory quality is distorted and is experienced as something unpleasurable, bordering on paresthesia. Again, this is reminiscent of the "pins and needles" we feel in a limb in which nervous conduction has been interrupted through pressure. The limb is felt as cold and numb. The "pins and needles" are the harbingers of returning sensation. They indicate that nervous conduction is not completely restituted and therefore cannot adequately cope with the stimuli with which it would deal under normal circumstances; but because of the interrupted conduction the otherwise normal stimuli become an overload.

takes place through the instrumentality of the oral cavity is still contact perception and thus basically different from distance perception, such as visual and auditory perception.

From Contact Perception to Distance Perception

Obviously a shift from contact perception to distance perception, from tactile to visual perception, is of paramount significance for the infant's development. This shift is mediated through the instrumentality of object relations. We mentioned how the infant stares *during nursing*[4] at the mother's face. Therefore, when the infant nurses at the breast, he *feels* the nipple in his mouth while at the same time he *sees* the mother's face. Here contact perception blends with distance perception. The two become part and parcel of one single experience. This blending opens the path for a gradual shift from orientation through contact to orientation through distance perception. The experiential factor in this shift is that during nursing, e.g., when the infant loses the nipple and recovers it, contact with the need-gratifying percept is lost and recovered, and lost and recovered, again and again. During the interval between loss and recovery of *contact* the other element of the total perceptual unit, *distance perception* of the face, remains unchanged. In the course of these repetitive experiences visual perception comes to be relied upon, for it is not lost; it proves to be the more constant and therefore the more rewarding of the two.[5]

---

4 At birth and in the weeks following it, nursing insures survival and is the best integrated of all directed actions—indeed, we may speak of it as the *only* directed, integrated action, though it is not a volitional one. We believe that the linkage between the principal survival-insuring *act* of nursing and the first learning situation for visual perception in man is of paramount importance.

5 Erikson would speak of the oral-contact experience as a zonal mode of functioning, the essential attribute of which is intake. It is then noteworthy that this zonal attribute becomes the hallmark of every function during the oral phase. I have discussed this aspect to a certain point (1955b) and called it cavity perception or primal perception. It also applies to visual perception.

This discrepancy between the two perceptual modalities (the discontinuous oral touch vs. the reliable, continuous, but not contiguous visual perception) probably has an even more fundamental significance than the establishment of visual perception as the leading perceptive modality in man. I believe that we have here the earliest beginnings of object constancy (Hartmann, 1952) and of object formation. From this modest beginning, object relations, both conscious and unconscious, progressively develop in the months and years to follow, involving not only the other perceptual modalities but also the vast variety of psychological functions.

The realization that the various modalities of perception (what we usually speak of as our five senses) are to a large extent inoperative at the inception of *perception as such* and have to be learned, opens up new avenues of investigation. We have seen in the case of visual perception that perceptive modalities follow each other in genetic sequence, so that distance perception (visual) develops later than contact perception (oral tactile). This could be (and in some mammals is) a function of maturation. In man, however, we were able to demonstrate this genetic sequence, beginning with the nursing situation, and to demonstrate the role of learning, of development, of object relations, in the course of the shift from contact perception to distance perception.

This finding prompted me to consider the heuristic proposition that development (both in the field of perception and in other areas of psychological growth) is subject to Haeckel's "biogenetic fundamental law" (formulated by Fritz Müller, 1864) according to which the organism, in its growth from the egg to the adult condition, recapitulates the stages which its ancestry passed through in the course of phylogeny.

It is a truism that eye and vision are a relatively late development in evolution and that they were preceded by contact perception and contact orientation. Realizing that such a principle may operate also in human psychological development, we may envisage the investigation of sequence, overlapping, and meshing in the development of the other perceptual modalities, hearing, taste, and also smell. There are many other possibilities to be investigated, for example, that some of these sensory modalities may have subclasses. To the attentive infant observer this is particularly clear in the field of visual perception, where some of these subclasses are evident at first glance. Among them we find, for instance, the category of color vision; that of spatial or depth perception; probably one of the earliest to become operative is the perception of movement; and probably simultaneous with it the perception of variations of luminosity. In the animal and in the adult these subclasses have been investigated extensively. There is as yet little known about their genetic sequence in man.

Under my guidance and supervision, my associates, P. Polak and R. Emde (1964a, b), have conducted a pilot study on the inception of three-dimensional visual discrimination (depth perception versus Gestalt perception). We have established that after the third month of life, depth perception begins to play a significant role. Between the ages of $0;2+0$ and $0;2+20$ (these are averages) the infant responds to stimuli which fulfill certain Gestalt qualities which are in motion, be they two- or three-dimensional. After the third month of life, the infant shows in his responses that he now distinguishes a three-dimensional Gestalt from the same Gestalt in two-dimensional projection.

Our findings also suggest that the progression from one subclass of perception to the next one is closely connected with and dependent on the particular conditions of the individual nursing situation. For nursing is that function which insures survival at this early age; therefore relatively small variations of the conditions of this function will exert a high degree of adaptive pressure. This very minor example points to the numerous possible lines of investigation within the *visual* field. Various of these aspects are under study by other investigators (Fantz, 1961; Gibson and Walk, 1960; Wallach, 1959; among others).

Research has also been going on in the other sensory modalities. We will only refer here to the sense of hearing. Goldfarb (1958), working with schizophrenic children, exposed them to delayed auditory feedback. They went into a panicky state corresponding to what Mahler (1960) called "disintegration." It would seem that these children experience this particular stimulation as a threat to the integrity of their person. One wonders whether the development and the integration of perceptual modalities has been disturbed in these children during a "critical period," so that the integration of the various perceptual modalities with one another either was only partially achieved or not at all. I have the hunch that in these children the shift from contact perception to distance perception, and more specifically to auditory perception, may have been delayed or severely disturbed in the course of infantile development.

The shift to distance perception does not supersede and even less abolish the role of contact perception, it only narrows it down. The addition of distance perception enriches the spectrum of perceptual sectors; it facilitates orientation and mastery; it expands the autonomous functions of the ego; and eventually contributes importantly to the primacy of the reality principle.

As yet we have examined only one of the several primordial perceptual centers in some detail, namely, the oral cavity. At this developmental level it overshadows all other such centers such as hand, labyrinth, and skin surface, because it is the only one that is really integrated and therefore operational. One might say with a certain justification that, like so many other animals, man also begins his approach to the perception of the surround rostrally.

It should not be forgotten that emotional qualities, namely, pleasure and unpleasure, partake in this perceptual experience. In addition, there are also dynamic qualities involved, those of activity and passivity. All of them emerge in response to a need which produces tension. This tension is reduced by need gratification, which then leads to quiescence.

Our work with neonates and our findings on the successive stages of perceptual development have caused us to introduce a slight modification of generally accepted psychoanalytic propositions. It has been assumed that the first "object" is the breast; Lewin (1946) concluded that the dream screen is its visual residue and the same was tacitly assumed by many regarding the Isakower phenomenon. I believe that the neonate is not capable of distance perception, only of contact perception through the oral cavity. It follows that the breast is indeed the first percept, but it is not a visual one; it is a contact percept—more specifically, it is an oral-contact percept.

THE PERCEPTUAL ACT AND THE THREE ORGANS OF PRIMITIVE PERCEPTION

Freud (1925a) spoke of perception as an action conceived in oral terms. He advanced the proposition that perception takes place through the ego periodically sending out small amounts of cathectic investment into the perceptual system, by means of which it samples the surround. The term in the German original is *"verkostet,"* which in English would be "tastes"; that is a clearly oral model; and Freud considers perception as an active process. We can thus consider it an action, just as behavior is so considered, and describe it in the terms introduced by Craig (1918), dividing it into appetitive and consummatory behavior. However, the neonate does not distinguish primal perception from need gratification. The two occur simultaneously and form part of the same happening, so that appetitive and consummatory behavior coincide

—mainly perhaps because of the nature of contact perception. At a later stage, through the acquisition of distance perception, a time interval is interposed between the act of perceiving and the consummatory act. From then on perception will be primarily restricted to appetitive functions. Much later defensive functions are added. For the time being, however, perception becomes the auxiliary of consummatory behavior and achieves survival value.

How does this relation between the appetitive character of perception and the consummatory character of behavior serving need gratification operate in the three ancillary organs of rudimentary perception present at birth?

Let us begin with the hand. Anybody who has observed a nursing baby knows how actively the hand participates in the act of nursing. The hand of the baby rests on the breast, his fingers moving slowly and continuously, clutching, stroking, clawing, and scratching.[6] In the following months, this activity becomes more and more organized, and it would seem that the rhythm of the closing and the opening of the baby's hand around the mother's finger is in some way related to the rhythm of his sucking. It is impressive to observe how the rhythmicity of these hand movements becomes increasingly organized in the course of the first six months.

Inevitably autoperception also will be involved here, though its role cannot be conspicuous in the beginning. It is possible that in the nursing neonate the movements of the hands on the breast are only a reflex response to palmar stimulation. However, very soon the intaking activity of the mouth will overflow into the activity of the hand. We may assume that this activity will soon be proprioceptively perceived. We mentioned above that Hoffer (1949) extensively discussed this relation between hand and mouth in the infant. His theoretical approach is confirmed by the clinical,

---

[6] This is the homologue in man of what is known in mammalians as "pressor movements" (Spitz, 1957).

experimental, and neuroanatomical data gathered by Tilney and Kubie (1931) and Tilney and Casamajor (1924). They demonstrated that in man the neural pathways connecting stomach, mouth, upper extremities, and inner ear with the central nervous system are operative at birth. Consequently, stimulation of any of these organs of which the mouth is the leading one will initiate specific behavioral patterns.

Hoffer's findings refer to a stage beyond that of the cavity perception. In a second article on this subject Hoffer (1950) introduced the concept of the "mouth-self." He postulates that this is the earliest self organization. In his opinion, this earliest self organization will be progressively expanded through the activity of the hand. Hoffer claims that the hand thus libidinizes various parts of the body so that they become the "body self." I do not share this opinion. I consider the hand only *one* of the means through which this libidinization is achieved. In a later chapter we shall discuss some of the other means serving the separation of the self from the nonself.

We are, however, in agreement with Hoffer's proposition on the function of earliest coordination of hand and mouth and its contribution to the development of ego functions and ego integration. In this capacity it represents one of the ego nuclei described by Glover (1932).

It is not any easier to disentangle appetitive and consummatory behavior in the other perceptive organs which operate in the nursing situation. In the case of the labyrinth, for instance, we know from experiments that by the eighth day of life a change of position will elicit the rooting and sucking response in the newborn. Prior to this, the response could be elicited only by touching the newborn's cheek. Lifting the baby into the nursing position induces a process in the labyrinth which can only be perceived proprioceptively. Needless to say, this is not a conscious perception at this early stage. It is a percept to which the organism reacts after the manner of the conditioned reflex.

Least of all is known about the performance of the third of the perceptive organs, the outer skin surface. That it has a major role in survival-directed, adaptive behavior appears probable in the light of propositions advanced by M. F. Ashley Montagu (1950, 1953, 1963). From a series of observations on nonhuman mammals (Reyniers, 1946, 1949; Hammett, 1922) he concludes that the skin possesses unsuspected functional significance for physiological and psychological development. Laboratory evidence has shown that in nonhuman mammals the licking of the young by the mother activates the genitourinary, the gastrointestinal, and the respiratory systems. In experiments with so-called "sterile" rats (rats raised in a sterile, bacteria-free environment) the animals all died until it was discovered that the parent animals had to lick their offspring's genitals, for otherwise the young could neither urinate nor defecate. This discovery made it possible to raise "sterile" rats from birth by using moist cottonwool to replace the licking by the parent animals. It has not been investigated whether these findings are also relevant for the problems of infant care in the human. But we should keep these observations in mind when our findings on "infantile eczema" will be discussed in Chapter XIII.

It appears that the sensations in the three ancillary perceptual organs present at birth (hand, labyrinth, skin) are subordinate to the central perceptual system of the oral cavity. Furthermore, in the neonate, they still operate jointly because differentiation between the various sensory modalities has not yet taken place. That is to say, sensations mediated by them merge and combine so that they are "sensed" by the neonate as a unified situational experience with the character of "taking in," of incorporating. Each of the organs mentioned participates in this experience.

THE PERCEPTUAL EXPERIENCE

This unified experience is of consummatory nature. It provides need gratification and tension reduction in the wake of a period of unpleasurable excitement; it also ushers in a period of quiescence marked by absence of unpleasure.

Furthermore, it is an iterative experience. For we are dealing with a reality in which this same cluster of sensations recurs in the same sequence morning, noon, and night, every day, five and more times a day, throughout the first few months of the baby's life; and in one way or another to the end of the first year and beyond.[7]

It is fair to assume that this iterative experience will from the beginning leave some form of trace, a "record" in the baby's nascent mind. In what form this record is stored, how it is modified, whether and how it influences or colors the infant's later perceptual experiences or gratifications is not known at this time. But the fact that this identical situation will recur during the major part of the baby's first year must necessarily lead to some form of psychic record; we will speak further on of two phenomena which appear to bear out this assumption.

That the first mnemonic traces are established only when an experience of satisfaction interrupts the excitation arising from an internal need was stated by Freud already in 1900 (see also Freud, 1925a). This experience of satisfaction puts an end to the internal stimulus which had caused a rise in tension.

In the grownup, the four spatially separated organs, mouth, hand, labyrinth, and skin cover, mediate dissimilar perceptual modalities. In the neonate, this is not the case. In Chapter

[7] The substance of these arguments derives from Freud's statement on the initial helplessness of the infant as the original source of all moral motives (Freud, 1895). This was elaborated in various areas by Bernfeld (1925), A. Balint (1954), Benedek (1952), and others.

III, I have already referred to my proposition that man's sensory, effector, emotional, etc., organizations are composed of two systems which (paraphrasing Head, Wallon, and others) I have called the coenesthetic and the diacritic systems. The coenesthetic system's sensations are *extensive* and mostly visceral; its effectors are primarily smooth musculature, its nervous organization comprises among others the sympathetic and parasympathetic systems. The diacritic system's sensations are *intensive* and involve the sensory organs; its musculature is striated and its nervous organization is subordinated to the central nervous system. However, in the neonate, the diacritic system has not begun to function in any appreciable manner. He perceives and functions primarily on the coenesthetic level.

In the adult, coenesthetic functioning produces sensations of a protopathic nature. The grownup is apt to experience many (though not all) protopathic sensations in a most unpleasurable manner—witness the stimulation of the labyrinth through a ship's motion in a storm, which can lead to vertigo, dizziness, and nausea, and ultimately to vomiting. Not so the infant; he tolerates vastly greater amounts of vestibulary stimulation. As we will see later, for him, vestibulary stimulation can serve as a conditioning stimulus. But in the grownup who gets seasick, we see an impressive exemplification of the connection between labyrinth, gastrointestinal tract, skin surface, hand, and mouth. For the symptoms of seasickness are vomiting, diarrhea, sweating and pallor of the skin, palmar sweating, and heavy salivation.

To the neonate, the simultaneous sensations in the four sensory organs (oral cavity, hand, labyrinth, stomach) are a proprioceptive total experience. To him all four are mediated through contact perception. Even the labyrinthine changes, though they take place inside the body, are close to the body surface, and occur in response to stimulation comparable to touch. Therefore they also have to be considered as being of the same nature as all other contact perceptions.

In the preceding section I discussed how maturation and development combine to bring about the shift from contact perception to distance perception. I stressed the role of frustration (in the nursing situation) in this process and how distance perception of the mother's face becomes differentiated from the unified experience of contact perception during nursing.

This proposition can be confirmed observationally; beginning with the fourth week of life, there is only one percept which the infant follows with his eyes at a distance, and that is the grownup's face. No other visual percept will produce this response. Thus the nursing experience, the nursing situation is not merely an experience of gratification. It initiates the transition from exclusive contact perception to distance perception. It activates the diacritic perceptual system, which gradually replaces the original and primitive coenesthetic organization.

REGRESSIVE PERCEPTUAL PHENOMENA IN THE ADULT

These observations on the inception of the perceptual function in the infant are in good agreement with, and indeed confirm, certain theoretical conclusions regarding regressive perceptual phenomena observed in the adult, notably the discoveries made by Lewin and Isakower. Lewin (1946) suggested a model for the structure of the dream which was not only highly original but proved clinically useful. He postulated that the visual memory of the breast constitutes a "dream screen," onto which the content of the dream is projected. I have discussed elsewhere (1955b), this trail-breaking contribution together with Isakower's important discovery of the phenomena named after him. Lewin bases his proposition on the wish-fulfilling nature of the dream, on the wish to ensure the continuation of sleep. He postulates that the wish fulfillment is achieved through a regression to the emotional state of the infant who goes to sleep at the mother's breast after having drunk his fill.[8] Lewin adds that in the so-called "blank dream" the dream-screen-breast actually becomes the content of the dream. He supports this proposition by numerous examples of patients' dreams. His theory has found extraordinarily wide clinical confirmation.

The dream screen is derived from a visual percept, from a distance perception. Actually in several of his publications on the dream screen, Lewin implies as much. As he was concerned with the dream, which is put together primarily from memory traces of visual percepts, it was to be expected that the dream screen also would make use of a visual memory trace, if an archaic one.

Isakower's approach is a different one. The phenomena he reports are by and large contact perceptions, and visual sensations are the exception. That again was to be expected, for Isakower's observations refer to the predormescent stage, in which cathexis has not yet been withdrawn completely from

---

[8] These are hypothetical reconstructions. Stern in a recent article (1961) considers it improbable that the Isakower phenomenon (and, by implication, Lewin's dream screen) might be a regression to a blissful memory of the nursing situation. (I would prefer to speak of a state of tension reduction and quiescence.) On the contrary, he advances the proposition that it is a regression to mnemonic traces of deprivation in the same situation. This is a plausible idea, if for no other reason than that experiences cathected with unpleasure are more likely to leave memory traces than those cathected with the affect of pleasure. However, a regression to such unpleasure-cathected memory traces implies a fixation point. I see no objection to such an interpretation either—what seems essential to me is the regression to the nursing situation. It will be difficult to determine whether the regression occurs to the blissful state or to the state of deprivation, for the simple reason that the Isakower phenomenon, Lewin's dream screen, and the observations mentioned by Stern all refer to the adult, so that secondary elaboration according to the subject's individual history has already taken place. Under the circumstances, the occurrence of severe anxiety and terror is not surprising—we see the same phenomenon in guilt-provoking dreams such as those involving incest. Moreover, what is a regression to the nursing situation if not a fantasied return to the original incestuous situation?

the representation of peripheral sensory organs (i.e., from the skin, the hand, the mouth), and from the representations of the haptic processes mediated by these organs (Spitz, 1955b). Some of his patients reported that in the predormescent stage they experienced sensations partaking of the mouth, of the skin surface, and of the tactile perceptions of the hand; they frequently had these sensations also when they had an elevated temperature. The sensations were vague and seemed to be of something wrinkled, or perhaps dry and gritty, soft, as if filling the mouth; at the same time this was felt on the skin surface of the body, and also as if it were being manipulated by the fingers. These sensations might at times be perceived visually as shadowy, indefinite, round, approaching and growing to enormous size—and then shrinking to practically nothing!

Isakower's observations suggest that two different kinds of psychic representation occur in the course of perception. One is that form of representation of which we speak in psychology as "percept"; it is mediated by our sense organs, it has an objectively describable, graphic content, and may or may not include the representation of the sensing organ itself.

The other representation is vaguer and more in the nature of a sensation; it contains perhaps a presentation of the sensing *process* itself, and of what derives from it. This second category of representation becomes conscious when special circumstances direct the attention to the process rather than to the sensory organ's percept. Such processes are discussed by W. Hoffer (1949), as well as by M. B. Bender (1952).[9]

Typical of this kind of experience are the strange sensations attendant on dental anesthesia. The anesthetized sector (e.g., the nasolabial fold, the lip, the inside of the cheek, the hard palate) is experienced as enlarged and as a foreign body. These unfamiliar sensations, akin to paresthesias, make us

[9] See Appendix for Piaget's explanation of "affective permanence."

aware of the perceptual process through its dysfunction. When the nasolabial fold, the palate, the lip, have become numb, and we touch them with our finger or tongue, the haptic processes taking place in the unanesthetized organ do not recognize the familiar anatomical configuration of lips or palate. This is because touching one's lips, etc., is recorded in our memory traces as a combined experience of the sensing process of both finger and lip. When the lip is anesthetized, one element of the sensation, that which should arise in the labial region, is missing or distorted.

I believe that the experiments of von Holst and Mittelstaedt (1950) on the principle of reafference are excellent experimental illustrations of the psychic representation of perceptual processes.

Such considerations suggest that memory traces, at least those of bodily perceptions, are laid down in the form of a configuration with Gestalt qualities. It should be remembered that in the terms of Gestalt psychology it is not only the visual Gestalt which is endowed with such qualities; for instance, the Gestalt psychologists mention melody as possessing these attributes.

If this proposition (which I advanced thirty years ago in regard to the nature of psychoanalytic free association) is correct, then the memory of a percept becomes conscious only when closure takes place. When, as in the case of anesthesia, closure is precluded through the deletion of a sufficiently large portion of the Gestalt, recognition does not take place. Instead, one more memory trace is laid down, that of a hitherto unknown experience.

This process has an obvious parallel in the psychoanalytic free association. The patient's memories remain meaningless until either analytic reconstruction or interpretation provides the missing part of the Gestalt. Every analyst is familiar with the sudden flash of insight and recognition which accompanies such interpretations. It is only natural that the patient loses the feeling of discovery within days: the reconstructed Gestalt actually was always there, an unconscious, but effective part of his psychological substance. The "interpretation closure" reintegrates the missing portion into its rightful place and perspective, just as if it had never been missing. Before reintegration it exercised its influence outside of the checks and controls of the conscious ego, only subject to the regulation of the pleasure-unpleasure principle. Reintegrated into the fund of conscious memories, it will now be subject to the regulation of the ego and the reality principle. This proposition, though far from being the whole of the therapeutic process, seems to me to be a valid explanation of the effectiveness of emotionally correct analytic interpretation.

Furthermore, the proposition of the Gestalt quality of memory traces (and among these, of free association) and the necessity of closure to provide them with the quality of consciousness takes up again an old proposition of Freud, that of the different registration of the same content in different psychic localities (Freud, 1915a). Freud discarded this suggestion in favor of the dynamic proposition of hypercathexis of the thing-presentation. But like so many of his half-abandoned suggestions, it seems to me that, with some new light shed on it, it is not only viable but also fertile for our understanding of perception, of memory, of the thought process, and of therapeutic effectiveness.

Some of this new light derives from the Isakower phenomenon. The sensations his patients reported have much in common with those I have described in dental anesthesia. But without anesthesia, how do we account for the disappearance of one part of the memory Gestalt during the falling-asleep process? In a paper on falling asleep and waking up (Spitz, 1936b) I advanced the proposition that during the process of falling asleep cathexis is progressively withdrawn from the periphery and from the peripheral sensory organs. In that paper I used a hydrostatic model to explain what happens when the general level of drive investment is lowered. Certain sectors of the sensory apparatus remain invested, because the level of drive investment is still sufficiently high to supply them with cathexis. Others at the same time have already lost their cathexis, emerging like dry islands from the retreating flood of drive investment. Thus, while certain sectors of the sensorium, like the visual one, or olfaction, have already lost their sensibility, others remain operative for a while. Indeed, the latter may appear to mediate sensations of a different nature and to react more intensely (that is, to weaker stimuli) than when we are awake; these still operative sensory sectors appear both qualitatively and quantitatively modified in their sensibility. I further used this assumption to explain the sensibility increase in certain areas of sensory perception; this is very characteristic, for instance, for the excitation stage of general anesthesia. The areas I mentioned at the time were pain perception and auditory perception. One might speculate whether these areas refer to more primitive, more archaic sensory modalities which, in the course of this regressive withdrawal of cathexis, will be the last to be abandoned.

It should be added that this discussion of the representation of the perceptual process in the predormescent stage does not refer to Silberer's (1911) work on symbolic representation; he postulated that the *symbolic* representation of mental processes often forms the manifest content of hypnagogic and hypnopompic hallucinations. Symbolic representation plays no role in the Isakower phenomenon; it consists of traces of sensations experienced during the nursing process. The crude sensation itself is repeated without any effort on the part of psychic censorship to edit it and to achieve a secondary elaboration, making it conform to the demands of intelligibility and logic and ultimately to the reality principle. In Lewin's dream screen such efforts are discernible when the visual experience is translated into something that "makes sense."

My observations on infantile development suggest a modification of both Lewin's and Isakower's assumptions. Their propositions were achieved by means of extrapolation from the analysis of the dreams of adults and from hypnagogic or predormescent sensations. In my opinion, these extrapolations and the conclusions drawn from them are correct, except as to the degree of regression which these phenomena indicate. Both Lewin and Isakower based their propositions on Freud's assumption that the first object in life is the breast. They concluded that in the dream the regression to the breast would be indicated by the dream content. By and large the dream has a visual content and Lewin's examples, with the exception of the blank dream, are visual ones. Direct observation, however, shows that the first structured visual percept in life to be crystallized out from "the various kinds of light blurs—with no shape to anything or distance" (von Senden, 1932) is the human face.

As already mentioned, up to three months of life (and longer) a nursing baby will look not at the breast but at the mother's face. This is an observational fact. He does not look at the breast when the mother approaches him, he looks at her face; he continues looking at her face while he has her nipple in his mouth and is manipulating her breast. From the moment the mother comes into the room to the end of nursing he stares at his mother's face.

Accordingly I would modify also Isakower's proposition as follows: from the *visual* point of view the Isakower phenomenon does not represent the approaching breast but rather the *visually* perceived human face. The *tactile* phenomena reported by Isakower—the mouth feeling something which is also felt on the skin surface of the body and manipulated by the fingers, corresponds to the baby's experience of *tactile* contact with the breast, with *mouth, oral cavity, hand,* and *skin surface.* The Isakower phenomenon is to be considered a totality experience, the synesthesia of several sense organs.

Thus, in the beginning the oral cavity constitutes the cradle of perception. The unmodified memory traces of these perceptions will form the essence and the major part of the Isakower phenomenon. Modified and expanded they will also be instrumental in mediating memory traces, which will later become the template of the dream screen of Lewin. In the dream screen we have the baby's amblyopic perception of the face; in the Isakower phenomenon we have the baby's synesthetic contact perception in the oral cavity, the hand, and the skin.[10]

While the Isakower phenomenon is a reactivation of the record of early infantile contact perception, the dream screen re-evokes the inception of distance perception. How these beginnings are elaborated, developed, and established will form the subject of subsequent chapters.

AFFECTS AND EMERGENT PERCEPTION

Up to here I endeavored to acquaint the reader primarily with the little-understood observational material from this archaic developmental stage, as I and other authors have been able to gather it over the years. In my discussion I have so far advisedly not dealt with the role of affects in this early

---

10 This explanation, though slightly modifying Lewin's proposition on the dream screen, at the same time discourages specious argument. For in our age of the automated nursery, it could be objected that most babies have never seen the breast, only the bottle. But Lewin's concept of the "breast" actually is a code symbol for the totality of the oral experience as I have elaborated it above. Whether the food object actually is mediated by the mother's breast or through the rubber nipple of a disposable plastic bottle, the essential element of the cavity experience remains (though the rubber nipple does not convey the exquisitely human reciprocity response). Furthermore, even when bottle feeding her child, the mother's face still provides the visual factor, her hands and body the tactile experience, which go into Lewin's dream screen and into the Isakower phenomenon. But "modern progress," undaunted, has succeeded in overcoming these last vestiges of human relations with one's child by inventing the bottle propper and strapping the infant to a cradleboard. I will be interested in finding out what happens to the dreams of a generation whose upbringing has been automated in this fashion.

development, even though affects, observable and diversified, figure prominently in the content of this book.

It is true that in the neonate, affects are observable only in their crudest form; we are hardly justified in calling them "affects," which is why I spoke of excitement of negative quality and of its counterpart, quiescence—both in the nature of precursors of affects.

Yet the crudeness of these precursors of affects does not make them less effective. The pressure exerted by these archaic experiences may be brutal, but in effect it enforces adaptation. How brutal this pressure can be one only realizes in extreme cases. Since all neonates produce the "birth cry," we consider this an unimportant and normal detail of delivery. We rarely stop to think that this first vocalization of the neonate is at the same time his excruciated gasp to take air in before he chokes.

In this example the need and the need gratification are so conspicuous that it is impossible to overlook them. In examining the genesis of the infant's first perceptions we have been made aware that they arise as a function of need and need gratification. In the circadian rhythm of the neonate's life, needs recur repetitively at brief intervals in one form or another. Their gratification is not always immediately forthcoming.

Between the sensing of need and its disappearance through need gratification delays are frequent. These delays play a major role in adaptive development. The frustration attendant upon the delay is at the origin of adaptive behavior and of one of the most important adaptive devices, namely, memory traces and memory.

In discussing reality testing Freud (1925a) points out that this is a question "of whether something which is in the ego as a presentation can be rediscovered in perception (reality) as well"; he goes on to say a few lines further: "it is evident that a precondition for the setting up of reality testing is that objects shall have been lost which once brought real satisfaction."

In the earliest development of perception, in what I would call the primal perception mediated by the oral cavity, we witness a constant ebb and flow of the two primary affects, the affect of unpleasure and the affect of pleasure, in the wake of mounting need and of its gratification.

In the newborn the oral region and the oral cavity have two very different functions, both of paramount importance for survival. One is *intake,* which ensures the immediate physical survival of the *individual.* The second function is *perception,* which in the neonate also begins at the rostral end, the oral region and in the oral cavity. From here perception will branch out into its five executive modalities, into touch, taste, smell, seeing, and hearing. Therefore the central representation of the oral and perioral region becomes the leading adaptive organization serving the survival of the *species.* Small wonder that it becomes the field of operation for the earliest dynamic processes, for earliest drive activity—the observable indicators of this activity are the affects of which I spoke above.

It follows logically that the further development of perception will also be closely linked with affect. That this is so is evident from a series of developmental milestones in the genesis of distance perception, of diacritic discrimination, of the smiling response, and in their developmental sequence. As will be shown further on, affect is the trail breaker of development; that goes for the development of perception as well as for that of all other functions.

Independently from our own findings, however, experiments on adults (Bruner and Goodman, 1947; Levine, Chein, and Murphy, 1942; Sanford, 1936, 1937) have shown that need (which, of course, provokes the affect) intrudes on and distorts perception and warps reality into something approaching wish fulfillment. This, however, is only the far end of the spectrum of the influence of affect on perception.

Every psychoanalyst will confirm that perception is constantly influenced by the prevailing affective tone of the subject. This does not have to reach actual wish fulfillment. Affect colors perception, it makes perception important or unimportant, it endows the various percepts with valency; for instance, in scotomization (Laforgue, 1930), it excludes some percepts, while it enhances others. Ultimately affects determine the relation between perception and cognition.

This is the reason why in science we try to exclude the role of affects and try to reduce perception to the reading of a scale. This method, which I consider reductionistic, has produced extraordinary results in the physical sciences; indeed, it has been dubbed *"the* scientific method." But when this method of mensuration, of quantification is applied indiscriminately to the living subject, particularly to man, it will in the end arrest the advancement of knowledge. We are reminded of Augustine's lament quoted at the beginning of Chapter II. In the living subject, and particularly in man, affects, affects first and last, serve to explicate behavior and psychological happenings. And affects have so far defied measurement.

CHAPTER V

The Precursor of the Object

Incipe, parve puer, risu cognoscere matrem!
—Virgil, *Georgica*

THE SMILING RESPONSE

Beginning with the second month of life, the human face becomes a privileged visual percept, preferred to all other "things" of the infant's environment. Now the infant is able to segregate and distinguish it from the background. He invests it with his complete and prolonged attention. In the third month, this "turning toward" in response to the stimulus of the human face culminates in a new, clearly defined, species-specific response. By this time the progress of the infant's physical maturation and psychological development permits him to coordinate at least one part of his somatic equipment and to use it for the expression of a psychological experience: he will now respond to the adult's face with a smile. Except for the infant's following the human face with his eyes in the second month, this smile is the first active, directed, and intentional behavioral manifestation, the first indicator of the infant's transition from complete passivity to the inception of active behavior, which henceforth will play an increasingly important role.

In the third month of life, the baby responds to the adult's face by smiling if certain conditions are fulfilled: the face must be presented straight on, so that the infant can see both eyes; and the face must move. It is immaterial what part of the face or of the head moves, whether the movement is head nodding, mouth movement, etc. At this age level, nothing else, not even the baby's food, provokes this response. To be sure, if you present to a bottle-raised child the selfsame bottle full of milk, nipple and all, a marked change will frequently occur in his behavior. Infants advanced beyond their chronological age will stop their activity, at times they will perform sucking movements with their mouths. At times they will try to extend their arms in the direction of the bottle; but they will not smile at a bottle. Developmentally less advanced babies may not even change their behavior; yet to the face of the adult they will respond with a smile.

We made a detailed experimental study of this phenomenon (Spitz and Wolf, 1946). We investigated a population of 145 children from birth to twelve months. This population was diversified according to ethnic, social, and national background as shown in Table III. Each of these children was observed according to the method described in Chapter II. In addition, the infants were exposed to a number of stimuli and experimental situations at regular intervals.

It was established that the smiling response appears as an age-specific behavioral manifestation of the infant's development from the age of two months to the age of six months.

TABLE III

SMILING RESPONSE ACCORDING TO ENVIRONMENT
AND RACE

| | Institution | | | Private Home | | |
Response	White	Colored	Indian	White	Indian	Total
Smile	53	26	23	14	26	142
No Smile	1	1	—	1	—	3
TOTAL:	54	27	23	15	26	145

Under the conditions specified above, 98 per cent of the infants smiled during this period in response to the face of any individual, friend or stranger, regardless of sex or color (significant above the 0.1 percentile level of confidence).

Chronologically this response is strictly limited. Before two months of age, that is, between birth and the end of the second month, only 2 per cent of our infant population smiled in *response* to the presentation of *any* stimulus (significant above the 0.1 percentile level of confidence).

At the opposite end, after the age of six months, the vast majority of our infant population did not smile any more when the stimulus that had elicited their smile between two and six months was presented to them by a *stranger*. Thus in the second half of the first year indiscriminate smiling responses at the grownup's face ceased in more than 95 per cent of our population. In less than 5 per cent of the infants observed by us this smiling response continued. In other terms, children before the age of two months will not smile *reliably* at anybody, or anything; the same children, after reaching the age of six months, reserved their smiling response for their mothers, for their friends, in one word, for their love objects, and would not smile at strangers.

EXPERIMENTAL FINDINGS

We traced and investigated the elements and meaning of the stimulus which provokes the infant's smile between the end of the second month and that of the sixth month. We examined whether and how this smile is related to the infant's object relations. It was established that the smiling response of the infant in the third month of life, his recognition of the human face, does not indicate a true object relation. Actually, in this response the three-month-old perceives not a human partner, not a person, not a libidinal object, but only a sign.[1]

---

[1] A definition of the term "sign" will be given later.

True, this sign is provided by the human face, but, as our other experiments have shown, it is not the totality of the human face with all its details which constitutes the sign, but rather a privileged Gestalt within it. This privileged Gestalt consists of forehead, eyes, and nose, the whole in movement. This finding has since been confirmed by the investigations of Rolf Ahrens (1954).

That the infant responds indeed to a Gestalt and not to a particular person is proved by the fact that his response is not limited to one individual (such as the mother) but that the individuals to whom he responds with a smile are freely interchangeable. Not only the child's mother, but anybody, male or female, white or colored, can at this stage elicit the smiling response if he fulfills the conditions required by the privileged Gestalt which acts as trigger for the response.

An extremely simple experiment can be performed to show that what triggers the smile is a sign Gestalt which consists of a circumscribed part of the face. In this experiment contact is made with a three-month-old by smiling at him and nodding one's head; the infant will react by smiling, by becoming active and by wriggling (Fig. 5). One now turns one's head

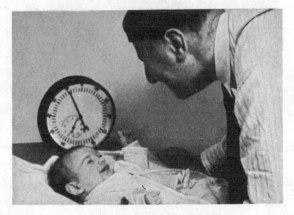

FIGURE 5
Reaction to the Smiling Face.

into profile, continuing to smile and to nod; the infant will
stop smiling, his expression becomes bewildered (Fig. 6). Developmentally advanced infants frequently seem to search
with their glance somewhere in the region of the experimenter's ear, as if searching for the eye which disappeared;
sensitive children appear to respond with a kind of shock, and
it takes time to re-establish contact. This experiment shows
that the three-month-old is still unable to recognize the
human face in profile; in other words, the infant has not
recognized the human partner at all; he has only perceived
the sign Gestalt of forehead, eyes, and nose. When this Gestalt
is modified through turning into profile, the percept is no
longer recognized; it has lost its tenuous objectal quality.

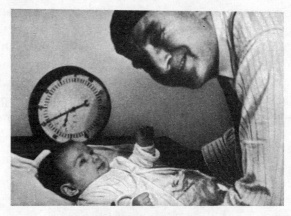

FIGURE 6
Reaction to the Face in Profile.

We studied the properties of the Gestalt which we considered to be the releasing stimulus. We did this by eliminating
one or the other single element composing it (e.g., by covering one eye, by presenting the infant with a nonmoving face,
etc.). We then replaced the human face with an artifact (a
mask made out of cardboard). This was found to be just as

effective as the human face in eliciting the smile of the three-month-old. It had the further advantage of lending itself much more easily to modifications, thus permitting us to isolate the essential elements of which the privileged Gestalt has to consist in order to be effective.

As a result of these experiments, we came to the conclusion that the smile of the infant between three and six months is elicited not by the face of a human being, but by a Gestalt indicator, a sign Gestalt.

If we relate this finding to the system of psychoanalytic theory, it is obvious that the sign Gestalt is not a true object; I have therefore called it a *preobject*. What the infant recognizes in this sign Gestalt are not the essential qualities of the libidinal object; not the attributes that motivate the object to minister to the infant's needs, to protect and gratify him. What he recognizes during the preobjectal stage are secondary, external, unessential attributes. He recognizes a sign Gestalt, which is a configuration within the human face—not within a specific individual face, but within any face presented to him straight on and in motion.

The recognition of an individual face is a later development; it will take another four to six months before the baby becomes able to single out one face among the many; to endow the face with object attributes. In other words, the baby then becomes able to transform what was only a sign Gestalt into his own unique individual love object. This is the outwardly visible indicator of the intrapsychic process of object formation, the observable part of the process of establishing a libidinal object.

The sign Gestalt, which the infant recognizes at the three-months level (as indicated by the emergence of the reciprocal smiling response) is a transition from the perception of "things" (which is our term for the "object" of academic psychology) to the establishment of the libidinal object. The latter is distinguished from the "things," and also from the preobject, by having been endowed with essential qualities in the course of mutual exchanges between mother and child. In these exchanges, the object, or rather what is to become the object, is progressively invested with libidinal cathexis. The individual *history* of these cathectic investments, that is, the genesis of the essential qualities, which characterize the libidinal object, distinguish it from the "things." The essential object qualities owe their relative immutability throughout the vicissitudes of life to this genesis. Their external attributes are unessential and therefore may be modified, as already mentioned. Conversely, external qualities *only* constitute the attributes of "things"; they do not possess the more essential historically developed attributes. Therefore any change, any modification, of these external attributes makes the recognition of the "thing" problematic or impossible.

Sign Gestalten actually are the hallmark of "things," their integral attribute. As such they are permanent; but this external permanency is incompatible with the characteristics of the libidinal object. It follows that the sign Gestalt to which the infant responds at the age of three months will not endure. However, because this sign Gestalt is elaborated into a signal in the course of the unfolding of object relations, it will be endowed with a quality transcending "thing" attributes. It is thus assured of a place in the "embryology" of the libidinal object developed from it.

In support of these propositions experiments just as convincing and simple as the profile experiment can be performed by presenting a cardboard Halloween mask to the infant. Motion pictures (Spitz, 1948a) of these experiments show that at three months, the infant smiles as readily at the Halloween mask as he does at the human face (Fig. 7) and that the smile will stop when the mask is turned into profile (Fig 8).

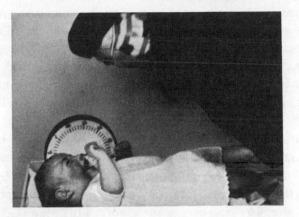

FIGURE 7
Reaction to the Mask Straight-On.

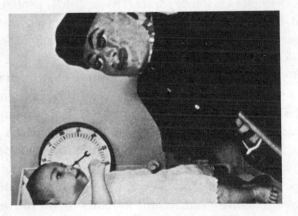

FIGURE 8
Reaction to the Mask in Profile.

We carried out further experiments with the purpose of discovering what elements in the facial configuration are indispensable to trigger the smiling response.

We concealed various parts of our face successively with a piece of white cardboard and then presented it (in motion) to the infant. When the lower part of the face was covered, the smiling response could be elicited as before. If, however, the upper part of the face, including the eyes, or only one of the two eyes was covered, the smiling response could not be elicited. If one or both eyes were covered while the infant was smiling at the experimenter's nodding face, the smiling response stopped abruptly.[2]

These experiments showed conclusively that it is not the individual human face as such, or even the human face as a whole, but a specific configuration *within* the face which triggers the infant's smiling response. This configuration consists of the forehead-eyes-nose sector. This sign Gestalt is centered around the eyes. It is my opinion that the eye part of this configuration is in the nature of the key stimulus of an IRM as defined previously (Spitz, 1955c, 1957), probably with survival value. This opinion has been supported by the experiments of Ahrens (1954) on man, and of Harlow on rhesus monkeys (personal communication, 1961).

Finally, it is of interest to mention here that in the course of our experiments we succeeded in working out a supernormal stimulus (Tinbergen, 1951). For the human infant the supernormal stimulus consists in replacing the smile on the nodding face of the observer by extreme widening of the mouth, somewhat after the manner of a savage animal baring its fangs. This supernormal stimulus elicits the infant's smiling response more readily and reliably than the nodding smiling face. It may be assumed that we have here an addi-

---

[2] My associates and I have continued this experimentation in view of clarifying further details in the natural history of the smiling response. The essential findings, like the age of onset and waning of the response, the stimulus which triggers it, etc., were supported by these experiments. Additional findings were made which may yield further information on the emergence and on the functioning of the infantile psyche. For instance, new information has become available through our recent experiments on the beginning of depth perception (see Chapter IV). For the discussion of some of our findings, see Polak, Emde, and Spitz, 1964, 1965).

tional stimulus which follows the law of *heterogeneous summation* (Seitz, 1940; Tinbergen, 1951).

It might be asked why the triggering stimulus has to be in motion. A detailed discussion of this question would lead us far into phylogeny and animal psychology. But in a general way I would be inclined to advance a tentative proposition. It is not so much that the triggering stimulus has to be in motion, but rather that motion is part and parcel of the triggering stimulus. Motion is the most effective way to separate figure from background. As was seen from the experiments reported, the triggering stimulus has Gestalt properties; motion appears to enhance them. This is why I consider it probable that motion is part of, and belongs to, the innate key stimulus of the IRM of the smiling response.

All this sounds quite mechanical: sign Gestalten, releaser mechanisms triggering innate responses. The reader may well ask: couldn't a mechanical doll, fitted with the sign Gestalt, rear our children just as well? No, it could not; and we will explain in the subsequent chapters why not.[3] Suffice it to say for the time being that, although the innate equipment is available to the baby from the first minute of life, it has to be quickened; the vital spark has to be conferred on the equipment through exchanges with another human being, with a partner, with the mother. Nothing less than a reciprocal relation will do. Only a reciprocal relation can provide the experiential factor in the infant's development, consisting as it does of an ongoing circular exchange, in which affects play the major role. When the infant experiences a need, it will provoke in him an affect that will lead to behavioral changes, which in their turn provoke an affective response and its concomitant attitude in the mother; she behaves "as if she understood" what particular need of the infant causes his affective manifestation (Spitz, 1962, 1963a, b, c). A rela-

---

[3] Harlow, in a series of experiments on Rhesus monkeys, has proved exactly this (Harlow, 1959, 1960a, b, c, d, e, 1962; Spitz, 1962, 1963a, b, c).

tion between a mechanical, automatic doll and the baby would be one-sided. It is the mutual give and take, its single elements constantly changing and shifting (though its sum total remains the dyadic relation), which represents the essence of what we are trying to describe and to convey to the reader.

The reciprocal feedback within the dyad between mother and baby, and baby and mother, is in continuous flux. The dyad, however, is basically asymmetric. What the mother contributes to the relation is completely different from what the baby contributes. Each of them is the complement of the other, and while the mother provides what the baby needs, in his turn (though this is less generally acknowledged) the baby provides what the mother needs.

FROM PASSIVE RECEPTION TO ACTIVE OBJECT RELATIONS

What we have stressed in the last paragraphs of the preceding section leads to an inescapable conclusion. From the beginning of life it is the mother, the human partner of the child, who mediates every perception, every action, every insight, every knowledge. We have brought some proof of this in the area of visual perception. When the eyes of the child follow each movement of the mother; when he succeeds in segregating and establishing a sign Gestalt within the mother's face—then, through the mother's instrumentality, he has segregated a meaningful entity within the chaos of meaningless environmental "things." Owing to the continuing affective exchanges, this entity, the mother's face, will assume for the child an ever-increasing significance.

The process of selecting a meaningful entity from the universe of meaningless things and establishing it as a sign Gestalt is in the nature of a learning process. It is a transition from a state, in which the infant perceives only emotionally, into a more differentiated state, in which he perceives in a discriminative or, as I prefer to say, in a diacritic manner. Our films show impressively how the mother's breast, her fingers, offer the nursling a host of tactile stimuli; how these stimuli give him the opportunity of learning and practicing perception and orientation; how the infant experiences superficial touch, deep sensitivity and equilibrium on the body of the mother, and in response to her movements; and it is hardly necessary to add that it is her voice which offers the infant vital acoustic stimuli which are the prerequisites for the development of speech.

In passing, it is worth mentioning that the acquisition of speech, which begins in the course of the first year of life, is a complex process. It involves both perception and energy discharge. As a psychological phenomenon, the acquisition of speech provides us also with further information about the infant's transition from a state of passivity (in which tension discharge obeys the pleasure-unpleasure principle), to one of activity in which discharge as such becomes a source of gratification. With this step, activity in the elementary form of play activity begins to contribute to development. The vocalization of the infant, which at first serves to discharge tension, undergoes progressive modification until it becomes a game, in which the child repeats and imitates sounds which he has produced himself. In the beginning the infant does not discriminate between the sounds coming from the surround and those which he produces himself. As a result of maturation, the various sectors of the perceptual organs become segregated from each other in the course of the first two months of life. At some point in this process, chronologically around the third month of life, the infant becomes aware that he can listen to the sounds he produces himself and that the sounds he makes are different from the sounds coming from the surround. The sounds from the surround he cannot influence. But he has it in his power to entertain himself by producing his own interesting noises or stopping to produce them.

It seems to me that this must be one of the first activities in which the infant experiences his omnipotence. Now the child begins to listen to his own vocalization. Vocalizing as such still retains its quality of discharge, of tension reduction, of pleasure. But a new pleasure has come into his life: the mastery of producing something which he can receive as a stimulation, in another sector of the sensorium. Now, after the third month of life, we can observe the infant's experiments with this mastery, his babbling monologues. Soon we notice how the infant produces sounds, mostly of the rhythmic, repetitive variety, linguals and labials, carefully listens to them and repeats them again and again, creating his own echo, the first acoustic imitation. Six months later, he will use this experience when he imitates sounds heard from his mother.

This sequence also illustrates a minor detail of the transition from the narcissistic level, on which the child takes himself as object, to the level of object relations proper. At the end of the first year, when the child repeats sounds (and words) originating in the mother, he has replaced the autistic object of his own person with the object in the outside world, with the person of the mother.

At the same time such games are the substratum of another aspect in the inception of developing object relations. The repetition of sounds, first those originating in the child and later in the mother, will, step by step, and hardly noticeable to the observer, assume the role of semantic signals. But before this comes to pass, major dynamic transformations have to take place and completely new structures have to be organized in the infantile psyche.

THE ROLE OF AFFECT IN THE MOTHER-CHILD RELATION

Once again we are compelled to return to the beginnings and to discuss the all-encompassing role of the mother in the emergence and unfolding of the infant's consciousness and her vital part in his learning processes. In this context the importance of the mother's feelings about having a child, and her own child in particular, can hardly be overrated. That these feelings vary over an exceedingly wide gamut is known, but not sufficiently appreciated, for the vast majority of women become tender, loving, dedicated mothers. They create what I have called the *emotional climate* in the mother-child relation, favorable in every respect for the development of the child. What creates this climate are the mother's feelings toward the child. Her love and affection for her child makes him an object of endless interest for her; and out of this unflagging interest she offers him an ever-renewed, rich, and varied gamut, a whole world of vital experiences. What makes these experiences so important for the child is the fact that they are interwoven, enriched, and colored by the mother's affect; and to this affect the child responds affectively. That is essential in infancy, for at this age affects are of vastly greater importance than at any time later in life. During his first few months affective perception and affects predominate in the infant's experience, practically to the exclusion of all other modes of perception. From the psychological point of view, the sensorium, the perceptive apparatus, sensory discrimination have not yet sufficiently developed. Indeed, much of this apparatus has not even matured. Therefore, the mother's emotional attitude, her affects will serve to orient the infant's affects and confer the quality of life on the infant's experience.

Manifestly there are endless variations from mother to mother. To make matters even more complex, within herself, each individual mother is different from day to day, from hour to hour, from situation to situation. The infant's individual personality impinges on this changing pattern in a circular process, influencing the gamut of his mother's affects by his behavior and by his attitudes. According to the mother's personality, it will make a vast difference whether

her child is precocious or retarded, whether he is an easy or a difficult child, whether he is compliant or obstreperous.

This is illustrated by the smiling response which appears in the third month of life. However, that age is just a statistical average. The earliest smiling response recorded in our films appeared already in a twenty-six-day-old infant. On the other hand, the smiling response may appear also much later, in some children only in the fifth or sixth month. It is self-evident that such differences will decisively influence the emotional climate of the mother-child relation. The smiling response is only one example, and a minor one at that, among the variety of behaviors and behavioral manifestations which govern the multiple relations developing between the infant and the mother.

Take, for instance, another example, the infant's feeding behavior. By and large the smiling response permits only of two alternatives: it is either there or it isn't. By contrast, the varieties of feeding behavior on the part of the infant are numberless. We have the good eater, who takes his meal rapidly, completely, with gusto, and falls asleep after the last mouthful. We have the bad eater, who has to be coaxed endlessly and does not seem to be eating what he should; or the child who is satisfied with his four or five meals daily and then sleeps through the night as against the brat who refuses his last evening meal but then demands repetitive meals in the course of the night; and so on and so forth. Obviously these differences in the baby's attitude will shape the dyadic relations. A permissive mother will react differently from a rejecting or hostile one; a secure mother differently from an anxious or a guilt-ridden mother. It is equally obvious that the mother's problem will reverberate in the infant's behavior, leading under certain conditions to an escalation of the conflict. An example of the pathology to which disturbances of the mother-child relation can lead will be given under the heading of the three-month colic.

It could be objected that the mother is not the only human being in the child's environment, not the only one who has an emotional influence, that his environment comprises father, siblings, relatives, and others, who all may have an affective significance for the child. Even the cultural setting and its mores have an influence on the child already during the first year of life. All this is self-evident; however, we do not always remember that in our Western culture these influences are transmitted to the child by the mother or her substitute.

For this reason I have concentrated my own research primarily on the problem of mother-child relations. Furthermore, throughout the first months of life and even in the first years, the mother-child relation is that psychological factor which is most readily amenable to a therapeutic and to a prophylactic intervention, and therefore deserves our most assiduous study and our special attention.

In the mother-child relation the mother represents the environmental givens—or one might say that the mother *is* the representative of the environment. From the child's side the givens are comprised in the congenital equipment of the infant, which consists of *Anlage* and maturation.

Under no circumstances can we neglect the significance of neural development, both embryologic and epigenetic, during the first months and years of life. Without maturation of the nervous system, behavior patterns and actions would be impossible. Many functions undergo changes as the result of the interaction of physiological maturation with psychological development. To a certain extent these changes are independent from the environment; for a considerable number of maturational sequences and series are innate. We will not discuss this here as the investigation of these problems is not germane to our present study.

For our present purpose, the relevant factors are: on the one side the mother, with her mature, structured individuality; on the other, the child, whose individuality is being progressively unfolded, developed, and established; the two are in an ongoing circular interrelation with each other. Both mother and child do not live in a vacuum, but in a socio-economic milieu, the primary referents of which are the members of the immediate family, whereas its more distant referents consist in the ethnic group, the culture, the technology, the national setting, the historical period and tradition. We will come back later to the discussion of the two really essential "factors" which form the symbiotic mother-child couple (Benedek, 1938, 1949; Mahler, 1952). All these considerations have made it amply clear that object relations lead from the emergence of the preobject to the endowing of the mother with the qualities of the libidinal object. We will now examine the consequences of establishing the pre-object and in the course of our further chapters discuss in greater detail the nature, the composition, and the vicissitudes of the object relations in preparing those psychological structures which ultimately lead to the establishment of the libidinal object.

THEORETICAL SIGNIFICANCE OF THE ESTABLISHMENT OF THE PREOBJECT

The consequences and the significance of the establishment of the first precursor of the libidinal object are the following:

a. This is the stage at which the infant turns from what I have called *reception* of stimuli coming from the inside to the *perception* of stimuli coming from the outside.
b. This transition is predicated on the infant's achieving the capacity temporarily to suspend the unconditional functioning of the pleasure-unpleasure principle, which demands his undivided attention to the stimuli coming from inside. Instead he can now suspend this demand long enough to cathect the presentation of external stimuli which are transmitted by the sensorium. In short, the reality principle has begun to function.

c. The fact that the infant is now able to recognize the human face and to indicate this by smiling in response to it shows that memory traces have been laid down. This implies that a division has taken place in the psychic apparatus. We call its constituent parts *Cs., Pcs., Ucs.* In other words, we now can begin to apply the topographical viewpoint.

d. It further shows that the infant has become capable of displacing cathectic charges from one psychic function to another, from one memory trace to the next. The recognition of the sign Gestalt implies a cathectic shift from the percept's sensory presentation (human face in the present) to the percept's comparable memory trace (human face perceived in the past).

e. The ability to shift cathexes from memory trace to memory trace (comparing "What is laid down inside as an image with what is perceived outside" [Freud, 1925a]) corresponds to Freud's definition of the thought process.[4]

f. This whole development also marks the inception of a rudimentary ego. A structuration has taken place within the somatopsyche. Ego and id are separating from each other and the rudimentary ego begins to function. The awkward, mostly unsuccessful, yet manifestly directed and intentional actions which the child begins to perform are the indicators of this functioning. From the beginning they serve mastery and defense. The rudimentary ego's steering operation is reflected in the increasing coordination and direction of the muscular activity. Freud (1923) called this rudimentary ego *body ego.* It will become part of what Hartmann (1939) called "the conflict-free sphere of the ego."

---

4 In his article "Formulation on the Two Principles of Mental Functioning" Freud (1911) described thinking as follows: "It is essentially an experimental kind of acting, accompanied by displacement of relatively small quantities of cathexis together with less expenditure (discharge) of them." In the paper on the Rat Man, Freud (1909) defined thinking as follows: ". . . processes of thought are ordinarily conducted (on the grounds of economy) with smaller displacements of energy, probably at a higher level [of cathexis], than are acts intended to bring about discharge or to modify the external world." Freud introduced this proposition in his "Project for a Scientific Psychology." He elaborated this in the same book in greater detail (1895) as well as in the Chapter VII of *The Interpretation of Dreams* (1900).

At the same time we can observe already in this archaic precursor of the ego a tendency to synthesis. This tendency has been described by various authors from different viewpoints. The most widely accepted description is that of Nunberg (1930), who called it the synthetic function of the ego. Hartmann's (1950) concept of the organizing function of the ego represents, I believe, only a different aspect of the same tendency.

As I have stated elsewhere (Spitz, 1959), I believe that this tendency is a general one in living matter. I have spoken of it for the first time in 1936, and called it "an integrative tendency"; it leads from the organic, that is, from embryology, into psychology and into the developmental sphere. My ideas were stimulated by Glover's (1933, 1943) proposition of the concept of ego nuclei. In his earliest formulation he spoke of a "model or prototype of an independent autonomic primitive ego-nucleus" (Glover, 1932). The example he gave was the oral system gratifying the instinct on the "object" (mother nipple). This concept agrees completely with my own; I think of constituent parts of the ego which have as their prototype innate, mostly phylogenetically transmitted physiological functions as well as innate behavior patterns. Later Glover (1943) appears to have revised his concept somewhat and eliminated from it all reference to a prototype, physiological or otherwise, defining it purely in psychic terms. However, he adds the idea that from the first the psyche has a synthetic function which operates with progressively increasing power.

Regarding the psyche's synthetic function I am again in complete agreement with Glover, though I place the age level of the formation of a rudimentary ego much earlier than he, namely, at three months of life. And I am still convinced that the transition from the somatic into the psychological is uninterrupted and that therefore the prototypes of psychic ego nuclei are to be found in physiological functions and somatic behavior. Examples of these are the IRM-like function of the percept of the sign Gestalt in bringing about the smiling response; or the rooting reflex and its different roles, on the one hand from the point of view of appetitive behavior, on the other from that of consummatory behavior (Spitz, 1957); or the sleep-waking pattern (Gifford, 1960); and many others.

These *prototypes* of ego nuclei, more or less autonomous at birth, will serve the neonate subsequently in his preobjectal interchanges with the mother. In the course of such interactions they are modified as a result of cathectic investment, endowed with psychic content, and transformed into *psychic ego nuclei.*

At the three-month level, a major integrative step takes place, which pulls many of the discrete ego nuclei together into a structure of a higher order of complexity, forming the rudimentary ego.

While being itself the product of the integrative forces which operate in living matter, the ego in its turn becomes a gravitational center of organization, coordination, and integration. Its gravitational power increases exponentially as a function of the increasing number of ego nuclei which it succeeds in integrating into its structure.

Isolated ego nuclei, relatively powerless at first, pulling at cross-purposes, become an ever-growing force when working jointly in the same direction, complementing, supporting, and reinforcing one another.

    g.   The protective function of the stimulus barrier is taken over by the emerging ego.

At birth the uncathected condition of the sensorium constitutes the stimulus barrier (Spitz, 1955b).[5] It follows that both progressive maturation of neural pathways and growing

---

[5] See also Freud (1917b), ". . . a complete emptying of a system renders it little susceptible to instigation. . . ."

cathexis of central representation of sensory receptors will gradually lower this threshold which protects against external perception. Concomitantly, cathectic processes set in motion through the activity of the ego nuclei lead to their synthesis, resulting in a rudimentary ego; that is, in a central steering organization. The rudimentary ego will now replace the crude threshold protection of the stimulus barrier by the superior and more flexible one of selective processing of incoming stimuli.

Energy charges evoked by incoming stimuli can now be fractioned, distributed among the various systems of memory traces, placed into storage; or, as the case may be, discharged in the form of directed action and no longer only as random diffuse excitation. The capacity for directed action leads the infant to a rapidly progressing development of a diversity of ego systems, beginning with the body ego, to which others are added later. Directed action proper becomes not only an outlet for the discharge of libidinal and aggressive energy, but also a device to acquire mastery and control through the psyche, thus expediting development. In the literature this function of directed activity, of actions as such, in promoting development during the first year of life has not been duly considered. We speak often enough of the aggressive drive; it is rarely spelled out that the aggressive drive is not limited to hostility. Indeed, by far the largest and most important part of the aggressive drive serves as the motor of every movement, of all activity, big and small, and ultimately of life itself (Spitz, 1953a).

That portion of aggression which is channeled into goal-directed action will have to overcome obstacles, but it may also encounter facilitations in achieving its aim. The manner in which this aim is achieved determines the action patterns that will emerge and their structure. In proportion to their success, such action patterns will be preferred to the random discharge of aggression; later on these action patterns will lead to the consolidation of a variety of ego apparatuses (e.g., locomotion, speech, etc.). It seems to me that a closer study of these early action patterns, how they are acquired in the framework of object relations, and how they influence them is desirable. The dynamics underlying the establishment of such action patterns might make a significant contribution to a psychoanalytic theory of learning.

   h. Even the naïve observer, unburdened by theory, cannot fail to be impressed by the infant's shift from passivity to directed activity at the stage at which the smiling response appears.

   i. Finally, the emergence of the smiling response initiates the beginning of social relations in man. It is the prototype and premise of all subsequent social relations.

I have listed nine aspects of a global phenomenon which can be conceived of as marking the point of transition from the primary narcissistic stage to the stage of the preobject. We will take as our point of departure the convergence of these nine facets of the phenomenon and in the following pages examine a few of them in detail. We must not lose sight, however, of the fact that at this point, at three months of life, psychic structure is still at its inception, the ego rudimentary, and object relations at the preobjectal stage.

CHAPTER VI

The Plasticity of the Infantile Psyche

The first year of life is the most plastic period in human development. Man is born with a minimum of preformed behavior patterns and has to acquire countless adaptive skills in the course of his first year. The adaptive pressure is powerful, development rapid and sometimes stormy. Never again in later life will so much be learned in so short a time.

During this period the infant passes through several stages, each representing a major transformation from the preceding one. The emergence of the smiling response marks the end of the first of these stages, that of nondifferentiation, which is also the stage of the newborn's greatest helplessness. I consider this very helplessness to be one of the reasons for the plasticity of the infantile psyche. Another is the absence, at least in the first six months of life, of a solidly established, dependably functioning ego organization.

After the stage of complete helplessness and passivity of the first three months the infant passes through a stage during which he explores, probes, and expands the territory gained up to this point. This probing is carried on through constant exchanges and interactions with the preobject. Not that these interactions were absent previously; but now they have acquired new characteristics, because the infant has progressed to directed activity and to structured action. Now action patterns are exchanged between the child and the libidinal object-to-be, and in these interchanges the infant experiences and establishes the limits of his current capacities. Step by step he expands the boundaries within the confines of which he translates the pressure of his aggressive and libidinal drives into directed actions.

TRANSITIONAL STAGES

In chemistry, the phenomenon of elements combining into compounds is spoken of as being *in statu nascendi,* for at this stage the bond between the compounds is labile. It is no mere figure of speech to say that, in spite of having already been born, in his first year the infant also is still *in statu nascendi.* Following the transition from the objectless stage of undirected activity to that of ego-directed structured activity, a second transition will usher in another, higher level of integration. The path from one such level to the next is of necessity one of trial and error, and therefore the transition is beset with pitfalls.

During a transitional stage, the infant's experiences have more far-reaching consequences than at other periods when his psychic organization is more stable. If the infant is exposed to a trauma during these transitions, specific and sometimes serious consequences will ensue. I am using the term "specific" with good reason. Each transitional stage is vulnerable to some traumata but not particularly vulnerable to others. In the most general terms, this is so because in each transitional stage, adaptive devices[1] are developed which are optimally appropriate for it. However, at the beginning of a transitional stage, the new devices are not quite ready; and so the organism must make do with the devices carried over from the previous stage even though they are no longer suit-

---

[1] "Adaptive devices" connotes here both behavioral patterns and psychological mechanisms for the processing of stimuli; it even covers the ego's mechanisms of defense.

able for the new tasks. The result is an interregnum, a sort of twilight zone in which the organism understandably will be more vulnerable than either during the period preceding it or in that which follows it. Relatively minor adversities, which would have hardly been noticed at, let us say stage two, and dealt with summarily at stage four, will assume the valency of a trauma during the transitional stage. Each successive (transitional) stage apparently has its own set of age-specific adaptive devices.

I shall return to the topic of age-specific vulnerability in subsequent chapters; for the time being I would like to illustrate the fact that one and the same stimulus takes on entirely different meanings, one and the same experience is differently perceived, experienced, interpreted, and responded to, according to the stage at which it is being encountered. This difference is often fundamental.

Changes in Meaning and Response

This is something with which the psychoanalyst is exceedingly familiar. A primal-scene observation at the oedipal stage, in puberty, or during climacterium has a completely different significance, from the point of view both of how it is understood and what its consequences are for the beholder. The differences are just as great for the infant if we compare one and the same experience at successive transitional stages of infancy.

We conducted the following experiment:[2] our standardized stimulus for eliciting the smiling response at the three-month level is a Halloween mask of a grinning face, presented in nodding motion. We presented this mask to Jessy when she was three months, seven and a half months, and fourteen months old. These age levels were not chosen at random: they are three successive periods at which the average infant

[2] This experiment was recorded in the film on the smiling response (Spitz, 1948a).

progresses from one level of psychological integration to the next higher and more complex one. Jessy responded as follows:

1. At the three-month level, the device provoked a smiling response.

2. When the mask was presented to Jessy at seven and a half months, the child laughed at the mask, approached it without fear, tried to pick the marbles serving as eyes off the mask, while actively attempting to climb onto the observer's knee.

3. At fourteen months Jessy was as usual in good contact with the female observer. The observer now placed the mask on her own face. The child's expression became terrified; she turned away screaming, and ran into a corner of the room. When the mask was removed from the observer's face, the child appeared reassured, but refused to touch the mask. Later, Jessy was persuaded to touch it, she handled it and started to bite the mask's eyes.

How should we interpret the difference between these three responses of one and the same normal, healthy child in the light of object relations and ego development?

In the first experiment, we see a child in transition from the objectless to the preobjectal stage. In this transition the sign Gestalt of two eyes, forehead, and nose, in motion, signals the approach of the need-gratifying object. The mask fulfills the conditions of this sign Gestalt. Accordingly, the response to the mask is positive: the child smiles.

In this same transitional period a first rudimentary ego has been integrated from a number of scattered ego nuclei.[3]

---

[3] Such as the ego nuclei relating to food intake combining the somato-psychic representation of the oral region, the hand, etc.; the ego nuclei created in relation to visual perception during the need gratification of food intake; the ego nuclei relating to tactile perception, particularly around the oral region, but extended to the whole of the body, connecting also with ego nuclei related to the equilibrium stimuli of change of position; and finally from the cross connections established between these and probably many other ego nuclei at this developmental level.

In the second experiment the child is just in the transitional stage from the response to a sign Gestalt to the stage of recognizing and distinguishing the libidinal object proper. The sign Gestalt has not yet lost its effectiveness, nor has the libidinal object proper achieved exclusiveness; the child smiles at the sign Gestalt (the mask), approaches it actively, and explores it. She involves the observer, whom she has accepted as a "friend," into her play with the mask and initiates a lively action exchange.

Jessy's ego has made enormous strides from the three-month level; through her experiences in the course of the intervening object relations, she has tested and expanded her limits. Now her ego has become a central steering organization. Her body ego obeys her volition and is instrumental in carrying out her intentions.

But this body ego is now only a part, an apparatus of a larger ego organization, an apparatus subservient in the unfolding conative sectors of that ego which in their turn are being activated by recently developed affective structures. We realize that what we are dealing with now has already become a surprisingly complex psychic organization, although it is rudimentary if compared to that of a mature person. Still, this is the inception of the ego proper, as we are wont to speak of it in psychoanalytic terms.

This development permits Jessy the freedom to use the mask in a reciprocal game with the observer. Such reciprocal action exchanges are now manifestly in the center of the child's object relations.

In the third experiment the picture has changed again and we witness an entirely new development. Object relations with the mother have now been firmly established. Furthermore, the dyad has begun to lose its exclusivity as a form of social relations. New layers are being added to the core of the original "mass of two"; subordinate object relations with various "friends" are emerging. But these "friends" are still recognized by their external attributes, foremost among these the familiar face. In the terms of Ferenczi (1916), the stage of omnipotence of thought has not completely lost its sway. It has not yielded its rule to that of the sense of reality. Magic is still the most potent force in the infant's universe. Causality, logical process, do not have the compelling power they will acquire later. Thinking operates instead on the lines of identification, introjection, projection, and similar mechanisms. As long as the child is convinced that he can and does change the world around through omnipotence of thought he will believe that everybody else can do the same. Witness the little two-year-old girl who, on seeing the sun disappearing after a spectacular sunset turns to her father: "Do it again, Daddy!" At this age every grownup is a magician, because the child himself is a magician, even though not quite as successful a magician as the grownup.

When at fourteen months Jessy had become the observer's "friend," it was no longer unimportant that the observer's face suddenly change into the mask of a "horrible stranger." The face (and the mask) as a sign Gestalt had already lost its effectiveness. Instead, the individual face of "mother," "father," "friend" had come into its own. And when the "friend's" individual face magically changes into a "stranger," the child runs away, screaming and terrified. Jessy has lost her "friend," a stranger has appeared out of nowhere; worse, the "friend" has turned into a changeling stranger.

When the mask is taken off again and the "friend" is restored, Jessy, after some cajoling, accepts her friend again. Leaning against her friend, secure in this body contact, she even accepts being cautiously introduced to the mask in the hand of the observer. But her feelings against the wicked sorcery of the mask persist and Jessy begins to bite the eyes of the mask.

In Piaget's terms, Jessy has only partially achieved *reversibility*. That is in agreement with Piaget's observations (1947);

the reversibility which the situation confronting Jessy would require will be achieved only at a much more advanced age than fourteen months, according to his experimental findings (see Appendix).

It is of interest to consider the ego's role in the three situations.

Situation No. 1: at the three-month level, the performance of the rudimentary ego was limited to perceiving, recognizing, and responding to the need-gratifying sign Gestalt with a smile. The rudimentary ego cannot discriminate between friend and stranger; even less can it protect the child from danger. Notwithstanding these limitations, the rudimentary ego is able to operate adequately because the mother acts as an *auxiliary ego,* external to the child (Spitz, 1951).

Situation No. 2: what has changed in Jessy's ego? At the age of seven and a half months, her ego is no longer just a rudiment, barely discernible, barely capable of coordinating a perception with some memory traces, and of responding with an expression of positive affect. At this stage the structure of the ego begins to show, and it has assumed the role of a central steering organization. Now it mediates between the child's instinctual drives, which have become more differentiated and are expressed in the form of affectively colored needs, desires, strivings, and avoidances. These are channeled into motor action and affective expression, for the ego begins to assume the role that it will retain throughout life: that of controlling access to mobility. In this sense the ego is in the act of assuming one part of the mother's role, that of achieving the baby's strivings. But it has not yet taken over mother's protective role. The strivings Jessy is carrying out in our little experiment are her wishes for closeness and exchanges with her friend, her exploratory curiosity about the new toy her friend offers her and which carries the magic sign Gestalt.

Situation No. 3: Jessy is now fourteen months and eight

days old. A radical change has taken place in her ego. Thought processes going far beyond the simple fulfillment of strivings are in evidence: the observer has remained her trusted "friend." When the observer dons the mask and turns into a changeling stranger, we witness the ego in its new role, as the *protector;* the ego now gives the signal of danger (Freud, 1926a); anxiety and flight ensue.

I believe that this series of observation illustrates well many aspects in the child's development. From a rudimentary beginning as a body ego we have witnessed its development first into the executive, and then at the next step into the protective organization of the child's person, the "watcher" as Anna Freud (1936) calls it.

A Basic Difference between Infant and Adult

But this series illustrates also the vast differences in the infant's response to one and the same stimulus in the successive stages. It is self-evident that a given percept or experience has an entirely different meaning at three, at eight, and at fourteen months. Each stage has an age-specific[4] set of problems to solve, and threats to cope with.

Not that the child during the first year of life is such a delicate, fragile being. It is clear from the aforesaid that at given stages only certain stimuli and not all stimuli, even if spectacular, are relevant. Correspondingly, only certain experiences have an influence fraught with significance at given stages during infancy.

What I am trying to convey is something not easily grasped by the adult. The infant is not comparable to the adult. His physiology is different; so are his sensations, his physicochemical reactions, his way of experiencing the surround. Indeed, what the infant can take in his stride may be fatal for

---

4 Actually we should call it "stage-specific"; the age at which a given stage is reached varies individually in rather wide limits.

the adult and vice versa. To deprive an adult of oxygen for fifteen minutes is a catastrophy, resulting in death. To the infant during delivery, this is a normal and even necessary condition.

The confusion arises from the fact that this difference is selective, it does not apply equally to every sector of the organism, it is not even uniform within a single sector. It does not mean, for instance, that the newborn is protected from all harm and suffering. He cannot tell what he suffers; but that does not imply that he does not suffer. Indifference, lack of empathy, and lack of imagination have resulted in unbelievable cruelty to infants. I have learned some years ago, for instance, that surgeons in leading hospitals routinely perform mastoidectomy without any anesthesia on defenseless infants.

We may suspect, though we have no proof for it, that such thoughtless brutality has consequences going beyond its immediate effects. I believe that it was Claude Bernard who said, "La douleur tue comme l'hémorrhagie." This may not fully apply here, for the infantile psychic organization appears to tolerate pain better than that of the adult. But it is my conviction that such traumatization can leave unsuspected psychological scars which make themselves felt at a later age. One is reminded of Phyllis Greenacre's propositions in her articles on the predisposition to anxiety (1941). I would suggest, however diffidently, to surgeons and pediatricians at large that they at least make an attempt to work out a physiologically harmless method of anesthesia which should be used as a matter of course in any surgery on infants.

If some experiences which are catastrophic for the grownup are reacted to far less severely by the infant, the opposite is also true. Modifications of the surround, seemingly of minor significance to the adult, can under certain well-defined circumstances (Spitz, 1950b) exert a profound influence on the infant, with serious consequences which sometimes even lead to major pathology. The moving scenes in Robertson's film *A Two-Year-Old Goes to Hospital* (1953) convey some idea of the milder consequences of hospitalization of infants.

Beginning in 1944, I have reported, both in motion pictues and in articles, a series of observations on emotional traumatizations which are even more severe than those recorded by Robertson. For the adult, such experiences would seem to present no threat; but in infancy they may constitute a traumatization which can endanger the helpless infant's life, particularly during critical transitional stages, such as occur toward the end of the first year of life.

Development in the first year of life does not proceed in a smooth, even curve. Instead, we can note at certain regularly recurring specific stages a change of direction in this curve. These changes correspond to a reorganization of psychic structure, which is followed by the emergence of new aspects and capacities of the personality. Each of these successive stages reflects a transition from a given level of development to the next higher one, and is marked by more elaborate differentiations of the mental apparatus. My study of these fundamental transformations led me to introduce a new concept to account for the factors which govern this process. I have called these factors "organizers" of the psyche, a term borrowed from embryology (Spitz, 1954, 1959).

THE EMERGENCE OF THE FIRST ORGANIZER AND ITS CONSEQUENCES

In embryology the concept of organizer refers to the convergence of several lines of biological development at a specific location in the embryonic organism. This leads to the induction of a set of agents and regulative elements called the "organizer" which will influence subsequent developmental processes. Needham (1931) speaks of the embryological organizer as a pacemaker for a particular developmental axis; it is a center radiating its influence. *Before* the emergence of such organizers, a piece of tissue can be transplanted from one part of the body, say from the eye region, to a completely different part, for instance, to the dorsal skin, where it will develop identically to the surrounding epidermis; that is, it will also become epidermis. However, if the same tissue is transplanted *after* the organizer for the eye region has been established, the transplant will develop as eye tissue, even in the midst of the dorsal epidermis.

About thirty years ago I advanced the proposition that analogous processes with *concomitant critical nodal points* were operating also in the *psychic* development of the infant. The findings made since in my longitudinal studies on several hundred infants have lent support to my proposition, so that I have attempted to formulate it more precisely and to apply it to subsequent age levels.

Independently from my own research, the existence of critical periods in the course of development has been confirmed by the work of Scott and Marston (1950) with the help of animal experimentation. I believe that Glover was the first among psychoanalysts to introduce the concept of "critical phases." He applied this concept to drive vicissitudes in adult instinctual life. Later Bowlby (1953) applied this proposition to the growing organism.

My observations show that during these critical periods the currents of development will be integrated with one another in the various sectors of the personality as well as with the emergent functions and capacities resulting from the processes of maturation. The outcome of this integration is a restructuration of the psychic system on a higher level of complexity. This integration is a delicate and vulnerable process, which, when successful, leads to what I call an "organizer" of the psyche.

In the preceding chapter I described the visible signs of the establishment of one of these organizers; its *indicator* is the appearance of the reciprocal smiling response. I repeat: the smiling response as such is merely the visible *symptom* of the convergence of several different developmental currents within the psychic apparatus. The establishment of the smiling response signals that these trends have now been integrated, organized, and will thenceforward operate as a discrete unit within the psychic system. The emergence of the smiling response marks a new era in the child's way of life; a new way of being has begun, basically different from the previous one. This is a turning point which is clearly visible in the child's behavior.

These turning points, these organizers of the psyche, are of extraordinary importance for the orderly and unimpeded progression of infantile development. If the child successfully establishes and consolidates an organizer at the appropriate level, his development can proceed in the direction of the next organizer.

However, when the consolidation of the organizer miscarries, development is arrested. The psychic systems which should have been integrated through interaction with the surround will remain at the inchoate, less differentiated level of development prior to the establishment of the organizer. Meanwhile, however, maturation continues at the steady rate and on the path prescribed in the inherited Anlagen. The latter are far less susceptible to the influence of, and better protected against, external interference than are developmental processes.

Therefore a disturbance in the unfolding of the infant's personality will ensue: for an imbalance in the equilibrium between the forces of development and those of maturation has arisen. This type of imbalance is, to a large extent, limited to the first years of life and arises most frequently in them. With advancing age its incidence decreases, to disappear completely after puberty. The maturation-development imbalance is greatly facilitated by the plasticity of the infantile psyche.[5]

THE ROLE OF THE EGO

Another reason for the plasticity of the infant's personality during the first year of life is the lack of well-established and well-differentiated psychic structure. Psychoanalytic theory states that the ego is that sphere of the psyche which mediates the relations between inside and outside, the transactions between internal world and surround. A variety of psychic systems and apparatuses in the ego serve mastery and defense, that is, they accomplish the discharge of unnecessary or even harmful tensions, the exclusion of unwelcome stimuli, the intake of desirable stimuli, the adaptation to stimuli, the removal of stimuli, and numberless other possible interchanges with the environment.

The newborn, however, has no ego (Freud, 1914b). He cannot deal with incoming stimuli and is protected against them quasi automatically by the high perceptive threshold of the stimulus barrier. However, when the incoming stimuli are sufficiently powerful, a break-through of the stimulus barrier occurs which may modify the as yet undifferentiated personality of the infant.

In the further course of development, rudimentary beginnings of ego constituents arise in connection with the primordia of the ego. On the one hand, ego nuclei are integrated, on the other a progressive lowering of the perceptive threshold takes place. Stimuli coming from outside now begin to modify this rudimentary personality organization. They compel it to react and to initiate a formative process. In its course the infant's responses are gradually coordinated and integrated into a loosely coherent structure. This process precedes

[5] For a more detailed discussion of this topic see Spitz (1959).

the beginnings of the rudimentary ego, on which will devolve the task of subsequently dealing with stimuli arising from outside and inside. The further development of the ego's structure, of its effectiveness, of its reserves in tenacity and strength, will be slow and gradual. In the course of months and years of constant interchange, the ego deals with the incoming stimuli and masters them. How a given ego is structured and organized is determined by the manner in which the environmental and internal stimuli are mastered; the experiences which impinge on the still plastic personality of the infant are used to modify this selfsame personality. An unending and gradual process of modifications unrolls here, which we have hardly begun to explore. However, it is not easy to convey the manner in which the infantile personality is molded. The formative forces are not violent ones; in the following chapters we will examine them in greater detail.

CHAPTER VII

The Role of Mother-Child Relations in the Infant's Development

In the preceding pages we have explored the neonatal and infantile personality from various viewpoints. These viewpoints cannot be separated from one another; actually they are only different aspects of an indivisible whole. In exploring these various aspects in succession, it is this whole which we are exploring from different angles: from the angle of maturation, when we are speaking of sequences and of the progression from sequence to sequence; from that of structure, when we speak of an ego; and lack of structure, when we speak of the infant's plasticity; from the viewpoint of development or that of adaptation, when we examine the inception of a psychic organization. What we call "infant" comprises much more: in the first place, the congenital equipment, which is then subject to dynamic processes; we have referred to these when we spoke of their manifestations in the form of affects—the very elements which will confer life and initiative on the totality "infant."

ACTION EXCHANGES IN THE MOTHER-INFANT DYAD

The formative influences originating in the surround (i.e., in the mother) are directed at this living, responding, and developing totality. We shall now turn our attention to the

122

interrelations and interchanges operating between the totality "infant" on the one hand and these formative forces on the other. We shall first examine actions and responses of the infant elicited by the mother. I use the term "eliciting" not only in the sense of a conscious intention of the mother, but rather in the sense of the mother as an ever-changing stimulus, an opportunity, a gradient. The existence of the mother, her mere presence, acts as a stimulus for the responses of the infant; her least action—be it ever so insignificant—even when it is not related to the infant, acts as a stimulus. Within the framework of object relations, those activities of the mother which provoke observable responses from the infant are the grossest and more easily noticed forms of stimulus interchange within the dyad. We shall speak of more subtle forms later. Meanwhile we can begin by stating that during the first year of life experiences and intentional actions are probably the most important single influence in the development of the various sectors of the infant's personality. The infant derives pleasure from the process of discharging his instinctual drives in the form of actions. Anyone who watches an infant's behavior is familiar with his manifest delight when he is released from the constriction of his swaddling clothes; and the baby's pleasure is further increased when a partner, the mother, participates in his antics. His striving toward the partner is obvious and with the passing weeks becomes increasingly directed. Success increases his pleasure; and he will repeat and ultimately master success-specific behavior. On the other hand he will abandon actions which lead regularly to failure.

This is a mode of learning. It is analogous to the process known in academic psychology as "trial and error," reinforced by "reward and punishment." A further reinforcing factor is that those actions of the infant which are pleasing to the mother are facilitated by her; and it follows that her preferences will have a directing influence on the baby's development. If her attitude is maternal and tender, she enjoys practically all of her baby's activities. Her affects, her pleasure, her own actions, conscious or unconscious, facilitate innumerable and varied actions of her baby. I believe that the largest measure of facilitation for the infant's actions is provided not by the mother's conscious actions but rather by her unconscious attitudes.

These attitudes stem from two different sources. One of these might be termed, with a felicitous concept coined by the Hampstead Nurseries, the "sector of controls."[1] This sector shows, on the whole, a close affinity to the demands of the mother's superego. The other sector largely expresses the aspirations of the mother's ego ideal. I have spoken of the latter attitude as the facilitations offered by the mother for the child's activities and his development. The sector of controls, as its name implies, is a restricting influence; the sector of facilitations is a liberating, encouraging, progressive force.

This is by no means a hard and fast division. Unquestionably the demands of the superego will impel the mother to encourage achievements also. In the same way the aspirations of the ego ideal persuade her to withhold the facilitations from activities of which she disapproves. But on the whole one can say that, while controls restrict, facilitations encourage. Though controls and facilitations are essential for development, the proportion in which they are applied depends on the inborn personality of the child. The controls as well as the facilitations provided to the child from the outside will enable him to develop and establish his own controls, some of which lead to defense mechanisms. The controls and defense mechanisms developed by the child are indispensable for his becoming a social being.

But despite these reservations we have been guilty of over-

1 See G. Bibring et al. (1961) and Sandler (1961).

simplification. No mother is "either-or"; in psychic life there can be no black and white. What we have attempted to describe so far are the contradictory currents operating in the relations which the "good, normal mother" establishes with her child.

Yet there also exist mothers whose deviant personalities may have a pathogenic influence on their children's development. In subsequent chapters we will have occasion to speak of such deviant maternal character structures, particularly of their pathogenic aspects.

Returning to the "good, normal" mother-child relations, it must not be overlooked that there is a gradient not only from the mother to the child, but there is also one going from the child to the mother. As stated above, the very presence, the very existence of the mother calls forth responses in the baby. But so do the baby's existence and presence evoke responses from the mother.

A significant part of these responses does not conform to the popular image of motherhood. The psychoanalyst is well aware of the struggle, the effort, the turmoil involved in bringing under control infantile behavior, wishes, fantasies. These the child must conquer to become an accepted member of his society. For the mother, witnessing and condoning infantile behavior reactivates all the guilty and at the same time delectable fantasies which she has had to conquer.

When I was working in an orphanage where foundling babies were cared for by Catholic Sisters of Charity, I listened with amusement to the scandalized exclamation of one of the Sisters who on diapering a baby had found him in erection: "Oh, look at the little pig!" The admixture of gaiety in the tone of indignation was unmistakable. Far from being innocent in the sense in which the term is used for grownups, the child gives free expression to his drives, whether socially acceptable or not. That goes for sexuality as well as for aggression, for oral as well as for anal behavior. Therefore the sanctimonious slogan of the "innocence of childhood" simply reflects a denial of facts. We are denying that witnessing infantile activities places a strain on our superego. For the grownup, the road back to the instinctual freedom of infancy is prohibited and perilous.

It follows that the mother has to defend herself against the gamut of seductions offered by her baby. Her relations with her child mobilize the entire armamentarium of devices offered by the defense mechanisms; she will deny, displace, turn into the opposite, scotomize, repress, and her behavior toward the baby's "innocent" activity will vary accordingly. In the course of this process, the mother prevaricates, consciously or unconsciously; she says one thing and does the other, and ends up with the well-known injunction given to the school child: "Don't do as I do, do as I say!"

One of the most effective ways of exercising such control consists in expressing concern about "dangers" which threaten the child. This can take many forms, verbal or nonverbal, avoidance, prohibition, overprotection, and countless others, and will be justified by claiming that "it is for the good of the child." This starts with the battle waged against thumb sucking and reaches its high point in the extraordinary variety of sanctions imposed on masturbation (Spitz, 1952) and the efforts expended to delay the beginning of sexual relations.

In a film called *Shaping the Personality* (1953c), I have presented ten examples of maternal influence on development. I chose unsophisticated and conspicuous examples to permit their demonstration in motion pictures. Nevertheless, they do transmit the flavor of this intangible element in the mother-child relations. They illustrate some of the ways and means through which such influences shape and mold the developing personality of the child.

We shall now examine the elements which are not immediately evident in this formative process, which I have called a molding process (Spitz, 1954). It consists of a series of interchanges betwen two partners, the mother and the child, which reciprocally influence each other in a circular manner. These interchanges have been called by some authors "transactions" within the framework of the mother-child couple. Freud (1921) called this duality a "mass of two." For brevity's sake I will use the term "dyad." The relationship in this dyad is a very special one, as evidenced by the variety of terms which the different investigators have coined for it. It is a relationship that in a certain measure is insulated from the surround, and held together by extraordinarily powerful affective bonds. If love could be called "an egoism of two" by a French philosopher, that applies a hundredfold to the mother-child relation.

What occurs within the dyad remains somewhat obscure. How, for example, can we explain the near-clairvoyant manner in which a good mother seems to divine the needs of her baby, to understand what his crying means and what his babbling? We speak of maternal intuition, of the mother's intelligence, and of her experience; but essentially we know little of what goes on in her in this respect. We are faced with a heightened awareness and sensitivity of which the best example is probably what Freud (1900) described as "nurse's sleep": the type in which a mother will sleep calmly through the noises of metropolitan traffic but wake up at the slightest moan of her baby. One must assume that here a far-reaching and selective process of identification has taken place; but with this statement we have barely classified the phenomenon, and only further investigation may provide the details and their explanation.

The counterpart to the mother's capacity for empathy is the baby's perception of the mother's moods, of her conscious as well as of her unconscious wishes. How are we to explain what goes on in the baby? For, if indeed he molds himself according to his mother's wishes, he must first perceive them.

And perceive them he does, for it is a truism that the channel of communication which goes from the child to the mother has its counterpart in a similar one which goes from the mother to the child. It will be our task to examine what this communication[2] consists in.

COMMUNICATION WITHIN THE MOTHER-INFANT DYAD

> *Hypotheses non fingo.*
> —NEWTON

Freud, in one of his earliest, posthumously published writings, the "Project for a Scientific Psychology" (1895), discussed how communication arises in the dyad. I have referred to this statement elsewhere (Spitz, 1957) and will paraphrase it here:

Speaking of an effort to discharge an impetus released along motor pathways, Freud discusses the process of discharge which becomes necessary as a result of stimuli originating inside the body. The example he uses to illustrate his thesis is the need for food. He explains that in order to remove the hunger tension, a change in the outside world has to be effected, but that the newborn is helpless and cannot achieve this. The newborn can only discharge the tension arising from his need by diffuse, random manifestation of emotions, by screaming, by innervation of blood vessels, etc. This discharge cannot permanently relieve the tension. The stimulus can be removed only by a specific intervention coming from the outside, such as providing the newborn with food. Outside help is necessary and that is obtained by arousing the attention of an individual in the surround, through the non-

---

[2] What is communication? Any perceivable change of behavior, be it intentional or not, directed or not, with the help of which one or several persons can influence the perception, the feelings, the thoughts, or the actions of one or several persons, be that influence intended or not (Spitz, 1954).

specific random discharge manifestations of screaming, diffuse muscular activity, etc.

A sentence of Freud's follows here which, in a monumental condensation, unfolds a whole sector of psychoanalytic thought: "This path of discharge thus acquires an extremely important secondary function—viz: of bringing about an understanding[3] with other people; and the original helplessness of human beings is thus the *primal source* of all *moral motives*" (italics mine).

Insight into the nature of communication in the preverbal stage between mother and child is extraordinarily important from the theoretical, the therapeutic, and the prophylactic point of view. In psychoanalytic literature this topic has not found the attention which it deserves. Philosophers, psychologists, and even some psychoanalysts have at times voiced unconfirmed hypotheses which assert that communication between mother and child is based on extrasensory perception or telepathy. I do not feel competent to express an opinion on extrasensory perception. I have limited my investigation to the method of experimentation and observation. Accordingly, I have approached the phenomenon of communication between mother and child from the viewpoint of the experimental observer. Many more such investigations will have to be added in the future. It is possible—even probable—that future studies of this phenomenon will greatly profit from the propositions advanced in communication theory. An increasing number of investigators, mostly mathematicians and physicists, more recently also neurologists and psychiatrists, apply cybernetics and communication theory in their work. My own technique in this investigation is more elementary and barely reaches the threshold of these highly sophisticated methods.

[3] In the original German, Freud (1895) used the term *"Verständigung"* which in this context refers primarily to communication.

ANIMAL AND HUMAN COMMUNICATION

In my attempt to achieve some insight into the means and channels of communication between mother and infant, I was inspired by studies made in animal communication. Experimentation with animals enjoys a license which we do not possess for investigation of the human child (nor do we wish to possess it). Therefore ethologists and animal psychologists succeeded in making highly significant and informative findings from which they derived certain general principles; in some measure these may also be useful for the study of the communication which goes on within the dyad.

Animals communicate on a level of psychological integration which could very crudely be called an affective-conative level. As such it differs fundamentally from the cognitive and abstractive functions of verbal communication. Communication between mother and child during the first six months of life and even up to the end of the first year also takes place on the nonverbal level, using devices comparable to those prevailing in the animal world.[4]

Animals possess means of communication which vary according to the species. Bees, as von Frisch (1931) demonstrated, communicate with the help of something which he called "dances." Ethologists like Konrad Lorenz (1935) and Tinbergen (1951) demonstrated on fish, birds, and a number of mammals how communication takes place with the help of certain forms of behavior. Such behavior consists of postural signals as well as of certain sounds; both have Gestalt characteristics. These behavior patterns do not contain a message from the subject directed specifically to another individual. The messages belong to the most elementary forms of manifestation, called expressive by Karl Bühler (1934). The behavior patterns express what I will call, for want of a better term, a state of mind, a mood, an affective attitude which

---

[4] For a detailed treatment of this question see Spitz (1963a, b, c, 1964).

reflects the immediate experience of the subject. It is an uncontrolled, undirected reaction to a stimulus perceived by the subject.

The reaction to the perception of this behavior pattern by a second animal subject may look as if he had understood this behavior *as a message directed to him.* That appearance, however, is deceptive. In reality, the second animal subject also reacts only to the perception of a stimulus and *not* to a message. The perception of the stimulus as such provokes a behavior in the second subject which will be the counterpart, or the homologue, or a complementation of the perceived stimulus.

This is the kind of communication which Bierens de Haan (1929) distinguished from human language by calling animal language egocentric and human language allocentric. Bierens de Haan's term "egocentric" has nothing in common with the psychoanalytic concept of the "ego." This author, like Piaget, means by "egocentric" anything which is "centered in the subject." Therefore, when he calls animal language egocentric, he means that it is not addressed to another animal, but that it is the expression of an inner process. The same situation obtains in the neonate, in whom the ego does not exist. His vocalizations are the expression of inner processes and are not addressed to anyone.

George H. Mead (1934) conveyed the singularity of this form of communication (although already on a higher level) by the following example: when dog A barks and at a distance dog B responds by barking, dog B does not know whether his barking has any meaning for dog A, let alone *what* meaning it may have. We, as the observers, know that dog B's barking is a stimulus for dog A and that dog A will respond by expressing his feelings about being thus stimulated. But that is exactly what dog B does not know, for his barking is egocentric and not allocentric as human language would be.

In the development of human speech this primitive form of communication represents that phylogenetically determined portion which we all possess already at birth in the form of an Anlage. Later, a specifically human ontogenetic development will be grafted onto this phylogenetic Anlage. The ontogenetic graft will consist in allocentric (directed) volitional communication which operates via semantic signs and signals. Its highest achievement will be the development of the symbolic function.[5]

ELEMENTS OF COMMUNICATION

The forms of communication within the mother-child dyad, however, which are established before the formation of object relations in the first months of life, are based on the above-described phylogenetic Anlage. As noted already, these forms of communication have expressive characteristics; that is to say, they originate from affects and they are not directed. They make use of what has been referred to as "organ language" (Kris, 1953; Jacobson, 1964; see also Abraham, 1916).

What are the expressive characteristics, the affective and the nondirected aspects of these forms of communication? In assuming forces which mold the plastic personality of the child we have also assumed that these forces are transmitted through some system of communication. Such communication takes place within the dyad and consists of circular, reverberating processes. It is obvious that this is a mode of communication which differs considerably from that which is usual between adults. In the following chapters I shall attempt to describe the way in which its operation may be visualized. First, however, a brief definition of the terms used in this discussion of communication is indicated.

Sign is a percept which is empirically linked with the ex-

[5] The role of the symbolic function is not limited to allocentric communication. It also operates within the individual, for instance, in the thought process, as intracommunication (Cobliner, 1955).

perience of an object or a situation. It can substitute for the
perception of an object or of the situation itself. The best
examples of what is meant are to be found in medical literature. For instance, Koplik's sign consists of red buccal macules
with a white center in the prodromal stage of measles. Or
McBurney's sign, a tenderness between umbilicus and the
anterior superior spine of the ilium (bone), informs us of
the presence of appendicitis.

Signs and signal are hierarchically related: sign is the
generic term; signal is the subordinate term, it is the specific
usage of a sign. Therefore, the term *signal designates a con-
ventionally accepted connection between a sign and an experience, be the connection an accidental one, be it arbitrary,
or be it objectively present.* Railway signals and road signs
(e.g., narrowing of the road indicated by parallel lines narrowing down and continuing in parallel; or "Main thorough-
fare" indicated by a triangle), are good examples of this.

*A symbol is a sign which stands for an object, an action, a
situation, an idea; it has significance beyond its formal aspects.*
Gestures and words are the most elementary symbols. Therefore, in this study, we will not discuss the symbolic attributes
in detail.

Communication between mother and child is basically different from communication between grownups, on several
counts. The most important of these consists in the fact that
the means used in communication between two or several
adult partners belong on the whole to one and the same
category, namely, the category of verbal or gestural symbols.
Not so in the case of mother and child; here there is conspicuous unequality in the means of communication. For
while the message proceeding from the infant, at least during
the first months of life, are signs and signs only, the messages
which originate in the infant's adult partner are volitionally
directed signals and perceived as such by the infant.

The Role of Reception and Perception: Coenesthetic and Diacritic Modes of Functioning

When we speak of a system of communication, we tacitly assume that any message transmitted will be perceived by the recipient partner. This assumption, however, creates a logical difficulty. In the foregoing I have posited that in the neonate, perception in the sense in which we apply the term to adults is nonexistent, and that it will be acquired step by step in the course of the first year of life.

Particularly during the first six months of life, and, to a certain extent even later, the perceptual system, the sensorium of the infant is in a state of transition. It shifts gradually from what I have called coenesthetic reception toward diacritic *per*ception. Unlike that of the diacritic organization, the operation of the coenesthetic organization is not localized, not discrete—it is extensive. The relation between the coenesthetic and diacritic organizations is reminiscent of that between primary and secondary process. Derivatives appearing in the secondary process inform us about the working of the primary process. Similarly we mostly become aware of the muted operations of the coenesthetic system either through the distortions it imposes upon diacritic functioning or through its influence on the primary process. The sensorium plays a minimal role in coenesthetic reception; instead, perception takes place on the level of deep sensibility and in terms of totalities, in an all-or-none fashion. Responses to coenesthetic reception also are totality responses, e.g., visceral responses (Spitz, 1945b). This *"reception"* and the corresponding responses are evoked by signals and stimuli which are completely different from those operating in adult perception and communication. The coenesthetic system responds to nonverbal, nondirected, expressive signals; the resulting mode of communication is on the level of "egocentric" animal communication.

Three questions now arise:

1. How and why does the infant manage to receive coenesthetic signals at an age at which he is unable to perceive diacritic signals?
2. In what categories of adult human behavior can such signals be found?
3. Why is it that grownups usually do not seem to respond to them?

The answer to the first question is not easy. The most elementary level of learned communication is the conditioned reflex, in which a stimulus (acting as a signal) evokes a response of the vegetative system. It has been demonstrated experimentally that the earliest conditioned reflex in the infant arises as a response to change of equilibrium, that is, to a deep sensibility stimulus. This is a stimulation of the coenesthetic system. Furthermore, perception through the sensorium (diacritic perception) does not yet operate; this absence of diacritic perception intensifies coenesthetic "reception," since only coenesthetic signals will be received, experienced, and become effective. Finally, if the infant is to survive, the coenesthetic organization must function from birth. It follows that in the neonate coenesthetic functions are more mature and reliable than all others.

The second question is easier to answer. Signs and signals that reach and are received by the infant in the first months of life belong to the following categories: equilibrium, tension (muscular or otherwise), posture, temperature, vibration, skin and body contact, rhythm, tempo, duration, pitch, tone, resonance, clang, and probably a number of others of which the adult is hardly aware and which he certainly cannot verbalize.

This brings us to the third question, namely, why the adult seems so unaware of the signals of coenesthetic communication. If we consider the categories enumerated above, we will readily realize to what extent these sensory categories are missing from the conscious communication system of adults. Adults, in their communication, have replaced the use of signals belonging to these categories by diacritically perceived semantic symbols. Adults, who have retained the capacity to make use of one or several of these usually atrophied categories of perception and communication, belong to the specially gifted. They are composers, musicians, dancers, acrobats, fliers, painters and poets, and many others, and we often think of them as "highstrung" or labile personalities. But it is true that they invariably deviate somehow from average Western man. Average Western man has elected to emphasize in his culture diacritic perception both in regard to communication with others and with himself. Introspection is discounted as unwholesome and frowned upon, so that we are hardly conscious of what goes on in us, unless we be sick. Our deeper sensations do not reach our awareness, do not become meaningful to us, we ignore and repress their messages. Indeed, we are fearful of them and we betray this fear in many ways. It may be expressed directly; we find premonitions distasteful; if they happen to come true, we consider them uncanny.[6] We try to deny them, or at least to rationalize them.

The soothsayer, the hypnotist, the medium, are all lumped together as disturbing and threatening our rational universe; they are relegated to a twilight zone and avoided. We even condemn intuition, we scoff at it in scientific discourse. And this scoffing, the sarcasm, the jokes in such matters, betray our uneasiness before what we cannot explain.

Therefore, far from being on the alert for autonomous changes in others, we do not even notice them and even less can we interpret them. Any animal knows as a matter of

[6] This is not the place to go into the unconscious processes underlying such phenomena as the uncanny. I refer the reader to the numerous articles on the subject in the psychoanalytic literature, beginning with Freud's papers "The Uncanny" (1919), "Fausse Reconnaissance" (1914a), "Dreams and Telepathy" (1922), and "Dreams and the Occult" (1932).

course when somebody is afraid of him, and acts without hesitation on this knowledge. Most of us are unable to duplicate this simple feat. We consider the psychiatrist a singularly gifted individual when he perceives anxiety, anger, longing, trust, in a patient unable to verbalize these affects.

The capacity for such perception and its use mostly undergoes repression around the period of latency. Therefore we find it difficult, if not impossible, to imagine the kind of world in which a being lives whose *total* sensing system, whose mode of relating, takes place in categories from which we have become estranged. This cleavage between the diacritic perception and expression belonging to the age of infancy may explain many seemingly supernatural gifts, for instance, the so-called mystical vaticination of primitives. In preliterate societies individuals retain to adulthood and practice the very sensibilities which Western man represses; or at least they are often able to regress to such modes of perception. This appears to be a regression in the service of a culturally determined ego ideal.

What is more, adjuvants are freely used in preliterate society to facilitate such regression. Such adjuvants either inhibit the functioning of the diacritically oriented ego, or alternately may reinforce the functioning of the coenesthetic organization. Among such adjuvants we may count fasting, solitude, darkness and abstinence—in one word stimulus deprivation. Or drugs, rhythm, sound, alcohol, breathing techniques, etc., may be enlisted to achieve a regression which is hardly any more in the service of the ego and may well be a part of a cultural institution. Similar conditions obtain probably in hypnotic trance; perhaps in some of the mystics; surely in the case of certain psychotics.

For the infant, however, the coenesthetic signals originating in the affective climate of the mother-child relationship are obviously the normal, natural means of communication, to which he responds with a totality reaction. And the mother in her turn perceives the totality responses of the infant in the same manner.

I have already referred to the quasi-telepathic sensitivity of the mother in relation to her child. In my opinion, during pregnancy and during the period immediately following delivery, mothers activate their potential capacity for coenesthetic response. Unquestionably a number of regressive processes take place in the course of pregnancy, delivery, and lactation (Benedek, 1952, 1956). It is regrettable that experimental psychology has never made the attempt to investigate differences in coenesthetic perceptive sensitivity between a mother who is nursing her child and that of a woman who was never pregnant. I am convinced that a nursing mother perceives signals of which we are unaware (see also Spitz, 1955a, 1957).

AFFECTS, PERCEPTION, AND COMMUNICATION

Affective signals generated by maternal moods seem to become a form of communication with the infant. These exchanges between mother and child go on uninterruptedly, without the mother necessarily being aware of them. This mode of communication between mother and child exerts a constant pressure which shapes the infantile psyche. I do not say that this pressure produces anything in the nature of unpleasure for the infant. I speak of "pressure" only because the words to convey these extraordinarily subtle and intangible exchanges have never been coined. I am trying to describe a process of which only the most superficial manifestations can be apprehended. Pressure and giving way alternate and combine to influence now one function, then another among those which unfold with maturation, retarding some, facilitating others. That is what I tried to capture in my film *Shaping the Personality* (1953c). What I could show there was surface only. Below this surface the ebb and flow of affective energies move the tides which channel the current of personality development into one direction or the other.

I cannot emphasize sufficiently how small a role traumatic events play in this development. What we see again and again are the cumulative results of iterative experiences and stimuli, of endlessly repeated sequences of responses. The same principle of cumulation holds for the etiology of possible later neurosis. Isolated traumatic events rarely play a decisive role in bringing about neurosis. I have repeatedly stressed that in neurosis it is the effect of cumulative experiences which is responsible for the pathological outcome. I have introduced the term *affective climate* (Spitz, 1947b), to designate the totality of the forces which influence development in the infant. The affective climate operates according to a psychic principle which I have formulated in a paper presented in the Vienna Psychoanalytic Society in 1936 and called the *cumulative principle*.

At this point I do not propose to discuss the role of affects in psychic processes, in sensation, perception, thought, or action. It should be pointed out, however, that most academic psychologists sidestep these questions, as well as the whole problem of affectivity, by speaking of "motivation." Psychoanalytic theory, on the other hand, has insisted from the beginning that all psychic functions, be they sensations, perceptions, thought or action, are predicated on shifts of libidinal cathexis, which are perceived both by the individual and by the surround as affects and affective processes. In other words, affective manifestations are the indicators of cathectic shifts; these provide the motivation for activating the psychic functions of which we have spoken above. In infancy, affects play the same role for the purpose of communication as the secondary process plays in the grownup.

Consciously or unconsciously, each partner in the mother-child couple perceives the affect of the other, and in his turn responds with affect, a continuing reciprocal affective exchange. These exchanges are fundamentally different from those which we have occasion to observe in adults, for instance, in our patients. In earliest infancy affective processes are not yet contaminated by elements originating in diacritic perception; nor have they been subjected to secondary elaboration by thought processes. Furthermore, the consequences of affective exchanges between mother and child are accessible to direct observation; that is the exception in adults. For in the infant we are dealing with affective processes *in statu nascendi,* observable, as it were, *in vivo.*

It is of special interest for our research that the unfolding of affective perception and affective exchanges precedes all other psychic functions; the latter will subsequently develop on the foundations provided by affective exchange. The affects appear to maintain this lead over the rest of development at least until the end of the first year of life. It is my personal opinion that they will maintain it a good deal longer.

Since affective experience in the framework of mother-child relations acts in the first year of life as trail breaker for development in all the other sectors, it follows that the establishment of the precursor of the libidinal object initiates also the beginning of the relatedness to "things." After the infant has become able to perceive and respond reliably to the human face, it will take another two months until he succeeds in recognizing the bottle, which surely is a most familiar "thing." He sees it, he handles it several times a day; and, furthermore, he derives need gratification from it. Nevertheless, he recognizes the bottle much later than the human face.

Like all our chronological dating about the inception and duration of a phenomenon in infancy, we can only indicate an average from which there are considerable temporal deviations. However, it is not so much the time of appearance or the duration of a specific phenomenon in infancy which is essential, for that may vary; the essential is the sequential order of development in the different sectors of the personality. This remains invariant. It is of paramount importance that the infant's first relation is with a human partner, for all later social relations will be based on this relation. Here begins the process which will transform the infant into a human, into a social being, into the *zoon politikon* in the human sense.

This relation, which is based on affective exchanges, makes the difference between the human *polis* and the termite colony, where the relationship is based on chemical and physical agents, on smell, taste, and touch.

BODY ORGANS, COMMUNICATION, AND EVOLUTION

Man's achievement became possible when upright posture liberated his hand, greatly facilitating social exchanges, for at the same time it freed the mouth and the oral region for communication (Freud, 1930; Bell, 1833; Spitz and Wolf, 1946).

Phylogenetically mouth, jaws, and perioral region had the task of food intake. In the course of evolution a vast number of other tasks were added, such as defense, aggression, exploring and grasping, carrying, vocalization, personal hygiene. As for the hand, its original function was support and locomotion, as long as the on-all-fours position was practically exclusive. This changed when the course of simian evolution aboreal life forced grasping onto the locomotor limbs. As a result some functions of the mouth were transferred to the locomotor limbs, particularly to the upper ones. Now the functions of the mouth became greatly impoverished, especially in animals with a mixed diet. Vocalization became more important, as evidenced in the incessant chatter of monkeys in the wild. To a large extent both food intake and vocalization involved the mimetic musculature of the perioral region. In the course of primate and human evolution, vocalization and mimetic expression proved increasingly useful as instruments of social expression, exchanges, and contacts.

Concomitantly the hand, liberated from the task of supporting the upper part of the body, took over many tasks which the mouth had performed up to then. Among these tasks there were also some social ones, such as the care of the young, grooming, positioning in the sexual act. Nursing and mothering the young in a face-to-face position became not only possible but routine. Any observation of vertebrates shows that the face-to-face situation does not occur in the care of nursing of the young, except in those animals which have developed vocalization on a large scale, namely, the birds, the primates, and man. However, in birds, facial anatomy is more or less rigid, unsuitable for expressing emotions. Therefore, though it does provide a signal during the feeding of the young (though vocalization, at least by the young, accompanies feeding), the facial signal remains unmodified during ontogenesis.

In the primates and in man, however, the facial, buccal, and pharyngeal region underwent phylogenetic modifications, which greatly enriched their neuromuscular endowment. This not only made the expression of affects possible in this region, and with much less expenditure of energy, it also opened the way for much more rapid changes in the expression of emotions. The facial region thus became a suitable instrument for producing affective signals; and the same applies to vocalization. This, I believe, is how the evolution of affective facial expression, vocalization, and their use for semantic purposes began; it was to lead ultimately to the emergence of speech.

In speech, semantic symbols replace postural and behavioral Gestalten, which act as signals. In speech, semantic symbols become the ego's main instruments for conducting object relation. This leads progressively to the discarding of postural signals in communication and to their atrophy. In our culture, posture is hardly noticed any more. The psychoanalyst has to learn anew to understand even the most elementary messages contained in the postural signals provided by his patients and to translate them into semantic signals (Freud, 1921; F. Deutsch, 1947, 1949, 1952).

Affective development is not limited to affects of pleasure or sign Gestalten promising need gratification like the mother's face. Unpleasure affects play an equally important role; for this reason they have also been investigated in this research.

THE NATURAL HISTORY OF AFFECTS OF UNPLEASURE AND THEIR DYNAMICS

Affects of pleasure emerge in the course of the first three months of life, the smiling response being their most impressive manifestation. Manifestations of unpleasure follow a closely parallel course; they become more and more specific in the course of the first three months of life. Beginning with the fourth month, the child expresses unpleasure when his human partner leaves him. But just as the infant at this age will not smile (reliably) at anything except the human face, he will not show unpleasure either when we take away his toy or other familiar objects—he cries only when his human play-*partner* interrupts their game and leaves him.

By the sixth month the specificity of the smiling response and of the unpleasure response becomes more marked and is extended to a growing number of stimuli, including those connected with "things." Now the child will cry not only when left by his play-partner, but also when you take away his toy. In the second half of the first year, he becomes able to select his favorite toy among several other things.

Our observations and experiments support the proposition that affectively invested experience expedites and insures the storing of memory traces. We demonstrated the validity of this proposition in our exploration of the natural history of

the smiling response, as well as in that of unpleasure responses
in the first year of life.

Affects are the perceived end results of discharge processes
(Freud, 1915a). The smiling response is the affective indicator
of expected need gratification, that is, the indicator of a tension discharge. Crying when the partner leaves is the affective
indicator of the expectation of mounting tension. In both
cases the infant's memory traces, stored during the occasion,
are those of the external situational givens associated with
subjective tension shifts, that is, changes in drive economy;
tension reduction in the first, mounting tension in the second
instance.

The memory traces of these two experiences will serve to
recognize the recurrence of similar givens, similar external
constellations in the future. These two experiences, that of
pleasure and that of unpleasure, are the two major affective
experiences in early infancy. All other experiences of the
neonate are either affectively neutral: that is, they do not provoke either positive or negative observable manifestations of
affect; or they are endowed only with minimal quantities of
affect. The two cases described above are the exceptions. They
stand out like two solitary peaks in the flatland of the infant's
indifference to most other experiences.

One of these two outstanding experiences is the appearance of the preobject, heralding gratification and the smiling
response which ensues; the other is the removal of the partner, initiating frustration expressed by crying. Essentially the
efficacy of these two experiences lies in their iteration of gratification or frustration which recurs in the identical setting
of external givens, every day, many times a day.

Memory Storage and Affectively Colored Experience

The proposition that affectively invested experiences ex-
pedite and insure the storing of memory traces of the accompanying external situational givens is in good agreement with

our assumptions on the function of the two sensory organizations in infancy, the coenesthetic and the diacritic. Discharge processes and their indicators, the affects, belong to the realm of coenesthetic functioning. The *extensive,* affectively invested coenesthetic perception is the only bridge over which the newborn can move forward and achieve *intensive* diacritic perception.

In animals the enormous acceleration of memory storage under conditions of emotional stress has been observed by ethologists. This acceleration stands in stark contrast to the laborious, slow, endlessly repetitive process of learning in the classical conditioning experiment.

It was to be expected that rapid, affect-invested learning would be more prevalent in animals, because their coenesthetic responses are much more conspicuous than those of man. They have to be, because of their survival value.[7]

Animal observations appear to show that acceleration and reinforcement are proportionate to the magnitude of the affect charge and this, in turn, is predicated on how much the situation provoking the affect pertains to the animal's survival.

In the affective phenomena discussed above the role of the underlying drive activity (of which affect is an indicator) in the implementation of thought processes is of great interest. Freud (1911) postulated that thought processes represent an experimental kind of action accompanied by displacement of relatively small quantities of cathexis. The displacement takes place along the pathways leading to memory traces (Freud,

7 The vapidity of most animal experimentation of the past, including learning theory, is perhaps due to the antropomorphic approach of animal psychologists. Since the coenesthetic system is so inconspicuous in the adult, they overlook it in their approach to the animal. It would seem that the increasing weight and import of findings made by ethologists and psychoanalytic infant observation has brought about a change: recent animal psychology has been able to offer more rewarding information. This influence is apparent in stimulus research, from Hebb to Harlow on the one hand, in the stimulus overload experiments of Calhoun (1962) on the other.

1895). Obviously, to make these cathectic processes possible, memory traces must first be laid down. The smiling response which is based on the recognition of the preobject exemplifies Freud's postulate on the connection between memory traces and thought processes. In regard to this phenomenon I have discussed the role of energy displacements in initiating, facilitating, and organizing memory storage and that of drive energy underlying the affect manifested on these occasions. I consider the smiling response phenomenon to be an example also of the operation of earliest thought processes.

Even later on, between the eighth and tenth month of life, the role of the two primary affects of pleasure and unpleasure is not difficult to detect in the infant's development. But subsequently their role becomes more obscure by the month, because from then on the two affects seem to interact in intricate and unexpected ways. This is particularly evident in ideational operations, such as the function of judgment, symbol formation, abstraction, and logical operations of all kinds (including Piaget's [1947] "reversibility").

An example is provided in Freud's (1925a) investigation of the function of judgment. Here Freud deals, among other things, with the operation of the two primary affects; he states: "A precondition for setting up reality testing is that objects shall have been lost which once brought real satisfaction." It follows that the affect of pleasure, which is one of the prime moving forces in the establishment of the object, as well as the affect of unpleasure, called forth by the loss of the object, both have to be experienced before the function of judging can crystallize. What is more, this crystallization can occur only if the two affects arise in succession at chronologically separate periods.

In a study on the origin of the semantic "No" gesture (1957), the details of which will be reported later, I have explored the developmental role of the two primary affects of pleasure and unpleasure. The conclusions of this investigation are not too dissimilar from Freud's propositions on the function of judgment. It became evident that in the process of acquiring the semantic "No" gesture the two affects operate in a complementary fashion. What one of them bestows, the other withholds, and vice versa.

THE ROLE OF FRUSTRATION IN LEARNING AND DEVELOPMENT

It follows that to deprive the infant of the affect of unpleasure during the course of the first year of life is as harmful as to deprive him of the affect of pleasure. Pleasure and unpleasure have an equally important role in the shaping of the psychic apparatus and the personality. To inactivate either affect will upset the developmental balance. This is why raising children according to the doctrine of unqualified permissiveness leads to such deplorable results. The importance of frustration for developmental progress cannot be overestimated—after all, nature itself imposes it. To begin with, we are subjected to the formidable frustration—Rank (1924) mistook it for trauma—of asphyxia at birth, which enforces the replacement of fetal circulation by pulmonary breathing. The repetitive and insistent frustrations of thirst and hunger follow it; they force the baby to become active, to seek and to incorporate food (instead of passively receiving food through the umbilical cord), and to activate and develop perception. The next major step is weaning, which enforces separation from the mother and an increasing measure of autonomy; and thus it goes on, step by step. What makes the modern educator, child psychologist, parent, imagine that they can spare the child frustration?

Frustration is inbuilt in development. It is the most potent catalyst of evolution of which nature disposes.[8] Dr. Johnson's

---

[8] Freud, of course, was well aware of this; witness his statement: "Sensations of a pleasurable nature have not anything impelling about them, whereas unpleasurable ones have it in the highest degree. The latter impel towards change . . ." (1923).

remark, that it is amazing how the knowledge that he will be hanged next morning can accelerate a man's mental processes, is true if brutal. Nature is not concerned with ethics but with evolution, and applies the pressure of frustration, of unpleasure, unmercifully. In present-day child rearing, the child usually is spared those frustrations which make the parent, the educator, the psychologist feel guilty. In reality their concern is not so much the child's welfare as the desire to avoid guilt feelings, conscious or unconscious.

For the child's welfare does require frustration. Freud's above-quoted statement shows *one* role of the affect of unpleasure in achieving reality testing—and reality testing is one of the vitally important functions of the ego. Without unpleasure, without that measure of frustration which I would call age-adequate, no satisfactory ego development is possible.

That is shown impressively in one of Harlow's experiments on rhesus monkeys: those which he called the "together-together" animals. In this experiment he took advantage of the monkey's instinctual clinging behavior by raising two baby monkeys together. He thus raised a pair of monkeys which never developed any adult monkey activity, be it social or sexual. They spent their days clinging together—a closed system which neither communicates with the surround nor accepts any interference from outside, pleasurable or unpleasurable (Harlow, 1958). We have here a most instructive illustration of what happens when an infant is not frustrated. It is obvious that under natural conditions, when raised by a rhesus mother, the rhesus baby will not be permitted unlimited gratification of his urge to cling. Similarly in the human infant, in the course of normal mother-child relations, the situations in which unpleasure is imposed on the child and frustration ensues are numerous and increase with age. This is as it should be.

I am not advocating child beating when I speak of frustration. I am referring to those frustrations which come naturally in rearing a child and which can be avoided only by unreasonable permissiveness. In dealing with these repetitive frustrations, the child achieves a growing measure of independence in the course of the first six months and becomes increasingly active in his relations with the outside world, animate and inanimate.

CHAPTER VIII

The Establishment of the
Libidinal Object

THE EIGHT-MONTH ANXIETY

A decisive change in the child's behavior to others occurs between the sixth and the eighth month. No longer will the baby respond with a smile when a chance visitor steps to his cot smiling and nodding. By this age the capacity for diacritic perceptive differentiation is already well developed. The child now clearly distinguishes friend from stranger. If a stranger approaches him, this will release an unmistakable, characteristic and typical behavior in the child; he shows varying intensities of apprehension or anxiety and rejects the stranger. Still, the individual child's behavior varies over a rather wide range. He may lower his eyes "shyly," he may cover them with his hands, lift his dress to cover his face, throw himself prone on his cot and hide his face in the blankets, he may weep or scream. The common denominator is a refusal of contact, a turning away, with a shading, more or less pronounced, of anxiety. May we assume that the differences in individual behavior are somehow connected with the affective climate in which the child was raised? A number of the observable behavior patterns have been presented in the film, *Anxiety: Its Phenomenology in the First Year of*

150

Life (Spitz, 1953b). I have called this pattern the *eight-month anxiety* (see Fig. 9) and consider it the earliest manifestation of *anxiety proper.*

FIGURE 9

The Eight-Month Anxiety.

What do we mean by "anxiety proper"? Based on our observations I have been able to distinguish in the first year of life *three stages in the ontogenesis of anxiety.* The first of these stages is the infant's reaction to the process of delivery. Freud (1926a) spoke of this reaction as the physiological *prototype* of all later anxiety. Other authors, Rank (1924) in the first place, made much of the so-called "trauma of birth" and tried to make this so-called "trauma" responsible for all later psychiatric problems. Freud never accepted this hypothesis.

During the neonatal period, in the first week or so after delivery, we see unpleasure manifestations occurring in situations which at a more advanced age might cause anxiety. These unpleasure manifestations are not anxiety in the sense in which we use the term in psychoanalysis. To call them anxiety is misleading. While they have all the characteristics of physiological tension states, with diffuse physical discharge phenomena, they have no psychological content.

As the child grows older, the nature of these tension states progressively loses its diffuse character; now they occur in response to ever more specific unpleasure situations. By the eighth week of life the manifestations of unpleasure become increasingly structured and intelligible, not only to the mother, but also to the experienced observer.

A few shadings begin to appear, replacing negatively tinged, generalized excitation, transforming the simple manifestations of unpleasure into something like two or three "coded" signs. Viewed from the mother's side, this is already the beginning of simplest communication. Viewed from the child's side, this is still only a sign of his discomfort; it is not yet an appeal for help; it remains on the level of expression, even though this manifestation now has become volitional and articulate. By now the surround has slowly learned to distinguish when the child is hungry, when he has a bellyache, and when he expresses the wish to be entertained.

As the child's manifestations become more and more intelligible, so the responses of the surround become better adapted to the needs he is expressing. Because he can now provoke need-gratifying responses, the child becomes able to grasp a connection between what he does and the responses of the surround. By the third month of life, memory traces of a series of signals directed by the child to the surround are encoded in his psychic apparatus. With this the child has mastered what Karl Bühler (1934) called "the appeal," the capacity to turn to the surround and signal his need.

Prior to this the child reacted in an archaic manner, with a reflex, as it were, to sensations coming from inside or to stimuli coming from the surround. Now the child can send out signals, both volitionally and deliberately, to which the surround responds more or less consistently by gratifying his need. The child's active expression of a need is followed in close temporal sequence by the gratification from the surround. This sequence is the same as that which operates in the conditioned reflex; however, the capacity to establish a conditioned reflex is probably based on innate neurophysiological pathways.

In the conditioned reflex the cue is given from the outside, from the other, and the response comes from inside, from the subject. In the stage of appeal this is reversed. Now it is the subject, the child, who gives the cue by his hunger screaming, and it is the other, the surround, which responds; it is the surround which is being conditioned by the child.

This sequence recurs with great regularity many times a day in every child's life. Therefore the two parts of the experience, the hunger screaming and the gratification which follows it, become linked in the child's memory. An association is established between two clusters of impressions in the form of a set of two memory traces laid down and reinforced by an affective connection. This development should be understood in the terms of Ferenczi's (1916) propositions on the stage of infantile omnipotence. Hunger screaming, followed by gratification, forms the basis of the feeling of omnipotence, which according to Ferenczi is an early stage of the sense of reality.

However, paradoxically, the same experience also prepares the basis for an ideational development which is the diametrical opposite of omnipotence. In my belief the sequence of gratification following hunger screaming is the earliest experience to which we can trace the inception of the ideational category of causality.

In this achievement of enlisting the mother's help for his needs through screaming, the human being experiences for the first time the *post hoc ergo propter hoc* in connection with his own action. Of course, this is a forerunner only and not the principle of causality proper. The *post hoc ergo propter hoc* principle will subsequently branch into two directions. One of them will remain in its crude form as a basic mode of functioning of the primary process. The other will be progressively refined until it becomes one of the most potent ideational tools of man in the form of the principle of determinism. In terms of the infant's experience this sequence might be expressed as follows: when B always comes after A, it is because A is the force, the power, which produces B, so that A is the cause of B.

The child now can influence the surround to relieve his discomfort; at a somewhat later stage he learns also to influence his surround to offer him desired gratification. Here we have the transition from the stage of the pure manifestation of *what he feels* to the stage of appeal for *what he wishes*. This is the first important step with which communication begins —it will eventually lead to communication with the help of semantic signals.

After the third month an ever-increasing number of memory traces is laid down in the child's *Mnem.* systems. They are mostly memory traces of the simplest kind and connected with pleasurable and sometimes unpleasurable shadings of affect. The memory traces related to certain recurrent and to the child particularly unpleasant situations are singled out. They are structured in such a manner that their reactivation will reliably elicit a specific unpleasure affect. This affect is manifested in the form of withdrawal behavior (e.g., in the case of repeated preventive inoculation). We speak of this response as *fear*. It emerges between the fourth and the sixth month of life. This is the second step toward the establishment of *anxiety proper*.

In the first stage, that of physiological tension states, an unpleasure reaction is manifested when inner tension disturbs the state of equilibrium. In the second stage, the reaction of *fear* is provoked by a percept which the child has connected with a previous experience of unpleasure. When the child re-experiences this unpleasure-cathected percept he responds by flight. This is flight from a reality threat and marks the beginning of what Freud (1926a) called "reality anxiety."

Like Freud we shall use the word "fear" rather than "anxiety" because it has found an object.

The eight-month anxiety which I described before, and which appears in the second half of the first year of life, is quite different from the behavior of fear. In the reaction to the stranger, the child is responding to something or somebody with whom he never had an unpleasure experience before. We carefully followed from birth a large number of children who later showed this behavior in the second half of the first year. They all had the usual experiences of unpleasure which are unavoidable in child care. But they had them with their mothers and not with strangers. Why then do they manifest anxiety or at least apprehension when approached by a stranger?

In view of all we have learned in the course of direct observation of infants, the hypothesis that the child responds to the absence of the mother with unpleasure is most plausible. In following the ontogenesis of unpleasure we found that between the third and sixth month the child manifests unpleasure when an adult partner leaves him. At the stage of the eighth-month anxiety the child is already more advanced in every respect. What he reacts to when confronted with a stranger is that this is not his mother; his mother "has left him."

This is in contrast to the three-month-old, for whom one human face is as good as another, for to him it only represents a sign Gestalt of need gratification. However, when a stranger approaches the eight-month-old, he is disappointed in his wish to have his mother. The anxiety he displays is not in response to the memory of a disagreeable experience with a stranger; it is a response to his perception that the stranger's face is not identical with the memory traces of the mother's face. This illustrates the operation of apperception; in this operation a percept in the present is compared with memory traces from the past. In psychoanalytic terms we say: this is a response to the intrapsychic perception of the reactivated wishful tension and the ensuing disappointment. Accordingly I have called this response the first manifestation of *anxiety proper*.

Like the smiling response at the age of three months, the eight-month anxiety marks a distinct stage in the development of the psychic organization. In the case of the smiling response the sign Gestalt of the face seen straight on is experienced as the homologue of a human partner. In the case of the eight-month anxiety the percept of the stranger's face *qua face* (and not as a sign Gestalt!) is confronted with the memory traces of the mother's face. It is found to be different and will therefore be rejected.

We assume that this capacity of cathectic displacement on reliably stored memory traces in the eight-month-old child reflects the fact that he has now established a true object relation, and that the mother has become his libidinal object, his love object.

Before this, we can hardly speak of love, for there is no love until the loved one can be distinguished from all others, and there is no libidinal object as long as it remains interchangeable. At the same time the child modifies his ways of dealing with his environment and mastering it. He is no longer limited to archaic forms of defense; he has acquired the function of judgment, of deciding. This represents an ego function on a higher, intellectual level of psychic development and opens up new horizons.

A word of advice is in order: if one wishes to observe the phenomenon of the eight-month anxiety—and to experiment with it—this should not be done in the mother's presence. Where manifestations of the eight-month anxiety are mild, the mother's presence will suffice to make them quite inconspicuous whereas in her absence they will show up unmistakably.

AN OBJECTION TO OUR EXPLANATION OF THE EIGHT-MONTH ANXIETY

A critique of this proposition from a "biological viewpoint" was published by Szekely (1954). He ingeniously reinterprets my observations on the smiling response and on the eight-month anxiety and arrives at conclusions diametrically opposed to those I published. According to him, the eye-forehead Gestalt is a "releaser stimulus" in the terms of Lorenz, Tinbergen et al., and represents the phylogenetic survivor of the "enemy" pattern in the animal world. Szekely claims that the infant reacts to the mother's face in the first months of life with anxiety.[1] He postulated that this "anxiety" is inspired by the "enemy" pattern of eyes and forehead. Szekely considers the third month's reciprocal smile to be the earliest mastering of this archaic anxiety. He posits that this mastery is achieved by the infant through a libidinal cathexis which transforms the "eyes-forehead" Gestalt into a part object. According to Szekely, the subsequent eight-month anxiety would then indicate that this part object has reverted to the original status of the archaic fear-producing stimulus. This, in brief, is the argumentation of Szekely, who emphasizes repeatedly that up to now there has been no experimental proof of his hypothesis.

From the beginning of my research on the smiling response I was impressed by the similarity between the operation of the releaser stimulus (Lorenz, 1935) in animals and that of the sign-Gestalt function of the eyes-forehead configuration in the case of the human infant. Therefore I systematically examined whether the "releaser stimulus" for the reciprocal smile is innate, whether it is activated by the newborn after the manner of imprinting through a few perceptual experi-

[1] Throughout his article Szekely uses the terms "fear" and "anxiety" interchangeably. As stated already, we make a clear distinction between *fear* and *anxiety* (Spitz, 1950b, 1955c).

ences, or whether it is learned. Clinical observation and experiments showed that all three factors are involved; it is a complex process.

Investigations by my associates and myself, as well as a study published by Ahrens (1954), make it appear probable that, within the total configuration of the sign Gestalt, the eyes and the motion may represent innate factors.

Recent studies (Polak, Emde, and Spitz, 1964, 1965) show, furthermore, that a learning process takes place through which the totality perception of the face is gradually endowed with three-dimensionality, size characteristics, and color characteristics. In the course of this development the infant gradually begins to distinguish the approaching face from the approaching bottle, the person from the food. Initially, reward and punishment play a conspicuous role in this learning process (Spitz and Wolf, 1946; Spitz, 1955c); later after the third month this is complemented by certain specifically human learning sequences.

Szekely's central hypothesis is that already during the first weeks and months of life the infant reacts to the mother's face, to this IRM (which represents the "enemy") with anxiety or fear. This is a phenomenon I have never been able to detect.

In the many hundred infants, to each of whom we presented the stimulus of the face at least once a week from birth to the age of three months, nothing suggesting fear has been observed. What is more, no observation of this kind can be found in the extensive literature on the subject.

In the years intervening since the publication of my reply to Szekely (Spitz, 1955c) I continued to explore the question raised by him in three different contexts:

1. I systematically observed all infants that I had occasion to study subsequently with Szekely's propositions in mind.

2. I reviewed my extensive motion picture material from this angle.

3. I had extensive discussions with a large number of ethologists and observed their experiments.

Despite this systematic review I found no evidence to support Szekely's central hypothesis. However, I did find support for his proposition that the eye configuration is an innate releaser. My own observations have shown that the eyes of the experimenter do provoke the infant's response at an extraordinarily early age, sometimes in the first few days of life, supporting the thesis that this response is not learned. This finding is in agreement with the careful observations and investigations of Ahrens (1954).

Although ethologists do concur with Szekely's opinion that eyes can indeed be an enemy signal for adult animals, I have not been able to find out whether this applies also to the animal young before weaning. With regard to the human infant, a further argument suggests that the eyes do not provoke fear but rather its opposite.

As noted in Chapter V, the child ceases to smile at the observer's face when the observer turns his face into profile. The reaction can go from loss of contact to bewilderment; it sometimes even includes a startle response. In the latter event it is quite difficult to re-establish contact with the child, and to elicit his smile again takes much longer than originally. If the eyes (and face) were indeed a fear stimulus, then the child should show *relief* when released from the observer's hypnotic stare by the turn into profile. But instead of showing relief, quite a few of the children are bitterly disappointed. Some show resentment in their face and they reject the observer's efforts to resume contact. Others simply ignore him, with a sullen expression.

Much of Szekely's argument is derived from the well-established fact that in phylogenesis the eyes are mostly the signal of a threat, a danger, an enemy. My knowledge in the field of phylogenesis is not adequate to confirm or refute this argument. However, it seems risky to apply to human behavior conclusions drawn from observations made on animal behavior. Modern scientific methodology (Novikoff, 1945) does not admit the transposition of laws valid on an organizational level of lower complexity to an organizational level of higher complexity. Therefore, as long as conclusive proof is not forthcoming, Szekely's thesis remains an ingenious but speculative conjecture.

THE SECOND ORGANIZER

The eight-month anxiety, placed into the conceptual framework elaborated earlier, indicates the emergence of the second organizer of the psyche. That means also that one of the critical periods (Scott and Marston, 1950) is situated around the eighth month of life. This marks a new stage of infantile development, in the course of which both the child's personality and his behavior will undergo a radical change.

Now both the form in which unpleasure is expressed as well as the perception and recognition of the stimulus which provokes unpleasure become ever more specific. The stimulus began at birth as an unspecific inner need which produced unspecific tension and its random unspecific discharge. Three months later the random expression of tension became more specific and was manifested when any (still unspecific) human partner left the child. Finally, at the eight-month level, the unpleasure takes the form of a specific anxiety, when the child is approached by a stranger. This specific unpleasure is caused by the child's fear of having lost his mother (the libidinal object). It is of the greatest interest to the psychoanalyst to note that the successive phases of this sector of development closely parallel the phases of two other sectors of development. One is that which leads to the integration of the ego. The other sector is that of progressive development of object relations which culminates in the constitution of the libidinal object.

Let me remind the reader that these three developmental currents, namely, the crystallization of affective response, the integration of the ego, and the consolidation of object relations, are interdependent though different aspects of the total personality. I have treated them separately only to facilitate their presentation. Actually they are interdependent parts of the total personality.

Let us briefly review the two major steps leading to the constitution of the libidinal object: (1) The establishment of the presentation of the human face in the memory system as a cue informs us of the emergence of the precursor of the object; this marks the first major step in the development of object relations. (2) Three to four months later the eight-month anxiety appears. It signals that the child has singled out the face of his mother and conferred on it a unique place among all other human faces. Henceforth, and for some time to come, the child will prefer the mother's face and reject all the other faces which differ from it.

In my opinion, this is the indicator for the establishment of the libidinal "object" proper. For the behaviorist, no doubt, the manifestation of the eight-month anxiety means only that a "thing" has been established in the optic sector and has achieved cognitive constancy. But once we go beyond the limitations set by the behavioristic method and search for the *meaning* of the behavior displayed in the eight-month anxiety, we realize that the affect, namely, anxiety, has the decisive role in this phenomenon. It is evident that the object has been established not only in the optic (cognitive) sector but also—and perhaps we should say *primarily*—in the affective sector.

As stated above, it follows from the establishment of a libidinal object that the person endowed with object attributes can no longer be interchanged with any other individual. Once the object is established the child can mistake nothing else for it. This secure exclusiveness enables the child to form the close bonds which confer on the object its unique properties. The eight-month anxiety is the proof that, to the child, everyone is a stranger, with the exception of the unique object;[2] that is to say, the child has found *the* partner with whom he can form object relations in the true sense of the term.

Let me outline other changes entailed by the establishment of the second organizer.

1. In the *somatic sphere,* the myelinization of neural pathways is now sufficiently advanced to make the diacritic functioning of the sensory apparatus possible; to achieve coordination of the effectors; to place groups of skeletal muscles in the service of directed action sequences; and to permit adjustments of posture and equilibrium which serve as the basis for muscular action.

2. In the *mental apparatus,* an increasing number of memory traces has been stored, so that mental operations of growing complexity can be carried out. These mental operations in their turn permit the performance of an increasing number of ever more diversified directed *action sequences.* The activation of mental operations and the resulting action sequences provide one of the conditions which makes the functioning of ego apparatuses possible.

3. Finally, in the *psychic organization,* maturation and development of the congenital equipment have made it possible to place the effectors in the service of sequences of directed actions. These action sequences permit the infant to discharge affective tension in an intentional, directed manner, that is, volitionally. Such directed discharges lower the level of tension within the psychic apparatus; an improved distribution

---

2 This is an oversimplified statement. Obviously the other members of the family also are endowed with a privileged position, not quite as privileged as that of the libidinal object, but still preferred over other individuals.

within the psychic economy is achieved, facilitating its regulative function and permitting not only a more efficient gratification of needs but also volitional, directed achievement of pleasure gain. The ego organization will now be enriched from a variety of sources; it becomes structured, and boundaries are being established between ego and id on the one side, the ego and outer world on the other. This enrichment of the ego is achieved as more and more ego apparatuses become functioning units. This activation is triggered by affectively cathected action exchanges between the infant and the nascent libidinal object. In infancy much of what we loosely call object relations takes place in these action exchanges with manifold effects, among which is the creation of boundaries between ego and id, ego and reality, I and non-I, self and nonself. But of these later.

In this integration and structuration of the newly established ego, in the delimitation of its boundaries through action exchanges, a decisive role is played by the progressive differentiation of aggression from libido and by the vicissitudes of these two instinctual drives. This is conspicuous in the latter part of the first year of life. In Chapter IX we shall examine the differentiation of the drives, their fusion, and their defusion. Suffice it to say for the moment that there is a close connection and interdependence—a feedback—between the early vicissitudes of the drives and the vicissitudes of object relations that lead to the establishment of the libidinal object. The entire process goes hand in hand with the progressive development of other ego functions, such as bodily coordination, perception and apperception, directed and volitional exchanges of action. The culminating point of this process of differentiation and integration is, to repeat, the establishment of the object, revealed by the appearance of the eight-month anxiety.

Following the establishment of the second organizer and dependent upon the developmental changes enumerated above, the inception of some of the ego's defense mechanisms can be observed. In their beginnings these serve primarily adaptation rather than defense in the strict sense of the term. But with the establishment of the object and the beginning of ideation their function changes. As will be seen later, once the object is established and the aggressive and libidinal drives become fused, some of the defense mechanisms, notably identification, acquire the function they will serve in the adult.

I wish to stress again that the organizer of the psyche is a construct, a model which I found useful in apprehending certain phenomena of psychic development (Spitz, 1959); it is a model like that of the psychic apparatus divided into id, ego, and superego, which also is not a concrete entity. As other hypotheses, such models have to follow the principle of parsimony and are justified by their usefulness.

Introducing the organizer concept is justified by the observation that the successful negotiation of the transitions from one phase to the next acts as a catalyst for a spurt in the infant's development. The interdependence of the sectors of development (of which I discussed three), the apparent feedback operating between them, makes the organizer concept most adequately suited to explicate the complexity of the maturational and developmental milestones achieved by the infant. This construct permits us to condense the multiplicity of maturational and developmental achievements of the infant into a manageable form rather than to enumerate them in every instance.

THE CULTURAL DETERMINANTS OF THE DYAD

As is the case with all other phenomena of infancy which I have discussed, the age at which the eight-month anxiety emerges varies considerably. One might even say that it is more variable than in the earlier phenomena. That is due to its special nature, for it is the result of relations between *two* individuals, namely, the dyadic universe, and therefore depends on the capacity of these two individuals to establish and maintain such relations, on the individual personality, but also on a number of other environmental or cultural conditions.

Most of our observations were made in the Western cultural sphere and our subjects were white, Negro, and American Indian. I stress this because I believe that cultural institutions have a significant part in personality formation. They provide the range of opportunities which delimit the expression of intrapsychic processes, in both mother and child. One of the institutions of the Western cultural sphere, the family, insures close contact and relations between the infant and *one single* mother figure throughout the first year of life. In the chapters dealing with pathology, we shall see how much this relation can be modified and how this influences the nature of object relations and the establishment of the object.

It follows that a cultural tradition in which contact between mother and child is regulated differently from the way we do it will have a significant bearing on the age at which the object is established as well as on the nature of the object relations themselves. Evidence of such modifications can be found in anthropological studies, for instance, those done by Margaret Mead (1928, 1935; Mead and McGregor, 1951) on cultures with infant-rearing institutions very different from our own. To mention only two: in Bali the father replaces the mother very early in the infant's life; in Samoa multiple mother figures replace the single mother of our culture. I believe this may lead to object relations of a diffuse nature. Anna Freud describes similar modifications of object relations among infants raised by a series of different nurses in rapid succession. These children could not form close relations with *one* maternal person—they did not have one; they replaced the missing dyad by forming what we might call "gangs" (A. Freud and Dann, 1951).

The importance of these observations and their implications for our own culture can hardly be overestimated. Patient and careful investigation of the consequences of modified mother-child relations in various cultures promises to yield valuable information. It will tell us in the first place what *not* to do; we will thus profit from the errors of others on the one hand, recognize the consequences of our own mistakes on the other. It will provide us with suggestions for prevention, that is, how to avoid conditions leading to malformations of character and personality; and with hints for the most favorable conditions for child rearing and education.

The concept of organizers and the above-described stages of object relations are but a crude draft which offers a few orientation points for the understanding of development in the first year of life. The details of this draft still have to be filled in, for they are still unknown and will require patient study of individuals and groups as well as cross-cultural comparisons.

CHAPTER IX

The Role and Evolution of the Instinctual Drives

In the preceding chapters we have viewed the phenomenology of object relations primarily from the topographic and from the structural viewpoint, both in the infant's and in the mother's personality. We shall now examine them from the dynamic viewpoint and attempt to shed some light on the role of the instinctual drives in this process. We noted that the libidinal and the aggressive drives participate in equal measure in the formation of object relations. At birth, however, and during the narcissistic stage following birth, the drives are not yet differentiated from each other; they will do so through a process of gradual development. I have elaborated the details of this process elsewhere (Spitz, 1953a; see also Jacobson, 1954), and here I will merely outline the manner in which I see this development.

The libidinal and the aggressive drives are differentiated from each other in the course of the first three months of life, as a result of the exchanges which take place between mother and child. At first these exchanges take place in the form of discrete, disconnected experiences in the specific sector of each of the drives and the two do not fuse or connect with each other. This is true during the narcissistic stage up to the age of three months, when the preobject will become established.

167

In the next months, development progresses step by step from the preobjectal stage to the stage of true object relations. Both during the narcissistic stage and during this transitional stage, the drives "lean onto" the gratification of the infant's oral needs. Freud designated the relationship growing out of this structure of the drives an "anaclitic attachment" (Freud, 1905b, 1914b). The mother is the person who gratifies the infant's oral desires; she becomes the target of the infant's aggressive and libidinal drives. This target, the mother, is not yet perceived as a unified, consistent, unchanging person, or rather, a "libidinal object."

The "Good" Object and the "Bad" Object and Their Merger

Following Hartmann, Kris, and Loewenstein (1946) and Abraham (1916), I assume that at this stage the infant has *two* objects: the bad object against whom aggression is directed; and the good object to whom libido is turned. With Abraham (1916) we can call this period *the preambivalent stage*.

At the beginning of this transitional stage, a rudimentary ego emerges, which acts as a central coordinating steering apparatus. This ego, however rudimentary, permits a drive discharge in the form of directed action. These directed actions, this very functioning, will progressively bring about the differentiation of the drives from each other. Due to the functioning of the developing ego the child learns to distinguish between the "bad" object, which refuses to gratify his needs and against which his aggression is directed, and the good object, which gratifies his needs and toward which his libido is directed.

Around the sixth month of life, a synthesis takes place. The ego's growing influence makes itself felt by integrating the memory traces of innumerably repeated experiences and exchanges which the child had with his mother. Eventually this results in the fusion of the images of the two preobjects, the "good mother" and the "bad mother." A single mother, the libidinal object proper, emerges.

This process can also be expressed in terms of the ego's memory systems. An endless chain of action exchanges with the mother lays down a growing number of memory traces, primarily the percepts of the mother changing roles. At the same time, perhaps even as a result of this very process, the retentiveness of the infant's memory is increasing—a fact which can be demonstrated experimentally (Hetzer and Wislitzky, 1930). There comes a point when the mother as unit, as a "whole" person, ceases to be perceived only as an element of the specific situation in which she is experienced. It is because of this situational determination of the percept that one and the same person is perceived by the infant as a number of discrete persons or rather percepts. Some of them are sensed as "good," others as "bad." After the sixth month the multiple percepts of the mother are fused due to the increasing retentiveness of the infant's memory function and his ego's integrative tendency. Underlying this achievement is an ideational process: successive memory traces of the preobject are recognized as identical with each other, independent of the situation, and the object is synthesized.

I might add here what I have said elsewhere (1957), that the secondary, inessential attributes of the percept are now disregarded; the percept is recognized by virtue of its essential attributes. With this, the percept "mother" becomes a single one, will no longer be equated with any other person playing her role in identical situations. From now on she will focus on her person the infant's aggressive as well as his libidinal drives. The fusion of the two drives and the fusion of the good and the bad object into one, namely, into the libidinal object, are therefore the two facets of one and the same process. The "good" aspects of the mother immeasurably outweigh the "bad" aspects. And in the same way the child's libidinal drive outweighs the aggressive one, for his libidinal drive is proportionate to his need. Consequently the good object appears to predominate in this fusion, which is probably why the libidinal object was also called the love object.

Now that the two drives are directed toward the one single, emotionally most strongly cathected, object we can speak of the establishment of the libidinal object *proper* and of the inception of true object relations. This is how I conceive of the collaboration of the aggressive and libidinal drives in the formation of object relations.

FEEDING SCHEDULES: THEIR IMPACT ON MOTHERING

If we accept this proposition regarding the role of the two drives in the process of object formation, it becomes abundantly clear that whether we suppress the expression of one of the drives or facilitate it to the detriment of the other, we are initiating a malformation of object relations. In general, it is the mother who suppresses or facilitates; it is her behavior, therefore, which will determine the way in which object relations will be formed and conducted. She can, in her choice, stress the "good object" or, at the other extreme, the "bad object." Of course, there is a wide spectrum of possibilities between these two extremes. But it is obvious that differences in maternal attitudes are quite dependent on cultural institutions and cultural processes, and are even subject to cultural fashions. I will mention two instances of the latter as an example:

Probably due to the influence of the school of behaviorism, the bad object was stressed in child rearing in the United States in the period following the First World War and until approximately 1942. During this period, infants were nursed on a rigid schedule, according to the clock, with a prescribed quantity of food, without considering whether the child was satisfied or not. The mothers were instructed not to "spoil" their children, not to handle them in a "mawkish," sentimental way, to be objective, kindly, and firm, never to hug and kiss them, never let them sit in their laps. To quote one passage from Watson (1928): "Treat them as though they were young adults. Dress them, bathe them with care and circumspection. . . . If you must, kiss them once on the forehead." This attitude was taken over by the United States Children's Bureau, which in its pamphlet *Infant Care* as late as 1938 recommended "training in regularity of feeding, sleeping and elimination" practically from birth, maintaining that through this method "the tiny baby will receive his first lessons in character building."

In other words, mothers were instructed to abstain from following their natural urge to express their love for their babies as they would wish to. Needless to say, even in those meager years, quite a few mothers continued to love their children "against doctor's advice"—and we can congratulate them and their children for this. Fondling and cuddling one's child could not be suppressed.

A complete reversal occurred around 1940; witness the radical revision of the 1942 edition of *Infant Care* of the United States Children's Bureau. The text of this new edition is so understanding of the child's needs, and perhaps also the mother's, that it can be called practically human. However, at the same time the so-called self-demand schedule had been "invented" and became popular. This method consists of nursing or feeding the infant whenever he expresses a "desire" for this—that is, whenever he manifests unpleasure. In many instances this led to an extraordinary measure of overfeeding amounting to gavage. This was going to the other extreme, and as ill-advised and unreasonable as the opposite procedure.

FRUSTRATION TOLERANCE AND THE REALITY PRINCIPLE

The two examples speak for themselves. At the same time one senses how, in the course of the progressive fusion of the two instinctual drives, the reward offered by the "good object" can serve as a compensation for the misdeeds of the "bad object." In their turn these compensations will enable the infant to withstand greater frustration—greater both in regard to the amount of frustration imposed and in regard to its duration. That is of vital importance, for ultimately the capacity to tolerate frustration is at the origin of the reality principle. The reality principle is the formulation of a detour function: immediate drive gratification has to be relinquished, so that, by postponing it, more adequate gratification may later be achieved (Freud, 1916-1917; but see also 1895, 1900, 1911). This capacity to suspend drive gratification, to tolerate a delay in the discharge of tension, to give up immediate and perhaps uncertain pleasure, in order to gain this certainty of later pleasure is a momentous step in the humanization of man. It made possible the progress from internal reception to external perception;[1] from "passive" perception to motor discharge in the form of action, eventuating in active appropriate alteration of reality, that is, alloplastic adaptation.

In the next step restraint of motor discharge provides the delay required for a process as complex as thinking and judgment. Thought permits a regulation of the drives by channeling their discharge into directed volitional action. Hence the directed discharge of aggression becomes possible, ensuring pleasure gain. Thus mastery over the "things" in the physical world becomes possible. It should not be overlooked that at the inception of the reality principle the compensation provided by the "good" object for the misdeeds of the "bad"

---

[1] From coenesthetic reception to diacritic perception.

object facilitates the inception of the reality principle and makes the delay not only bearable but rewarding. This makes it understandable why, as the late Katherine Wolf[2] so sensitively observed: "Normal object relations with the mother are a prerequisite for the child's capacity to relate to things and to master them." Finally, it shows again how indispensable it is for the infant to succeed in fusing aggressive and libidinal drives and to be able to discharge them onto *one* single partner, namely, the mother.

[2] Personal communication.

CHAPTER X

Further Development After the
Establishment of the Second Organizer

The extraordinary significance of the second organizer for the infant's further development is reflected in the rapid unfolding and structurization of his personality. In the weeks immediately following the first signs of the eight-month anxiety, many new behavior patterns, performances, relations make their first appearance. Foremost and most conspicuous among these is the emergence of new forms of social relations, on a signally higher level of complexity than those present earlier. The understanding of social gestures and their use as a vehicle of reciprocal communication begins. This is most impressive in the child's understanding of, and response to, prohibitions and commands.

Progress in understanding social relations is also evident in the child's growing participation in reciprocal social games. Roll a rubber ball to him and he will return it; offer him your hand saying "Hello" and he will put his hand into yours. If you intrude on his activities by energetically saying "No! No!" and at the same time shake your head or wag your finger in sign of prohibition, he will stop whatever he is doing. His face may even express consternation (see Figs. 10 and 11).

174

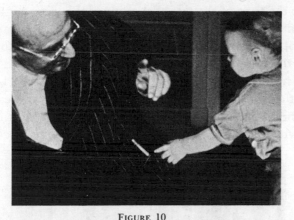

FIGURE 10

The Observer Wags His Finger While Saying "No, No"
to the Child Who Tries to Grab the Pencil.

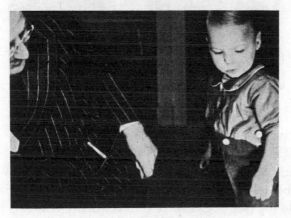

FIGURE 11

The Child's Response.

PROGRESS IN PERCEPTUAL, MOTOR, AND AFFECTIVE SECTORS

At the same time significant changes occur also in the
child's dealings with his inanimate environment. To begin
with, his "territory," his relation to the space surrounding
him is modified.

Up to the time of the establishment of the second organizer, the infant's orientation in space seems limited by the bars of his cot, his "crib space." Within his cot he grabs toys with ease. If the same toy is offered to him outside of the bars of his cot, he reaches for it; but his hands stop at the bars; he does not continue his movements beyond; he could easily do it, for the bars are sufficiently widely spaced. It is as if space ended within his cot (see Fig. 12). Two to three weeks after

FIGURE 12

The Child is Still Unable to Grasp His Favorite Toy
When it is Offered to Him Beyond the Bars of His Cot.

the eighth month, however, he suddenly sees the light and becomes able to continue his movement beyond the bars and to grasp the toy (see Fig. 13). It is noteworthy that this happens before the advent of erect locomotion.

In another sector, progress is made in the capacity to discriminate between inanimate things. We have noted that the ability of discrimination is acquired through exchanges with the partner, with the libidinal object. The role of affective relations as trail breakers for perceptual development is particularly evident in regard to inanimate objects. Distinguishing the mother from strangers (that is, *one person* from

FIGURE 13

After the Eighth Month, Space Beyond the Bars of the
Crib is Understood.

another) precedes by two months the child's capacity to distinguish one *toy* from another. If after the emergence of the eight-month anxiety several toys are placed before the child, he will grasp his preferred toy and not, as previously, the toy or the thing which is closest to his leading hand.

Progress in ideation such as the inception of the child's understanding of the relatedness between things is evident in the following example: If one now attaches a string to a bell, then places the string inside the child's cot and rings the bell, the child quickly sees that he can pull the bell into his cot by pulling the string. This performance reveals that the child has achieved for the first time the use of a tool.

On the affective level, subtle shadings of emotional attitudes begin to emerge. Jealousy, anger, rage, envy, possessiveness on the one hand, love, affection, attachment, joy, pleasure, etc., on the other, can be observed toward the end of the first year of life.

The differentiation of these new shadings of emotions results from the unfolding of ever more complex object relations, which also prompt the formation of certain defense mechanisms toward the end of the first year of life.

IMITATION AND IDENTIFICATION

At this age level the operation of the mechanism of identification is conspicuous and easily observed. We shall therefore examine it more closely. Its first traces were seen in about 10 per cent of the infants in our sample already at the age of three to four months. These children were the exception. When presented with the adult's face they seemed to attempt to mirror his expression. To be sure, this is an extremely rudimentary form of imitation: just as perception at this stage is global (that is, a Gestalt perception), imitation will also be global. If, for instance, you offer the infant a widening of the mouth, the infant will try to widen his own mouth, and attempt lip movements that are the opposite of narrowing his mouth. Conversely if one narrows one's mouth as if to whistle, the imitating infant may narrow his mouth in the same way, or he may push his tongue out, so as to form a pointed shape (Kaila, 1932).

True imitation appears much later, between the eighth and the tenth month, that is, after the establishment of the second organizer. In several of my films I have recorded the beginning of imitation: for example, that attendant on social games, like rolling back a ball. Berta Bornstein[1] has called this behavior pattern "identification through the gesture." If I understand her correctly, her term means that the child imitates the gesture without understanding its ideational content. However, identification through the gesture is only a precursor of the mechanism of identification proper, with which I shall deal in Chapter XI.

The mother's attitude, the emotional climate which she provides for the infant, are of decisive importance for the de-

[1] Personal communication.

velopment of imitation. Her attitude is even more important for the dynamic process through which the mechanism of identification will be established. The emotional climate within the dyad is an influence which facilitates or impedes the infant's attempts to become and to act like his mother. I have mentioned this influence earlier in connection with the development of action patterns and their development.

The acquisition of action patterns, the mastery of imitation, and the functioning of identification are the devices which permit the child to achieve increasing autonomy from the mother. Imitating the mother's actions enables the child to provide himself with all that his mother had provided before.

We have now followed the child to almost the end of the preverbal stage. In the course of the last steps leading to the formation of the second organizer, reciprocal communication, directed, active, and intentional, has developed between the child and his mother. Though the child is active in this process of communication, he does not yet use semantic signals and, even less, words. In the phase which now follows, these directed and reciprocal communications are gradually organized into a kind of system of semantic gestures, which in their turn will later be transformed into verbal ones. I speak advisedly of verbal *gestures*. The words which the child uses at the turn of the first year of life, the so-called "global" words, are still very much in the nature of gestures. They encompass much more than any specific thing, they indicate a direction, and a need, and a wish, and a mood, and the thing or object in question, all at the same time. This is a decisive turning point in the evolution both of the individual and of the species. Once this progress is achieved, the character of object relations undergoes a fundamental change. From here on they will be carried on more and more by means of words. Soon speech will become the principal device through which exchanges within the dyad are conducted.

CHAPTER XI

The Origins and Beginnings of Human Communication: The Third Organizer of the Psyche

Among the most important transformations which set in with the advent of the second organizer is the child's progressive understanding of prohibitions and the emergence of the first traces of identification phenomena. The two developments are somewhat related, as we shall see later.

THE IMPACT OF LOCOMOTION ON DYADIC RELATIONS

Prior to the establishment of the second organizer maternal messages reach the child primarily via tactile contact (except for the visual sphere). Having acquired locomotion, the infant strives for autonomy and succeeds to get out of the mother's reach. He can wriggle out of her sight, but he cannot easily evade her voice. Consequently object relations hitherto based on proximity contact will undergo a radical change.

Independent locomotion is a maturational progress fraught with perils for the child. It presents many problems for his surround. As long as the infant was a prisoner in the cage of his cot, he was secure. Now he can walk; he does not hesitate

180

to satisfy his curiosity, his need for activity, and throws himself headlong into the most dangerous situations. At any moment the mother's intervention may become imperative. However, now the child's capacity for locomotion frequently puts space between himself and his mother so that maternal intervention will have to rely increasingly on gesture and word.

Inevitably the nature of the exchanges between mother and child must undergo an equally radical transformation. Until now the mother was free to gratify or not to gratify the needs and wishes of the child. Now she is *forced* to curb and to prevent the child's initiatives, just at that period at which the thrust of infantile activity is on the increase. Indeed, the shift from passivity to activity is a turning point (Freud, 1931); it coincides with the advent of the second organizer.

Accordingly the exchanges between mother and child will now center around bursts of infantile activity and maternal commands and prohibitions. This is in vivid contrast to the preceding period, when infantile passivity and maternal endearment and supportive action constituted the major part of object relations. Indeed, the very form and content of communication change drastically. At the preverbal stage, messages transmitted by the mother necessarily consisted mainly in action, primarily because of the child's helplessness. I have advanced the proposition that the mother is the child's *external ego* (1951). Until an organized structural ego is developed by the child the mother takes over the functions of the child's ego. She controls the child's access to directed motility. She cares for the child and protects him, she provides food, hygiene, entertainment, the satisfaction of the child's curiosity; she determines the choice of avenues leading into the various sectors of development; she has many other functions. In the course of this extensive activity, of which one might speak as the prototype for all altruism, sympathy, and empathy, the mother must act as the representative of the child both in respect to the outer world and to the child's inner world. In these roles she performs the baby's actions and carries out his wishes as she understands them. In their turn, her actions communicate her intentions to her baby.

This is not to say that during the preverbal stage vocal exchanges are absent in object relations—the contrary is true. Every mother speaks with her child; often her actions are accompanied by a running monologue, and frequently the child answers, babbling, lallating.

This species of conversation, in which the mother croons incoherent verbiage to her baby, inventing words—while the baby answers, lallating—takes place in the irrational realm of affective relationships. Such conversations are only vaguely related to expressions of physical desires by the child; they do not prohibit, they do not prevent, they do not obligate; yet they create a mood. They are, so to say, twitterings of reciprocal pleasure.

Negative Head Shaking:
The Infant's First Semantic Gesture

Once locomotion is acquired, all this will change. Crooning is replaced by prohibition, by command, by reproach, by invective. Now the word she uses most frequently is "No! No!" and saying these words, the mother shakes her head, while she prevents the child from doing what he wanted to do. At first the mother will necessarily emphasize the prohibiting gesture and word by some physical action, until the child begins to understand verbal interdictions.

The child understands the mother's prohibitions through a process of identification. The details of this identificatory process will be presented later. The manifest symptom of the presence of such identification is the fact that the child will in due time imitate the negative head shaking which routinely accompanies the mother's action. For the child, this head shaking becomes the symbol and the enduring vestige of the maternal frustrating action. He will adopt and retain this gesture even as a grownup. It becomes a stubborn automatism which even the best-mannered adult relinquishes with difficulty. Etiquette fails in uprooting this gesture even at the cost of great efforts. That is not surprising for it was acquired and reinforced during the most archaic period of consciousness, at the beginning of the verbal stage.

Perhaps some readers will challenge my opinion that the negative head-shaking gesture and the word "No" are the first semantic symbols to appear in the course of the child's semantic communication code; actually they are his first semantic symbols and words only from the viewpoint of the adult. In this they differ fundamentally, not only from the lallating monologues, but also from the first so-called "global" words which appear prior to the word "No"; I refer to words like "Mama," "Dada," etc. These global words represent a variety of wishes and needs of the child, ranging from "mother!" to "food!"; from "I am bored" to "I am happy." The negative headshake and the word "No" by contrast represent a concept: the concept of negation, of refusal in the narrow sense of this term. It is not only a signal but also a sign of the child's attitude, conscious and unconscious. It is the minus sign of mathematics, where such signs are called algorisms.

Imitation, Identification, and Negative Head Shaking: Three Propositions

But beyond this, the head-shaking "No" is also, and perhaps foremost, the first abstract concept formed in the mind of the child. How does the child acquire this concept? One might believe that the child apes his mother. But looking closer it becomes quite evident that this is not pure and simple imitation. True, the child imitates the mother's gesture *qua* gesture. But it is the child who chooses the circumstances in which to use this gesture, and, later on, *when* to use the *word* "No." He uses the gesture primarily when he refuses something, be that a demand or an offer.

As noted, this phase of development is marked by the conflict between the child's initiative and the mother's apprehensions. When in his turn the child refuses something which the mother wishes or offers, it looks as if he were imitating, as if the negative head-shaking gesture of the mother had been recorded in the memory of the child simply because of her repeated prohibitions. However, such an interpretation would have us assume that, after recording the association of headshake and refusal in his memory, the infant in his turn reproduces the gesture when *he* expresses refusal. This mechanical explanation is in good agreement with the reinforcement hypothesis of learning theory. But it does not explain how together with the memory traces of the association of percept with experience, the infant also is able to take over its meaning. How does he achieve the abstraction and generalization which are apparent when he refuses offers as well as requests, prohibitions as well as commands? The major intellectual feat necessary for such abstractions and generalizations cannot be explained through simple cumulation of memory traces. Quantitative explanations which disregard dynamics do not satisfy the psychoanalyst. Changes in quantities alone do not explain mental processes.

A somewhat better explanation of the phenomenon is offered by Gestalt psychology. In a series of very simple and clear experiments, Zeigarnik (1927) showed that unfinished tasks are remembered, while tasks which have been completed are forgotten. Accordingly, when the mother prohibits or refuses something, her "No" prevents the child from completing the task which he intended to carry out. The fact that the child could not carry out the task will thus reinforce its recollection and recall.

A far more comprehensive explanation and one that also sheds light on the cathectic shifts which underly the child's "No" gesture can be provided by psychoanalytic propositions. Careful study of the circumstances which lead to the child's mastery of the negative head-shaking gesture reveals that it is the result of a complex dynamic process.

In the first place, every "No" of the mother represents an emotional frustration for the child. Whether she forbids him some activity, or he is prevented from achieving a thing which he desires; whether one disagrees with the manner in which he wishes to conduct his object relations—it always will be the instinctual drives which will be frustrated. The prohibition, the gestures, the words through which the frustration is imposed will be invested with a specific affective charge, which has the meaning of refusal, of defeat, in one word, of *frustration*. And so will the memory trace of the experience. It is this affective cathexis which ensures the permanency of the memory trace, both of the gesture and of the word "No."

On the other hand, prohibition by its very nature interrupts an initiative, an action of the child, and pushes him back from activity into passivity. At the age when the child begins to understand the mother's prohibition, he also passes through a metamorphosis in another sector of his personality. A surge of activity begins which replaces the passivity characteristic of the narcissistic stage. This emerging outer-directed activity will be much in evidence in his object relations. He will not tolerate being forced back into passivity without resistance (Anna Freud, 1952).

The child's physical efforts to overcome the prohibitions as well as the obstacles put in his way do not tell the whole story. Another psychodynamic factor is added—namely, the affective charge of unpleasure which accompanies frustration, and which provokes an aggressive thrust from the id. A memory trace of the prohibition is laid down in the ego and will be invested with this aggressive cathexis.

Now the child is caught in a conflict between the libidinal bond which draws him to his mother and his aggression provoked through the frustration imposed by the selfsame mother. Between his own wish and the object's prohibition, between the unpleasure of opposing the mother and thus risking loss of object and later loss of love, he will have recourse to a compromise solution. This consists in an autoplastic change provided by a defense mechanism, that of identification, which, at this stage, is just emerging. However, he will make use of a rather special variant of this mechanism; this is the "identification with the aggressor" as described by Anna Freud (1936).

Anna Freud demonstrated this form of the mechanism in the school child, who uses it in dealing with conflicts between the ego and the object. In her cases, the superego, or at least its precursors, play an important role. In our fifteen-month-old child the superego plays no role because it does not yet exist. Moreover, in the phenomenon which we are discussing, the infant identifies with the frustrator rather than with the aggressor. But the difference between aggressor and frustrator is only one of degree.

The dynamics which lead to the acquisition of the semantic gesture of "No" are then the following: the negative head-shaking gesture and the word "No" spoken by the libidinal object are incorporated into the ego of the infant as memory traces.[1] The affective charge of unpleasure is separated from

[1] After the publication of the monograph *No and Yes* (1957) I was approached from several quarters with questions on the subject of memory traces operative in the acquisition of the gesture and the word "No." Those questions make it desirable to say a few words on the theoretical implications of this problem. Freud (1915a) suggested that memory traces referring to one and the same percept (experience) are laid down in different psychic "localities," that is, in topographically separated registrations ["*topisch gesonderte*

this presentation; this separation provokes an aggressive thrust, which will then be linked by way of association to the memory trace in the ego.

When the child identifies with the libidinal object, this identification with the aggressor, in Anna Freud's terms, will be followed, as she describes, by an attack against the external world. In the fifteen-month-old infant, this attack takes the form of the "No" (gesture first, and word later) which the child has taken over from the libidinal object. Because of numerous unpleasure experiences the "No" is invested with aggressive cathexis. This makes the "No" suitable for expressing aggression, and this is the reason why the "No" is used in the defense mechanism of identification with the aggressor and turned against the libidinal object. Once this step has been accomplished, the phase of stubbornness (with which we are so familiar in the second year of life) can begin.

Niederschriften"]. These "localities" are the system *Ucs.* and the system *Cs.* (or *Pcs.*). It would appear from this, as well as from some of his later statements on the subject, that what is laid down when the head-shaking "No" is acquired are several memory traces, differing in their qualities from one another. The gesture will first be laid down as a "thing presentation." Ultimately this will belong to the system *Ucs.*

However, it is probable—indeed, it is in accordance with psychoanalytic theory—that in the beginning of the process of acquiring the "No" gesture, the memory trace is equally available both to the system *Ucs.* and to the system *Pcs.* Freud's assumption is that the system *Pcs.* is composed primarily of word presentations which will derive their (sensorimotor) quality from the unconscious *thing presentations.* However, at the age at which the "No" gesture is acquired, around the fifteenth month of life, the separation between the systems is not as firmly established as it will be later. A variety of apparatuses are still being integrated into an ego; and ego systems are being delimited from one another and organized. Several months later, when the *word* "No" is also incorporated in the memory as a *word presentation,* the separation between the unconscious *thing presentations* and the preconscious *word presentations* will already be much more advanced. Now the sensorimotor qualities attached to the *thing presentation* of the prohibition can be linked with the "No" (gesture and word) and will activate the *word presentation* in the system *Pcs.*

It would appear then that in acquiring the "No" gesture the child begins to shift from exclusive reliance on the primary process to the gradual use of the secondary process.

The Third Organizer of the Psyche

The mastery of the "No" (gesture and word) is an achievement with far-reaching consequences for the mental and emotional development of the child; it presupposes that he has acquired the first capacity of judgment and negation. Freud (1925a) discussed this question in a masterly article of a few pages, "Negation." I shall touch only on a few of the most essential aspects of this milestone in development; for a more complete treatment I refer the reader to my monograph *No and Yes* (1957).

To begin with, identification with the aggressor is a selective process. Three factors can be distinguished in the mother's behavior when she imposes a prohibition. They are her *gesture* (or her word); her *conscious thought;* and her *affect.* Obviously the child incorporates the gesture. But how could a fifteen-month-old understand or even perceive the reasons which motivate the mother to impose her prohibitions? What happens is that the child does *not* incorporate the mother's thought. In this phase, the child is still incapable of rational thought, and therefore he does not know whether the mother prohibits because she is afraid that he will hurt himself, or whether she is angry because he has been bad.

As for her affect, the child at this age still understands affects only in a global manner. One might say approximatively that he distinguishes only two affects in the "other." I have called them the affect "for" and its opposite, the affect "against." Therefore what the child does understand is that the affect of the mother is: "You are not *for* me; you are *against* me." It follows that in identifying with the aggressor by means of the negative gesture, the child has only appropriated the gesture itself, together with the affect "against." Nevertheless, this is an extraordinary progress. Until now, the expression of the child's affects in the situation of object relations was limited to immediate contact, to action.[2] With the acquisition of the gesture of negation, action is replaced by messages, and distance communication is inaugurated.

This is perhaps the most important turning point in evolution, both of the individual and of the species. Here begins the humanization of the species; here begins the *zoon politikon;* here begins society. For this is the inception of reciprocal exchanges of messages, intentional, directed; with the advent of semantic symbols, it becomes the origin of verbal communication. This is the reason why I consider the achievement of the sign of negation and of the word "No" the tangible indicator of the formation of the third organizer.

The "No," in gesture and in word, is the semantic expression of negation and of judgment; at the same time this is the first abstraction formed by the child, the first abstract concept in the sense of adult mentation. The concept is acquired with the help of a displacement of aggressive cathexis; I believe that displacements of aggressive cathexis are characteristic of every abstraction. Abstraction is never the result

[2] Earlier, during the infant's period of helplessness, the period which Ferenczi (1916) called the stage of infantile omnipotence, fantasy replaces action. These fantasies, however, are not comparable to adult fantasy and even less to the lurid fantasies of the preschool child. The infant's fantasies must necessarily remain within the compass of his limited cognitive resources. At this stage cognition is unquestionably derived far more from physiological than ideational sources.

This statement calls for certain reservations. Cognitively, the infant in his first year is aware only of a minor part of the physiological functions that seem so obvious to the grownup. We certainly can assume the infant's awareness of intake and of the actions connected with intake, like chewing, swallowing, grasping, and hitting. It is questionable how much of elimination has already entered the infant's cognition. My observations led me to assume that by the end of the first year of life the infant is just turning his attention to the eliminative functions. I therefore hold that most fantasies during the stage of helplessness will be centered around activities connected with intake and culminating in introjection. This proposition is in part supported by the manifest beginnings of the child's identificatory performances in the latter half of the first year. Activities patterned on the functions connected with elimination and suggesting the mechanism of projection are less in evidence, though already noticeable. Such activities will come more to the fore in the course of the second year of life.

of identification as such; it is the result of a two-step process. The first step consists in our use of aggressive energy to detach certain elements from what we perceive. The second step is the result of the synthetic activity of the ego (Nunberg, 1930) in that the elements detached by the aggressive energy are synthesized. The product of this synthesis is either a symbol or a concept. The first such concept in the life of the child is negation.

As mentioned before, soon after the beginning of the second year, the child expresses negation by shaking his head, and thus communicates his refusal to his surround by a semantic sign. Head shaking as a sign of negation is extraordinarily widespread on the globe. It is *by no means* a universally understood sign. In some cultures other gestures are used for negation. It is, however, very probable that head shaking has been the most frequently used gesture for negation on our globe. To me, the ubiquity of the gesture makes it seem probable that its motor origin could be retraced in human ontogenesis, and perhaps even in phylogenesis. Behavior derived from very archaic and primitive experience has the tendency to become generalized in the species, for it is shared by all its members.

BIOLOGICAL AND NEUROPHYSIOLOGICAL ROOTS OF NEGATIVE HEAD SHAKING

We decided therefore to investigate the earliest behavior patterns of the newborn, to find out whether there was one among them which might be similar to the head-shaking gesture of negation. We did find such a behavior pattern; it is the reflex called "sucking reflex" by some and "orientation reflex" by others. It is triggered by touching the perioral region with the finger; with Bernfeld (1925) I like to call this region the "snout"; it is the region which includes mouth, chin, nose, and the major part of the cheeks. We will refer to this reflex as "rooting."

This is an exceedingly archaic behavior pattern. Our motion picture studies show that the newborn in the nursing position begins nursing by performing several rotatory head movements, with open mouth, until he succeeds in snapping the nipple. As soon as he has succeeded, rotation ceases and sucking begins. I have found that this behavior is very simply explained on the grounds of the rooting reflex. In the nursing situation, one cheek of the newborn, for instance, the right, touches the breast. The head, mouth open, is then turned to the right; if the mouth does not encounter the nipple, the infant continues the movement until his left cheek touches the breast. Thereupon he turns his head toward the left, and so on, until the nipple is located by the open mouth.

Minkowski (1922) was the first to demonstrate that rooting behavior in the human fetus is already present at three months after conception. In a beautifully precise study of an anencephalic teratoma Gamper (1926) demonstrated that this behavior is even present on the mesencephalic level in all its details. Davenport Hooker (1939) continued these observations and experiments, recording them in impressive motion pictures.

On the phylogenetic level Prechtl, Klimpfinger, and Schleidt (1950, 1952, 1955) studied rooting in human infants and lower mammals, as one example of the development of early infantile motor behavior. They summarize their conclusions as follows: asymmetric stimulation (unilateral stimulation) on snout or lips triggers rotating movements of the head. As soon as the stimulation becomes symmetric through the simultaneous touching of upper and lower lip, the rotating movement stops, the mouth is closed, and suction begins. Rotation and sucking are mutually exclusive. Tilney and Kubie (1931) demonstrated that already in newborn kittens, the neural pathways which connect stomach with brain, mouth, labyrinth, and extremities are sufficiently developed to coordinate these organs in the task of nursing.

The above investigations have proved conclusively that the "rooting behavior" is firmly established at the level of embryological development, both in phylogenesis and in ontogenesis.

In the weeks and months following the baby's birth, the rooting movement becomes increasingly certain and goal-directed; after the third month the newborn achieves the nipple with one short movement of his head. The rooting movements, the rotation of the head, are the visible manifestations of the effort made by the newborn to achieve food. Biologically, it is an anticipatory behavior (Craig, 1918), an approach movement which has a positive "meaning"; from the psychological viewpoint one might call it an affirmative movement.

CHANGE IN FUNCTION: BIOLOGICAL AND
PSYCHOLOGICAL ASPECTS

The rotatory movements ensure the tactile orientation of the head toward the nipple. Hand in hand with the increase in efficiency of visual orientation and of muscular coordination, the rotatory head movements are progressively extinguished. Yet, after the sixth month of life, the rotatory head movements reappear in a situation which is the diametrical opposite of the one in which they had originally appeared. The six-month-old baby, when he is satiated, when he has had enough, turns his head from side to side, avoiding the nipple, or the spoon, in one word, the food—with the very same rotatory movement which at birth served him to seek food. Now, however, this movement is transformed into withdrawal behavior, into refusal. The movement has acquired a negative "meaning." It should be remembered, however, that this is still behavior and not yet a semantic gesture. It will take more than half a year's development before the child succeeds in transforming the avoidance behavior into the semantic gesture of refusal.

These are the principal stages in the vicissitudes of the motor patterns which will be used in the gesture of negating. I wish to stress that throughout the first year of life, *only* the motor pattern exists; this pattern has a function—first, to achieve food, later to avoid it. It is only after the fifteen month of life that the motor pattern is invested with an ideational content by the infant—that it takes on the value of a gesture and that the gesture conveys an abstract idea.

In the course of its ontogenetic development, the motor pattern of the head-shaking gesture of negating passes through three distinct stages. At birth, rooting is an affirmative behavior. This is not surprising—Freud (1925a) stressed that there exists no "No" in the unconscious. This of course follows from the laws governing the primary process. As the newborn is not conscious during the first weeks after his birth, he functions only according to the primary process; his reactions, his activity, are the result of tension discharge which, in the absence of a psychic organization, cannot become conscious. It follows that his behavior cannot express negation.

The second stage in which the six-month-old refuses food by means of rotating movements of the head occurs at the time when the first rudiments of a conscious ego are established. At this stage, however, the child does not yet have the means or the capacity to direct a communication to the "other." When we look at it from the outside, in this situation his head-rotating behavior expresses refusal. But this refusal is not directed to a person; it is objectless and still only the manifestation of the psychophysical state of the child. In the third stage, around fifteen months, it becomes permissible to interpret similar head-rotating behavior as a message addressed to another person, and to state that the congenital motor pattern of rooting has been placed into the service of the abstract concept of negation, and is integrated into a communication system.

The readers might object that the opposite of the negative gesture, the affirmative gesture, the vertical head nodding, is probably just as ubiquitous in the world. However, nothing of what I have so far presented in regard to the negative gesture can be applied to the affirmative one. It is improbable, for instance, that identification with the aggressor, or even with the frustrator, operates in establishing head nodding as a semantic gesture—although identification with the object is certainly involved in this process. Indeed, one might say that in the development of negation the aggressive drive has a major role, although not an exclusive one. In the development of affirmation, one then could expect the libidinal drive to be involved. But while in the neonate and even in the fetus a motor pattern quite similar to the head-shaking movement of negation is clearly in evidence, it is difficult to see what motor pattern present at birth could resemble head nodding even distantly. There is no trace of nodding movements in the rooting behavior; what is more, at birth the musculature of the neck is not sufficiently developed to support the head freely and even less to perform voluntary movements in the sagittal axis.

But have we not insisted on the fact that in the beginning every behavior has an affirmative character, oriented toward the gratification of the need? Where do we find the archaic prototype of the motor pattern of head nodding?

Eventually we discovered that prototype also among the behavior patterns connected with the nursing. But it is not present at birth, and only appears three months later.

At the age of three to six months, the baby can already support his head and move it with the help of the neck musculature. At that time, he also begins to orient himself visually. If one withdraws the nipple from a three- to six-month-old baby during nursing, he will perform approach movements with his head, nodding it vertically toward the breast. These movements resemble closely the motor pattern of head nodding; they are its first prototypes. In the course of the following months, they are integrated into the approach behavior of the infant. Unlike the motor pattern of head shaking, which undergoes a functional change in the course of development to become the sign of negation, affirmative head nodding retains its affirmative function. In the course of the second year of life, it takes on its semantic meaning, and thus becomes the gesture of affirmation: it is very probable that this happens several months after the semantic gesture of negation is acquired.

The history of the development of the "No" and of the "Yes," and of their differentiation into diametrically opposed directions in the course of the first year, is a striking example of the basic importance of psychic development for the subsequent fate of archaic behavior patterns. At the same time it is a confirmation of Freud's hypothesis (1910) on the origin of the antithetical meaning of primal words.

Part III

Pathology of Object Relations

CHAPTER XII

Deviant and Disturbed Object Relations

In the preceding chapters I have attempted to outline what might be called a psychoanalytic psychology of the first year of life; in this presentation the genetic and developmental aspects have been especially stressed. Of necessity such a presentation must be based on the figment of the "normal" child and its "normal" development. "Normal," of course, is a construct, hardly encountered in real life. I have, nevertheless, attempted something in the nature of an approximation, which relies on two assumptions. The practical value of one has been demonstrated in academic psychology, the other involves a methodological postulate well rooted in psychoanalytic theory and practice.

The first of the two is the assumption that it is possible to "measure" developmental progress absolutely and relatively at successive stages during the first year of life and to present the findings in the form of numerical results. As mentioned previously, we use these numerical results not as actual yardsticks but as ordinal indications. The corollary of this approach is the establishment of norms of average development and average developmental progress. The details of the strategy in this respect were shown in Chapter II.

The second postulate is in good agreement with Freud's

basic thinking: namely, that by studying deviations and disturbances, the "healthy" functioning of the organism can be inferred. This is an idea traditionally derived from neurology. We assume that normal development can be reconstructed through a clinical approach.

In the present study our inferences were derived from the data of object relations. We tacitly postulated that a child having good object relations with his mother—other things being equal, i.e., when the child is medically sound—would develop in a "normal" manner.

These two assumptions govern everything relating to developmental progress. Their usefulness will now be put to a rigorous test. As we examine pathological conditions, these assumptions must be capable of explaining all phenomena. If it is possible to relate pathological phenomena in infancy —presented in the form of tables, graphs, and indices—to specific disturbances in dyadic mother-infant relations, the methodology and assumptions will have fulfilled their purpose.

Before turning to pathology, at least a few words need be said about what we as psychoanalytic infant psychologists consider normal object relations.

NORMAL OBJECT RELATIONS

As already mentioned, one of the approaches to infant development is that of measurement and indices; it describes normality in terms of the average achievement of the infant at a certain age level; and I have been careful to point out that the achievements at each age level vary in a wide range, often as much as plus-minus two months. In the infant's first year, this is indeed a wide range, for it can represent as much as the major part of his chronological age.

Within this statistical average, there is another criterion of normalcy. The tests divide the infant's achievements and performances in the first year of life into six sectors. It is characteristic of so-called "normal" infantile development that in each of these sectors the infant progresses at different rates during the first year of life. Accordingly the ratio between the performance scores in the different sectors will vary from month to month.

In a certain number of cases, however, we found—and I shall return to this later—that the ratio between the individual sectors remains relatively invariant from month to month in one and the same child. This indicates that development, as expressed in the reciprocal ratio of the six sectors (which normally varies in the course of the first year), has come under some influence which inhibits (or, in some cases, induces) variations. This influence originates mostly from the mother-child relations and its presence in any particular case should be an incentive to investigate it.

So much for statistical criteria. Notwithstanding the ease and clarity with which they can be obtained and interpreted, I believe that they merely complement the clinical picture. But how to describe this clinical picture?

Let us begin by saying that a normal child is a healthy-looking, active individual, who on the whole gives the impression of being happy, and who gives his parents little to worry about. He eats well, he sleeps well, he grows well, his weight increases regularly, as does his size, and month by month he becomes brighter and more active, and more and more of a human being. Emotionally he enjoys his parents and his surround more and more, and vice versa he is being increasingly enjoyed by them.

It is evident from these homely words that nothing is more difficult to describe than normalcy. However, the last statement has brought us closer to a psychoanalytic criterion. That the parents enjoy their child and that the child enjoys his parents is a layman's description of object relations. These object relations must to some extent be examined from the point of view of normalcy. In Chapter I, I mentioned that the relations between mother and child involve two completely dissimilar individuals, and that what satisfies the mother is wholly different from what may satisfy the infant. Yet it is basic for our concept of normal object relations that they have to be satisfactory both for the mother and for the child.

Let us begin with the mother: her gratification stems from the role which the facts of bearing, having, and raising a baby represent for her specific personality. It should be kept in mind that this relationship differs from every other one in the world, for the fact is that this selfsame baby she is holding in her arms had only recently been inside her and part of her own body. At that time her attachment to the baby was indistinguishable from the attachment she felt to her own body. The fetus was invested with narcissistic cathexis, ordinarily reserved for one's own body. When, through delivery, the newborn became separate from her, she had to go through a process of cleavage, of renouncing the feeling that the baby was still identical with her. This is a gradual process. For a long time any of the baby's achievements will be her own, any of the baby's shortcomings will be her failure. The psychoanalyst who has had the occasion to analyze pregnant or recently delivered women is exceedingly familiar with a mother's multiple and contradictory feelings. The fact that childbearing has caused her discomfort, the delivery pain, the nursing sacrifices and joys will all enter directly or indirectly into her feelings for the baby. Whether any of these factors will represent an asset or a drawback is determined less by what we would consider its physical reality than by its psychological reality, by what it means to her personality in terms of the dynamics of her own emotional history. It is not very surprising then that the child who has caused his mother more suffering, more anguish than the others can easily become the most cherished.

As one investigates these feelings of the mother more closely, one discovers an increasingly larger number of complex factors that enter the picture: the baby's sex; his personality; his place in the order of his siblings; the mother's age; her relations to her parents; *her* place among *her* siblings —we could go on and on with this enumeration. But I shall leave it to the imagination of the readers to envision the endless possibilities and limit my discussion to a single aspect only; the reader must surely have wondered why I did not mention that the baby also has a father; and the mother a husband!

After all, the father of the baby is the ultimate culmination of the mother's first object relation. He is the ultimate product of the vicissitudes which the mother's object relations have undergone, from the first preobjectal relations to the breast, from the formation of the libidinal object in the person of her mother, its transportation to her father, in the oedipal stage, and its crowning fulfillment in her lover and husband, the father of her child. Does the child resemble him? Do the two compete? The fact that I have so far mainly spoken of the way in which the infant experiences and responds in the circular exchanges within the object relations, is molded by them, and eventually achieves the libidinal object, should not let us forget or ignore that for the mother her baby is a prime love object; and like all love objects, it is for her foremost a source of gratification.

These gratifications are both narcissistic and object libidinal. Putting it in structural terms, we may say that the mother obtains from her child id, ego, and superego gratifications. It follows that the gratification which any mother can derive from her relations with her child are determined by a number of elements: (a) through the nature of the constituent elements of her personality; (b) through the transformation which these constituent elements have undergone until the time she had delivered her child; (c) from the manner in which the particular child, by virtue of his congenital equipment, has the capacity to bring about the synthesis of these various elements in the mother's personality as well as to fit into the circumstances of outer reality.

The needs which object relations are called upon to gratify for the infant are quite different. To begin with, the infant's organism is in the process of rapid unfolding and development. The very nature of what satisfies the infant will therefore undergo rapid changes. It follows that the nature and the form of his gratifications will change progressively at each successive level of development. At the most primitive level at which an ego is not yet functioning, satisfactory relations will be need gratifications, closer to physiology than to psychology. These gratifications offer the infant security, provide for the discharge of need tension, and, as the case may be, for the relief from unpleasure tension. After the emergence of the ego, the gratifications required by the infant can be satisfied only in a relationship which becomes progressively more varied and complex. To keep up with the infant's progress, the mother's responses to the initiatives of the child have to make the gratification of libidinal and aggressive drives possible in the form of circular interactions. These interactions reverberate between mother and child and become ramified and diversified as times goes by. The maternal responses to the infant's actions facilitate and make possible the integration of maturational processes in the baby. They provoke an increasing complexity in the structure of the child's ego and lead to the formation of multiple systems. At the same time this increasing complexity of the ego expands the spectrum of the gratifications which the child now demands from object relations.

I realize that my attempt to define normal object relations is vague, groping, and tentative. It is difficult, if not impossible, to find a formula to express the multiform, silent ebb and flow, the mute invisible tides, powerful and at the same time subtle, which pervade these relations. It can never be sufficiently stressed, nor too often repeated, that object relations take place as a constant interaction between two very unequal partners, the mother and the child; that each provokes the responses of the other; that this interpersonal relation creates a field of constantly shifting forces. Perhaps one might say that object relations which gratify both mother and child are relations in which an interplay of forces operates in a way to complement each other in such a manner that not only do they offer gratification to both partners, but the very fact that one of the partners achieves gratification will produce a gratification for the other also. It will not have escaped the thoughtful reader that this last statement would be an equally fitting description of a love relation and even of the mutual feelings between man and woman in the sexual act. But then, as I have said above, what is the love relationship if not the crowning fulfillment of object relations?

The very perfection of a relation between two beings as closely attuned to each other and linked by so many tangibles and intangibles entails the possibility of serious disturbances if they are out of tune. They do not even have to be out of tune with each other. It suffices if one of the partners of the dyad—and that will mostly be the mother—is out of tune with her surround. Her molding influence makes it inevitable that her own discord will be reflected in the child's development—and reflected, as it were, in a magnifying mirror. Disturbances in the relation between mother and child will therefore provide us with a great deal of information both in regard to pathology and its etiology, as well as in regard to normal development. In the following pages I will describe some deviant forms of infantile development and examine the nature of the object relations prevailing in such cases, as far as I have been able to study them.

Quantitative and Qualitative Factors in Disturbed Object Relations

In the mother-child relation, the mother is the dominant, active partner. The child, at least in the beginning, is the passive recipient. This leads us to our first proposition: *disturbances of the maternal personality will be reflected in the disorders of the child.* If we limit the psychological influences which become effective during infancy to the mother-child relation, we obtain our second hypothesis: *in infancy damaging psychological influences are the consequence of unsatisfactory relations between mother and child.* Such unsatisfactory relations are pathogenic and can be divided into two categories: (a) improper mother-child relations, (b) insufficient mother-child relations. Stated differently, in the first case, the disturbance of the object relations is due to a qualitative factor, while in the second case, it is due to a quantitative factor.

IMPROPER MOTHER-CHILD RELATIONS

These can lead to a variety of disturbances in the child. I have been able to distinguish several clinical pictures of such disturbances; each seemed to be linked to a specific inappropriate mother-child relation; indeed, the clinical picture appeared to be the consequence of a given maternal behavior pattern. Some of the clinical pictures have been described in the pediatric literature. I do not claim that the psychogenic etiology of these diseases has been adequately demonstrated through the fact that I succeeded in uncovering a linkage between specific disturbances of object relations and given clinical pictures. Indeed, in certain of these diseases one can demonstrate specific congenital elements which also seemed to play an etiological role. However, neither the psychological factor *alone,* nor the congenital element *alone,* would lead to the onset of the disease in question—only the conjunction of the two.

The clinical pictures which we observed in a statistically significant number of infants in the given environmental set-up were partly physical diseases, partly abnormal behavior patterns. In the etiology of these clinical pictures we could demonstrate psychogenic factors deriving from the mother-child relations. We were inspired in this approach by a statement of Freud (1911): ". . . the form taken by the subsequent illness (the *choice of neurosis*) will depend on the particular phase of the development of the ego and of the libido in which the dispositional inhibition of development has occurred. Thus unexpected significance attaches to the chronological features of the two *developments* (which have not yet been studied), and to the possible variations in their synchronization" (p. 224f.; italics mine).

Our work has been specifically concerned with the study of these two above-mentioned developments. However, our findings were made in given environments of the Western cultural sphere. Their validity will have to be checked in other such environments (and perhaps in cultures other than ours) before it is permissible to make cross-cultural generalizations on infant psychology.

Returning to our subject, the improper mother-child relations: I have stated above that by the nature of things, the mother's personality is dominant in the dyad. We may then assume that, where improper mother-child relations prevail, the mother's personality is unable to offer her child a normal relation, or that, for reasons of her personality, she is compelled to disturb the normal relation which a mother would ordinarily have with her baby. *In either case,* we can say that the mother's personality acts as the disease-provoking agent, as a psychological toxin. For this reason, I have called this group of disturbances in object relations, or rather their consequences, *psychotoxic diseases of infancy*. I was able to distinguish a series of damaging maternal behavior patterns, each of which appeared to be linked to a specific psychotoxic disturbance of the infant. These maternal behavior patterns are enumerated below:

a. Primary overt rejection
b. Primary anxious overpermissiveness
c. Hostility in the guise of anxiety
d. Oscillation between pampering and hostility
e. Cyclical mood swings of the mother
f. Hostility consciously compensated

INSUFFICIENT MOTHER-CHILD RELATIONS

Depriving infants in their first year of life of object relations is a major damaging factor which leads to severe emotional disturbance. Such infants present a striking clinical picture; they give the impression of having been deprived of some vital element of survival. When we deprive infants of their relations with their mothers, without providing an adequate substitute whom the baby is able to accept, we deprive them of libidinal supplies. In the event of partial deprivation, they obtain insufficient libidinal supplies. The analogy with avitaminosis suggests itself. Therefore I have called this second category *psychogenic deficiency diseases,* or, alternatively, *emotional deficiency diseases.* The consequences of emotional deficiency fall into two subcategories, according to the extent of the infant's deprivation (of libidinal supplies): (a) partial deficiency; and (b) total deficiency. Any of these deficiencies refers of course, only to deficiency of the libidinal supplies; food, hygiene, warmth, etc., must always be provided for the infant unless he is to die.

Table IV presents the relationship of maternal attitudes and the corresponding emotional disturbances:

TABLE IV

ETIOLOGICAL CLASSIFICATION OF PSYCHOGENIC DISEASES IN INFANCY
ACCORDING TO MATERNAL ATTITUDES

	Etiological Factor Provided by Maternal Attitudes	*Infant's Disease*
Psychotoxic (Quality)	Overt Primal Rejection	Coma in Newborn (Ribble)
	Primary Anxious Over-permissiveness	Three-month Colic
	Hostility in the Guise of Anxiety	Infantile Eczema
	Oscillation between Pampering and Hostility	Hypermotility (rocking)
	Cyclical Mood Swings	Fecal Play
	Hostility Consciously Compensated	Aggressive Hyperthymic (Bowlby)
Deficiency (Quantity)	Partial Emotional Deprivation	Anaclitic Depression
	Complete Emotional Deprivation	Marasmus

CHAPTER XIII

Psychotoxic Disturbances

PRIMARY OVERT REJECTION

PRIMARY ACTIVE REJECTION

In this syndrome the maternal attitude consists of a global rejection of motherhood; this rejection includes both pregnancy and the child, and probably also many aspects of genital sexuality. I have a motion picture of such a case; however, the follow-up is lacking. These cases are difficult to follow, for the child frequently dies ("accidentally" or through infanticide), is abandoned, or, at best, is given for adoption.

PRIMARY PASSIVE REJECTION

The reaction of the newborn to a mother who will not accept him was first described by Margaret Ribble (1938). In extreme cases, the newborn becomes comatose, with Cheyne-Stokes type dyspnea, extreme pallor, and reduced sensitivity. These cases appear to be in a state of shock; treatment consists of saline enema, intravenous glucose, or blood transfusion. After recovery, these babies have to be taught to suck by repeated and patient stimulation of their oral zone. The condition endangers the life of the newborn.

I have observed a few such cases and have filmed one of them (1953c).

Case 1. The mother of the child is a sixteen-year-old, unusually good-looking girl, unmarried. She was employed as a servant and seduced by the son of her employer. Allegedly only one intercourse took place, resulting in impregnation. The child was undesired, the pregnancy accompanied by very severe feelings of guilt, as the girl was a devout practicing Catholic. The delivery took place in a maternity hospital and was uneventful. The first attempt to nurse, after twenty-four hours, was unsuccessful and so were the following ones. The mother, allegedly, had no milk. We had no difficulty in obtaining milk from her by manual pressure. Neither was there any difficulty in feeding this milk to the infant from a bottle. During nursing the mother behaved as if her infant were completely alien to her and not a living being at all. Her behavior consisted in a withdrawing from the baby, her body, hands, and face rigid and tense. The nipples, though not inverted, were not protruding and nursing did not appear to provoke turgor.

This went on for five days, while the baby was kept alive with milk expressed from the mother's breast. In one of the final attempts (which was filmed), the baby was seen to sink back into the stuporous, semicomatose condition described by Ribble. Energetic methods had to be applied, including tube feeding and saline clysis, to bring the baby out of this condition.

Concurrently, an attempt at indoctrination of the mother was made, and she was shown how to treat her nipples to produce turgor, making nursing possible. From the fifth day on, after this indoctrination, nursing went on relatively successfully; the child recovered, at least for the subsequent six days during which I could observe him.

One may well ask how a child will develop when he is confronted with as massive a rejection from the beginning. I assume that it is highly likely in these archaic reactions that even when the danger to life has been overcome, other, perhaps less critical, psychosomatic sequelae will appear.

The following case of infantile vomiting is one of these sequelae, though in this case the mother's passive rejection of motherhood probably was admixed with *active* rejection of her child.

Case 2. This child was first breast-fed by his mother. Subsequently she refused to continue nursing and formula was introduced. Both during breast feeding and formula feeding, the mother was full of complaints and recrimination. Breast feeding, she said, was unsatisfactory, because the child vomited; but the formula was not right either, because the child vomited also. After three weeks, the mother contracted influenza, was hospitalized, and separated from her child. The child's vomiting ceased immediately. Six weeks later the mother returned. The child started vomiting again within forty-eight hours.

To date cases like these have not been sufficiently investigated. In my opinion, passive maternal rejection is not directed against the child as an individual, but against the fact of *having* a child. That is to say, it is a rejection of motherhood, it is objectless. This attitude can exist only during the first few weeks after delivery, and at most during the first couple of months. Later, when the child begins to develop, his specific individuality, his personality will begin to make itself felt, and maternal hostility will also become more specific, more directed to what her child is, namely, an individual different from all others.

The attitudes of these mothers, their generalized hostility to motherhood, originate in their individual history, in their relations to the child's father, in the manner in which they succeeded or failed to solve their own oedipal conflict and their castration anxiety.

The preceding considerations took into account primarily the hostile mother's response to her child; as for such an infant's response to a hostile mother, it must be realized that at the outset, at the very beginning of life the neonate has not even begun to develop the rudiments of adaptation, let alone of defense. The child, as Freud stated, is born helpless; he is in the primary narcissistic stage, the most archaic way of existence known to man. This archaic mode of existing slowly evolves into the earliest modes of oral behavior, which later gradually become integrated into behavior patterns associated with what is known in psychoanalysis as the oral stage. In this archaic period, the infant's contacts with his surround have only just been transferred from the umbilical cord to the mouth and have changed from transfusion to incorporation. It is quite logical that the manifest symptoms of the child's disturbance in the cases just described will be expressed through oral symptoms as a paralysis of incorporation during the first days of life—and as vomiting at a somewhat more advanced stage.

PRIMARY ANXIOUS OVERPERMISSIVENESS
(THE THREE-MONTH COLIC)

Primary anxious overpermissiveness is a maternal attitude which can be considered a subdivision, that is, a special form, of what Levy (1943) has called maternal overprotection. Unfortunately, maternal overprotection has become an omnibus concept, used indiscriminately by authors in different disciplines, to describe a wide scale of behavior patterns and attitudes without regard for the diversity of the underlying motives. In the following chapters I shall attempt to distinguish a number of different forms of this "maternal overprotection." I shall try to elucidate the motivation which leads to these different forms, and to relate these forms to the specific clinical pictures presented by the child.

Connected with anxious overpermissiveness is, I believe, the disturbance which Spock has called the "three-month colic."[1] In pediatric circles the "three-month colic" is a familiar clinical picture: after the third week of life, and continuing to the end of the third month, the infant begins to scream in the afternoon. Feeding may calm him, but only temporarily. Within a relatively short time, the baby again shows the symptoms of colicky pains. Whether one shifts the

---

[1] Personal communication.

baby from the breast to the bottle, or from the bottle to the breast; whether one changes the formula or leaves it alone—nothing seems to help. Drugs have been tried, among them atropine, mostly without result. The stools of these infants are not pathological, though in certain cases one may see some diarrhea. The pains of the infant last several hours, then stop, and begin again the next afternoon. Toward the end of the third month, the disturbance has the tendency to disappear as inexplicably as it appeared—to the great relief of mother and pediatrician.

THE WORK OF WEIL, FINKELSTEIN, ALARCON, AND SPOCK

The condition had already been described by Weil and Pehu (1900) and by Finkelstein (1938) under the name of *"spastische Diathese."* They attributed its origin to an incapacity to assimilate the mother's milk. I was struck by an interesting observation made by Spanish and South American pediatricians. Alarcon (1929, 1943) first, and later Soto (1937), remarked that the three-month colic is unknown in infants who are raised in institutions. They call the three-month colic *"dyspepsia transitoria del lactante"* and investigated it extensively.

I can fully confirm Alarcon's and Soto's finding from my own observations. In the different institutions in which I observed infants, three-month colic never presented problems. In those institutions in which the infants were deprived of maternal care, colic was completely absent. In the institution which I have called "Nursery," where mother-child relations were relatively at their best, it occurred occasionally. But in the case of children raised in their own families, three-month colic was frequent.

Soto's explanation for the absence of three-month colic in institutions is that there the infants are not "spoiled." He observed a considerable number of infants in an orphanage for dependent children and described the manner in which they were cared for as follows: "The nurse only takes the infant into her arms to feed him, and she does it with the indifference characteristic of somebody who is taking care of a child who is not her own." Only one of the many infants which Soto observed in this institution contracted three-month colic.

This single exception is instructive indeed. It was a child adopted at the age of six weeks by a lady whom Soto describes as being extremely solicitous and loving with the child, carrying him in her arms a good deal, playing with him all the time, and succeeding, in the course of a very few days, in making the infant weepy and colicky. In Soto's opinion, this was a consequence of her "exaggerated solicitude" and of her disregard of the regular feeding schedule, meaning that she did not adhere systematically to feeding the child according to the clock, as he had been fed before, but feeding him on demand.

In Soto's belief, the routine of feeding strictly by the clock which prevailed in the orphanage for dependent children, as well as the complete absence of maternal solicitude, explains the immunity to three-month colic of babies in this institution.

This observation is supported by a remark of Spock's who also thinks that the mother's overanxious solicitude must have a bearing on the etiology of three-month colic.[2] Spock's remarks intrigued me, and I wondered which one among the numerous forms of anxious oversolicitude was responsible for this reaction of the infant.

THE EXPERIMENTAL FINDINGS OF LEVINE AND BELL

A few years later, an interesting finding was published by Milton Levine and Anita Bell (1950) in a study on twenty-eight infants suffering from three-month colic. All were

2 Personal communication.

raised by their own mothers in their homes, on the "self-demand" schedule. This reminded me how Spock also had told me that he had observed three-month colic mostly in children raised in their own home. And Soto's observations that institutionalized children do *not* suffer from three-month colic support the data of Levine and Bell and of Spock.

These observations open the door to the understanding of this hitherto incomprehensible clinical picture. The self-demand schedule requires that every time the baby desires to be fed, the mother should offer him food, bottle or breast. To what extremes overenthusiasm about this idea can lead is well illustrated in the report of an obstetrician at a scientific meeting: he was enthusiastic about the idea of self-demand, introduced it into his hospital, and he reported that after the first day, some of the infants were nursed up to twenty-eight times in the course of twenty-four hours. In view of such extravaganzas I think that I can safely state that a mother who accepts self-demand does show quite some solicitude for her child—and that in some cases this solicitude can lead to anxious overpermissiveness.

Levine and Bell mention a second factor in the picture, not mentioned by Spock, though both Finkelstein and Alarcon seem to have suspected it. This is the fact that the twenty-eight infants whom they observed were hypertonic from birth. That is to say, they showed a strikingly higher muscular tonus in general, particularly in the abdominal musculature, and increased peristalsis. Finkelstein actually speaks of *spastische Diathese,* which means that he had noticed the spasticity, while Alarcon prescribes atropine, presumably to relieve spasticity. Levine's and Bell's therapy was simpler and more old-fashioned: they provided the infants with pacifiers, and suddenly the colic, which had resisted the best efforts of pediatricians, disappeared. How can we explain this surprising effectiveness of the pacifier? Is it possible to formulate a hypothesis on the dynamics which operate in this therapy?

THEORETICAL CONSIDERATIONS

From the findings of the various observers, two factors emerge which appear to me to be significant in the etiology of three-month colic: these are maternal overconcern on the one hand, and hypertonicity of the infant from birth on the other. I therefore advanced the hypothesis of a *two-factor* etiology: *if newborns with congenital hypertonicity are raised by a mother who is anxiously overconcerned, they may develop three-month colic.*

This hypothesis is in good agreement with Freud's postulate of a complemental series in the etiology of neurosis mentioned in our introductory remarks. The hereditary constitutional factor (Freud, 1916-1917) which predisposes these cases to the three-month colic is a somatic compliance (Freud, 1905a), namely, hypertonicity.

Unlike in the adult, conditions are rather simple in the infant; there is no conflict between ego and superego, since in the neonate neither the one nor the other is present. Instead, a vicious circle is established between the infant's hypertonicity and the mother's anxious overpermissiveness, and particularly so when the self-demand schedule is practiced. One surely may assume that an oversolicitous mother tends to react to *any* unpleasure manifestation of her infant by feeding him or nursing him. One may even surmise that the unconscious hostility to the child of some of these mothers produces guilt which they overcompensate. Due to this tendency to overcompensate they readily accept and even insist on the self-demand schedule. Clinically this looks as if they wanted to atone for their unwillingness to give anything to their child—and least of all the breast.

It is relatively easy to uncover the psychological factor of the complemental series and its dynamic aspects in the behavior of these mothers. It is rather more difficult to detect these factors in the undifferentiated personality of the three-week-old infant. Here, however, physiology helps us. Tension has to be discharged; a hypertonic infant will have to discharge much larger quantities of tension at more frequent intervals than a calm and placid child. During earliest childhood the principal organ of discharge is the mouth. David Levy (1934) demonstrated the need for this discharge through a series of experiments on puppies and through observation of children. When these dogs and these children could not suck at the nipple for adequate periods (because the milk was free-flowing and it came out too fast), they had the tendency to replace this insufficient amount of discharge by much more frequent sucking of available parts of their own body. In the case of the children, these parts were their own fingers —in the case of the puppies their own or other puppies' paws, ears, and tails. These findings show that we have to distinguish two functions in nursing: (1) the ingestion of food as such, which gratifies and assuages hunger and thirst simultaneously; and (2) the discharge of tension, or one could say, the gratification of the oral mucosa through the activities of lips, tongue, palate, and laryngopharyngeal space during nursing. I have elaborated elsewhere (1955b, 1957) on the far-reaching implications of the latter form of tension discharge for development in general and for the organization of the psyche in particular. It goes without saying that tension discharged through oral activity originates not in the oral zone but in the general libidinal tension existing in the newborn.

Conclusions similar to those worked out by Levy can be found in the psychological investigations of Jensen (1932). In a series of experiments made on several hundred newborn infants she demonstrated that immediately after birth, any stimulation, in whatever part of the body, will be responded to by the sucking reflex. The stimuli offered went from neutral to painful; among the painful stimuli were hair pulling, pinching, and even dropping the infant from a height of one foot. To all of these, the newborn responded in the significant majority of instances by the sucking response. It is therefore licit to conclude that during the first weeks of life rise of tension will be discharged through oral activity.

These observations provide a clue to the findings of Levine and Bell which we may now interpret as follows: the twenty-eight infants of their sample were hypertonic. Therefore they had an increased need for tension discharge. This need created unpleasure; at this age (the first weeks of life) unpleasure from whatever source is expressed by oral protest.

We may then assume that an overconcerned mother is less capable of distinguishing whether her child is really hungry, or whether he screams for other reasons, than a mother with less guilt feelings. Consequently she responds to his cries by feeding the infant.

At this point the constitutional hypertonicity, the somatic compliance of the infant, meshes with the mother's psychological overconcern. The digestive system of these infants is more active, peristalsis faster, possibly more violent, and excess food will produce excess intestinal activity. A vicious circle results: the hypertonic child is unable to get rid of his tension normally in the course of the nursing process. Instead he discharges it through the postprandial screaming and motor agitation typical of these children. The oversolicitous mother immediately feeds the child again, in an exaggerated compliance with the tenets of self-demand. During this unscheduled feeding, some tension will be discharged through oral activity and deglutition; for a brief period the child becomes quiet. However, the food which the infant has ingested again overloads the digestive system, increases tension and causes a recrudescence of the state of unpleasure, leading to renewed colic and screaming. The anxious mother is able to interpret the cries of the child only within the framework of self-demand, and will again feed the infant, and thus the vicious circle goes on.

How can we explain that around the age of three months of life the syndrome disappears?

In the first place, we may assume that, after three months, even mothers with guilt feelings or inexperienced mothers will tire of the constant sacrifice required by exaggerated self-demand. Or perhaps they will learn to interpret a little bit better the screams and vocalizations of their infants and will give up the all too single-minded interpretation of the child's demands.

But, more important, in the course of the third month of life the infant will develop his first directed and intentional responses, namely, volitional behavior directed toward his surround. This is the age when the first social responses emerge, the first precursor of the object appears, the first cathectic displacements on memory traces take place, and mental activity begins. Body activities multiply; we witness "experimental" movements, the inception of the first attempts at locomotion, the active striving of the child toward the things in his reach.

Theoretically speaking, a wide spectrum of activities, affective, mental, and physical, becomes available to the infant for the first time in the course of the third month. Not only is he able to engage in these activities, but they also serve to discharge tension. Therefore it is no longer the oral zone alone which serves for such discharge as it did in the beginning. And when the infant succeeds in discharging drive tension by other than oral means, his vocal demands on the mother diminish; and thus the vicious circle of tension, resulting in nursing on self-demand, self-demand then leading to colic, will be interrupted. But after the third month the infant's energies are channelized into his activities and the level of tension is lowered.

PRACTICAL CONSIDERATIONS

The therapy suggested by Levine and Bell, the much-maligned pacifier, is a simple and at the same time ingenious device, which interrupts the vicious circle I described. They discovered it by taking a leaf from the simple wisdom of our grandmothers. I do not know whether Levine and Bell would agree with my theory of the vicious circle or not. I do believe that the pacifier given to the child suffering from three-month colic cures him because it offers a means of discharge without introducing the irritant of unnecessary food into the digestive system. Our grandmothers knew very well that the pacifier quiets the infant; we have condemned it, hypnotized as we were by the dangers of infection, since allegedly the pacifier is not hygienic—as if one could not boil a rubber pacifier!

I certainly believe that there are also other methods of discharging the infant's drive tensions at this age, when he is unable to do so actively. I suspect that another antiquated device, which has become the subject of contempt, like the pacifier, served a similar purpose. I am speaking of the cradle and of rocking the infant.

Our grandmothers knew also that if you rock an infant, he will become quiet and will go quietly to sleep. Nevertheless we have discarded the cradle, and I know of no valid reason for doing so. Isn't it evident that the hypertonic infant will be able to discharge a great deal of tension if one rocks him during a relatively prolonged period? It seems to me that this becomes self-evident in the third month, when the infant succeeds in providing himself with discharge through the active movements of his own body, and thereupon stops the three-month colic.

I am also convinced that natives in less sophisticated cultures than ours, who cling to the ancient custom of carrying their infants all day on back or hip, confer blessings on them of which we are unaware. For they provide their children with extensive tension discharge as well as with perceptual stimulation on that level of receptivity which is most age-adequate during early life. I refer to the constantly transmitted movement, to the body contacts, to the cutaneous contacts, to the transmission of thermal stimuli, etc.

Hypnotized as we are by the more questionable blessings of technology, by the baby carriage, the elaborate baby cot, the bottle propper, etc., we do not seem to ask ourselves whether the distance we put between our children and ourselves does not deprive them of that cutaneous contact, of those muscular stimuli and deep sensibility stimuli, which less sophisticated people do provide for their babies. Rapidly increasing interposition of distance between the baby and his mother, culminating in our era in the banishing of the baby during his first week of life to a checkroom in the hospital, is a relatively recent development in our Western culture, going back less than one hundred years. It was introduced on the plea of safeguarding the newborn against infections. But there is reason to ask ourselves whether depriving our children of vital stimuli which nature has ensured for the young of all mammals, does not inflict on the newborn damage which far outweighs the hypothetical danger of infection.[3] It is quite possible that our much-vaunted "progress" may entail consequences which only now become increasingly evident because of the time needed for the general acceptance of customs and practices.

To avoid any misunderstanding, I wish to stress that I am certainly not condemning the self-demand schedule. I believe that its drawbacks are limited to hypertonic infants, who after all are in the minority. For other children this practice is admirable, as long as the mother does not pervert its use because of her own psychological problems. And as regards this last

---

[3] See my remarks on skin perception in the neonate in Chapter IV, specifically the propositions advanced by M. F. Ashley Montagu (1950, 1953).

point, it is clear that the self-demand schedule is not the only method and behavior through which the mother transmits anxious concern to her child, be he hypertonic or not.

CONCLUDING REMARKS ON THE THREE-MONTH COLIC

I therefore believe that we will find three-month colic also among infants who are not on self-demand; on the other hand I do not claim that the hypothesis advanced here applies in each and every case; there surely exist also other conditions which can produce three-month colic besides the combination of the infant's hypertonicity with the mother's anxious over-permissiveness.

The interplay of these two factors and their role in the etiology of the three-month colic is clear. This two-factor etiology is specific for this stage of infantile development, when differentiation between psyche and soma is still incomplete, and when the dynamics are more in evidence in the mother's psyche than in that of the infant. I spoke above of the infant's part in the etiology of the three-month colic as somatic compliance—which I consider to be at least partially psychological, because it consists in tension states. At this age, tension states are the precursor and, in a certain sense, the equivalent of affects. The latter will manifest themselves only after a rudimentary ego is established.

What we observe in the three-month colic is closer to the physiological than to the psychological; however, it is from these psychophysiological states, and from the responses in which they are expressed, that later purely psychological structures and functions will develop or be segregated. That is one of the reasons why I have dealt so extensively with this early disturbance of the mother-child relations. It has the virtue of presenting one of the most archaic forms, a precursor of disturbances of object relations. It is instructive to observe how much the somatic and the biological predominate at this stage in the difficulties encountered in mother-child relations; while later, after the inception of the ego, behavioral disorders proper will dominate the picture.

It should also be remembered that on these two different developmental levels (the one before the inception of the ego and the other after its inception) the laws of psychic function are completely different. The disturbance just described, the three-month colic, takes place during the first transitional period which goes from the purely somatic at birth to the inception of psychic functioning marked by the indicator of the first organizer of the psyche, by the smiling response. It is only after the establishment of the first organizer that a second transitional period begins in the course of which somatic function is separated from psychic function.

In the first stage, we are therefore confronted with an inextricable mixture of the two forms of functioning, so that we witness a nearly tangible meshing of somatic and psychological etiology. One might speculate whether, in disturbances taking place at a much later age, or even in the adult, partial regressions to such archaic stages occur. They may be facilitated through fixations which could be laid down at that period. These fixations would make possible, or at least, foster what we speak of as somatization,[4] that is the participation of the organic within the framework of neuroses or psychoses.

HOSTILITY IN THE GUISE OF MANIFEST ANXIETY
(INFANTILE ECZEMA)

THE FINDINGS AND CLINICAL DATA

The maternal attitude which we observed in the great majority of mothers whose infants suffered from infantile

---

[4] More correctly, we should say that such fixations foster resomatization (Schur, 1955, 1958).

eczema[5] was that of manifest anxiety, mainly about their child. It soon became clear that this manifest anxiety corresponded to the presence of unusually large amounts of unconscious repressed hostility.

We had occasion to observe 203 infants in an institution; 185 of these were observed for one year or more after birth. The remaining 18 were observed in the same institution for six months only in the second half of their first year. We were struck by the high incidence of infantile eczema among the children housed in this institution.

In the usual institutional environment and among children raised in their own families, the percentage of infants suffering from this syndrome ranges from 2 to 3 per cent. Among the 203 above-mentioned institution-raised infants, the percentage reached approximately 15 per cent during the second half of their first year. Thereafter, more precisely between the twelfth and the fifteenth month, the eczema tended to disappear.

The institution's attending physician tried a variety of treatments such as: modifying the food; prescribing vitamins; topical treatment, salves, applications of talcum, medicated or not, etc. A careful search was made to determine the possible presence of allergenes in the toiletries of the children, in the substances used for the laundry, etc. This was negative and the eczema continued unchecked. Finally the condition was accepted with a certain resignation, as the children recovered from it anyhow after the end of the first year of life.

At this point we decided to start a detailed psychiatric in-

---

5 Throughout this presentation I shall speak of *infantile eczema*. Consultation with different dermatological authorities did not show consensus in regard to the terms eczema, atopic dermatitis, etc. I have therefore elected to use the old-fashioned term: infantile eczema; the picture in question is that of a skin affection, beginning in the second half of the first year of life, localized predominantly on the flexor side, favoring skin folds (inguinal, axillary, popliteal, cubital, crease behind the ear, etc.) with tendency to weeping and exfoliation in the most severe cases. In the subjects studied it seemed to be self-limiting and to disappear in the first half of the second year.

vestigation of the data we had collected on the 28 infants affected with eczema, and on their mothers. We used as a *control group the remaining 165 infants* housed in the same institution who remained free of eczema, and their mothers. We compared the data collected on this control group with the data collected on the infants who developed eczema. (Ten eczema cases were excluded from our sample because the diagnosis appeared uncertain or because they had left the institution before the conclusion of our study.) We reasoned that, if after the exclusion of accidental somatic damaging factors, we still found such an unusually high percentage of eczema in this institution, so much higher than in others, there had to be a nonsomatic psychological factor.

We had valid reasons for such a hypothesis; for this was a penal institution, where delinquent girls, who had become pregnant, had been interned. These girls delivered their children in the institution, and raised them there during the first year of life, that is, during the period of their commitment. It follows that the group of mothers in this institution is not a random sample of the population of the city where this institution is located. It is rather a very specially selected group, a group of girls between the ages of fourteen and twenty-three years, who had come into conflict with the law, or at least with the mores of their cultural environment.

We proceeded to scrutinize the extensive amount of data which we had collected on these infants from birth, and those we had obtained on their mothers.

We had recorded the following data for each child: birth weight, length, head circumference, mode of feeding (nursing or bottle), age of the mother; and later the time of weaning.

The following reflexes were tested at birth: the Moro reflex, the sucking reflex, the grasping reflex, the digital extension reflex (Spitz, 1950c), and the cremasteric reflex.

At weekly intervals we described each child's behavior, with particular attention to the presence or absence of rocking, genital play, and fecal play. We noted the frequency and distribution of the cases in which one or the other or all of these manifestations were present, and, if so, their beginning, their frequency, and their duration.

We tested the presence or absence of the smiling response and the eight-month anxiety. We computed the developmental quotient of each child at the age of three, six, nine, and twelve months.

We noted whether or not a separation from the mother had taken place, the age at which a separation (if any) had occurred, and its duration. Finally we examined whether the child had become depressed in response to such a separation; and whether the depression had been severe or mild; or whether no depression had been observed, in which case we also noted the quality of mother-child relation prior to the separation.

The statistical evaluation of this material provided us with eighty-seven tables and curves. We proceeded to ascertain how infants who develop eczema in the second half of the first year differ from those who in the same environment remain free of it. Surprisingly enough, the difference between the 28 infants who developed eczema and the 165 who did not was reduced to only two factors: (1) a congenital predisposition; (2) a psychological factor originating in the environment, which in this institution was virtually limited to the mother-child relation. The remaining environmental variables were identical for the entire group of these infants.

Thereupon we examined in detail our data on the infants themselves. These included data on delivery measurements at birth, reflexes at birth, results of tests administered at regular intervals, clinical data, protocols of weekly behavioral observations, etc. We found that (with the exception of the sectors of learning and social relations [see below]) there was no significant difference between the averages of the scores of the infants in the control group. Indeed, in the vast majority of the items examined, there was no difference at all; the averages were identical. These identical items are therefore irrelevant for the etiology of the syndrome. In the area of reflexes, however, one difference is evident and striking. The response in the sector of deeper reflexes (such as the tendon reflexes) averages the same in both groups. There is, however, a statistically significant difference between the control group and the eczema group in the sector of cutaneous reflexes (such as the rooting reflex, the cremasteric reflex, etc.).

In the sector of cutaneous reflexes, the infants who six months later developed eczema showed a much higher average score of cutaneous excitability responses than the infants who did not develop eczema. I would say, borrowing a term from Michael Balint (1948), that infants who will develop infantile eczema in the second half of the first year of life are born with an "increased reflex excitability." Since reflexes at birth are unlearned behavior, we have here a congenital predisposition.

This might suggest that at birth the skin of these children is more than usually vulnerable. If that were true, however, eczema should appear already in the first few weeks of life, or at the latest a month or two after birth. But such is not the case, it actually begins in the second half of the first year. Therefore we may rule out the vulnerability of the skin, and say that the eczema of these children is due rather to an increased readiness for response; or, in analytic terms, an increased cathexis of cutaneous reception. That actually is another way of saying that at birth the group of future eczema children had an increased reflex excitability. And one may wonder whether the phenomena described by Greenacre (1941) in her article on "The Predisposition of Anxiety" as the consequence of a "dry birth" cannot be explained equally well by a higher excitability of the newborn's skin.

As to the second factor, influence of the environment, that is the influence of the object relations on these children, we found the following: in a subtle way their object relations were different from the average. In one sociopsychological area of the child's functioning, namely, in the manifestations of the eight-month anxiety, there was a statistically significant difference between the two groups. Of the children suffering from eczema, 15 per cent showed eight-month anxiety; in children without eczema eight-month anxiety was present in 85 per cent of the cases.

This might appear paradoxical to the psychoanalyst who is used to consider anxiety as a potentially pathological symptom. Our finding would then suggest that in the eczema group less children have pathological symptoms than in the non-eczema group. However, as I have stated in Chapter VII, the eight-month anxiety is not a pathological symptom. On the contrary, it is a symptom of progress in personality development: it indicates that the infant has achieved a step forward in the development of object relations, namely, the capacity to distinguish between friend and stranger. Here we have a striking example of one of the many differences between the psychology of the infant and that of the grown-up. Therefore it is not the presence but rather the absence of the anxiety reaction in the eight-month-old child which indicates pathology. The absence of this reaction warns us that the child has been retarded in his affective development. This retardation is evidently due to a disturbance of object relations. We therefore investigated the relations between mother and infant in our entire population.

The psychiatric exploration of the mothers of the eczema children yielded significant information. The majority of these mothers showed an attitude of manifest anxiety about their children. It soon became clear that unusually large amounts of unconscious repressed hostility were concealed behind this manifest anxiety. As could be expected, delinquent girls committed to a penal institution are not average personalities. Legally, they were committed under the Wayward Minors Act. The reasons for their commitment ranged from sexual delinquency to theft and even murder. The majority of these girls, however, had been committed because of sexual misdemeanor. In our era this is not considered a serious breach of the law; indeed, it is considered to be the average sexual behavior of a majority of our unmarried female population—if we are to believe Kinsey et al. (1953). However, they had been caught at it, caught in a rural environment which did not accept such a breach of mores. Therefore we can say that they represented a deviant minority in *their* cultural environment.

For those familiar with minors committed because of sexual misdemeanor, I state the obvious when I say that a high percentage of them are on the mental level of the dull normal, if not the feeble-minded. In such personalities the integration of the superego is mostly incomplete; after all, these girls have not even been able to achieve a satisfactory integration of the ego. In such a group one may expect to find many infantile personalities, and our group was no exception. But it was striking that among the 203 mothers investigated by us, the great majority of manifestly infantile personalities was concentrated in the group of the mothers of eczema children.

These mothers also had other notable peculiarities: they did not like to touch their children; they always succeeded in talking one or the other of their friends in the institution into diapering their child, bathing him, giving him the bottle, etc. At the same time they were concerned about the fragility, the vulnerability of their children; one of them used to say and this is characteristic: "A baby is such a delicate thing, the least false movement might harm it." This exaggerated concern is an overcompensation for unconscious hostility. The actions of these mothers contradict their words. Our interpretation is supported by the numerous instances in which the same mothers exposed their babies to unnecessary risk, to real danger. They often barely avoid inflicting serious damage on the baby, such as feeding it an open safety pin in the cereal; some of these mothers consistently and intolerably overheated the baby's cubicle on the plea that he might catch cold; one of them knotted the baby's bib so tightly that the baby became blue in the face and only my timely intervention saved him from strangulation. In this group one was not surprised to learn that this baby or that had fallen out of bed on his head more than once in the course of his stay in the institution.

Our study of the infants who develop eczema has thus revealed two anomalies. (1) They had mothers with an infantile personality, betraying hostility disguised as anxiety toward their child; mothers who do not like to touch their child or care for him, and who deprive him systematically of cutaneous contact. (2) We have a child with a congenital predisposition for increased cutaneous responses, leading to increased cathexis of the psychic representation of cutaneous perception —in loose analytic terms, to a libidinization of the skin surface. This is the very need which his mother refuses to gratify. Accordingly these babies' needs and their mothers' attitudes stood in an asymptotic relation to each other.

The developmental profiles plotted on the basis of the Bühler-Hetzer tests revealed another peculiarity in the eczema children. Unlike infants who do not get eczema, they show a characteristic retardation in the learning sector and in that of social relations.

In this test, the sector of learning represents the mastery of imitation and of memory. Retardation in the mastery of imitation becomes understandable if we consider the circumstances in which these children were reared; the anxious mothers, who do not touch their children during the first six months, during the primary narcissistic stage, will make *primary* identification difficult.

THE ROLE OF PRIMARY IDENTIFICATION

The term primary identification rarely appears in the literature. It is a construct of psychoanalytic theory which refers to the state of nondifferentiation (see Chapter III, n. 3) in which there is no differentiation within the infant, nor is he able to distinguish between inside and outside, I and non-I. Perhaps the best description of this state would be to say that it is lacking not only in psychic structure but also in psychic and somatic boundaries. The use of the noun "identification" in the term represents a measure of expediency, useful in pointing up the incorporative aspects due to the lack of boundaries and does not concern other aspects of the state of nondifferentiation.

The idea of infantile omnipotence fits well into this picture. When his needs compel the infant to scream or squirm, his need is gratified sooner or later. He has no reason to feel that this is not of his doing, that the food which assuages him has not been produced by his agitation.

Primary identification then consists in the infant's experiencing everything in his environment which pertains to need gratification (drive gratification) as part of his own person and body, outside of which nothing exists. Glover (1930) appears to be thinking on similar lines: "For the primitive mind, all states having the same pleasure tone tend to bring about identification with the objects connected with these states."

Primary identification is accordingly made difficult by those anxious mothers who withhold from their children the need gratification inherent in being touched.[6] They extensively restrict the occasions for primary identification through withholding tactile experiences. Yet, if the infant is to differentiate himself from his mother, these primary identifications, tactile and otherwise, have to be dealt with, severed and over-

[6] See Chapter IV for a discussion of Montagu's (1950, 1953) propositions on the role of perceptual experience through the outer skin surface for survival and adaptation in the neonate.

come. Action-directed motility first, and locomotion later, are the child's devices for dealing with primary identification and achieving differentiation. When differentiation from the mother has been accomplished, the infant can form those secondary identifications which pave the way to autonomy and independence.

Elaborating on Mahler's (1957, 1960) concept of "the process of individuation-separation" we would then say that the road to individuation leads through secondary identifications. For the child must acquire the mother's techniques of taking care of him, of watching over him (and he can do so only through identification), before he becomes able to separate himself from her and to become an independent individual. I believe that the process of individuation-separation which Mahler places after the eighteenth month of life has two precursor stages. The first of these stages I would call the process of *primary individuation,* in which the child deals with primary identifications, severs and overcomes them. Stage two is that of secondary *identification,* which begins in the second half of the first year of life. In the course of this stage the child acquires techniques and devices by means of which he achieves independence from his mother (Spitz, 1957).

Such relative independence is achieved somewhere around the eighteenth month of life, the period at which Piaget situates the acquisition of reversibility by the child and at which the child also acquires formal language as spoken by adults. At this moment, Mahler's process of individuation-separation can be set in motion.

In contrast with primary identification (which is a *state*), secondary identification is a *mechanism*. It is an unconscious process, the outcome of which is a modification of the ego. Secondary identification therefore presupposes that at least a rudimentary ego is already segregated from the undifferentiated totality which operated at the period of primary identification.

It follows that when the mother makes primary identification difficult by withholding tactile experience, she obstructs
two important developmental achievements—that of ego formation, and that of secondary identifications (Spitz, 1957).

PSYCHODYNAMIC PROCESSES

In the normal course of development, the libidinal and the
aggressive drives are discharged in the framework of physical
interaction between mother and child. Underlying these dyadic interactions are dynamic processes involving cathectic
displacements. Among other things, these lead eventually to
secondary identifications of the child. This age-adequate processing of the libidinal and the aggressive drives is not as
readily available to the eczema-afflicted child, for, as we have
shown, his mother does not give him sufficient opportunity
for such discharge. We may speculate whether infantile
eczema is not an autoplastic symptom which replaces the un-
available developmental process of alloplastic discharge followed by autoplastic identification.[7] On the basis of our find-

---

[7] That the manifestations of a disease appear at the very site at which
vital stimulation has been withheld should be weighed from the psychoanalytic point of view. Theoretically speaking, a damming up of drive energies
has taken place, because they were denied an outlet. Accordingly, the manifestation of the disease falls into the category of what has been loosely referred to as "somatization" in dynamic psychiatry and psychoanalysis. We have deliberately refrained from using this term in our conceptual framework, since,
with a single exception, neither the dynamics of the psychological process nor
the mode of its transformation into somatic manifestations had been eluci-
dated. However, in the past decade the work of Max Schur (1955, 1958) in this
area has greatly contributed to a clarification of the entire problem. In two
papers he distinguishes between the phenomena of "desomatization" and
"resomatization." The former is a developmental process, in which psychic
energies are increasingly mastered by *psychic* rather than by *somatic* devices.
When regression occurs, "resomatization" takes place, which is the reverse
process. Accordingly, desomatization corresponds to an increasing application
of secondary-process regulation, whereas resomatization is associated with a
return to primary-process regulation.

I cannot do justice within the scope of this book to the sophistication underlying this very creative contribution to psychoanalytic theory. It is, however,
of particular interest for my above-described findings that Schur (1955) extensively discusses a case of atopic dermatitis (eczema) as an example of resomatization.

ings, we have up to this point isolated two factors in the etiology of eczema: one is the congenital factor of the child's reflex cutaneous excitability, the other, the environmental factor of the mother's infantile anxious personality. However, this explanation is not completely satisfactory from the dynamic and the economic viewpoint.

A PAVLOVIAN EXPLANATION

Some further clarification was brought by a reflexological experiment, which could be interpreted in terms of learning theory. In Pavlov's Institute, experiments were being made to explore the effect of ambiguous signals in provoking what Pavlov calls "experimental neurosis." A conditioned reflex was established with the help of electrical stimulation on a given perimeter of a dog's thigh; his task was to discern a given sensory percept. The two points of electrical stimulation were brought progressively closer, thus forcing the dog to perform an increasingly difficult task of discrimination. The majority of the dogs complied with the prediction: when the signals became ambiguous, they developed an "experimental neurosis." One dog, however, was a maverick; he did not develop an experimental neurosis. Instead, when discrimination between the signals became impossible, he developed eczema in the perimeter of the electrical stimulation. Furthermore, when the experiment was interrupted, the eczema disappeared. In the further course of this particular research, the experimenter found other dogs who reacted to ambiguous electrical stimulation in a similar manner. He explored the difference between those animals who reacted with an "experimental neurosis" and those who reacted with eczema. He states that the latter have what he calls a "labile temperament."

I believe that it is permissible to draw a parallel between what the Pavlovians describe as "labile temperament" in these dogs and what I have called (with Balint) "reflex excitability" in the eczema-afflicted child. In the light of the similarity between the predisposition of the dog (labile temperament) and that of the neonate (reflex excitability) we now can evaluate how the learning process is affected in each of them when they are confronted with ambiguous cues.

The dog used in these experiments is an adult animal. He is endowed with a fully developed canine psychic organization functioning at the usual level of a dog. Consequently, he is able to perceive and use signals according to the learning capacity of adult dogs, namely, to use the signals for establishing a conditioned reflex. In the particular experiment described, the adult dog is faced with ambiguous cues in the form of cutaneous electric stimulation. Hence, what the Pavlovians are studying is, in effect, the disruption of the normal learning process. In this instance, the learning process was replaced by one of two disturbances: the majority of the dogs developed an "experimental neurosis"; the minority, dogs with a "labile temperament," developed eczema.

By contrast, when we began to observe the study children, they did not yet have a psychic organization and still were in the process of developing an ego. Normally the child acquires his rudimentary ego in the manifold interchanges with his mother, in the course of which he progressively organizes his responses to the consistent signals coming from her. He reacts to these signals with a mental development which goes beyond that of the dog. During the first trimester of life the infant begins to form a number of conditioned reflexes. Thereafter, a new factor enters the picture: instead of the conditioned reflex which is based on a reward *following* the correct answer to a signal, the child now produces *"anticipatory* reactions." These lead to a form of learning which, for lack of a better term, I call "learning according to the human pattern." It parallels the organization level of the child's ego.

There is a second important difference between the child's

learning process and that of the dog in Pavlov's harness. The cues offered to the dog are linked to one single affective situation, and to one *only*, namely, to hunger. The cues offered to her child by the mother, on the other hand, range over a wide gamut of affective needs and over many shadings of affectively colored situations. These signals originate in the mother's affective attitude. Though they may be scarcely perceptible to the adult observer, these signals serve to elicit anticipatory affective responses in the child.[8]

The same affective signals ought to operate also in the eczema-afflicted children's interchanges with their mothers. However, this was not the case. Direct observation demonstrated that these mothers offered only inconsistent and unreliable signals to their children. Psychiatric exploration of these mothers' personality and their Rorschach both revealed an inadequately integrated ego as well as excessive amounts of uncontrolled unconscious anxiety. This is in striking contrast with the findings made on the 165 mothers of the control group who showed a much better integrated ego and no indication of excessive amounts of unconscious anxiety.

The inadequately integrated ego of the eczema children's mothers made it particularly difficult for them to develop devices for controlling and compensating their unconscious anxiety in a consistent manner. This difficulty obviously is at the root of the chaotic affective signals which they presented to their offsprings.

That such anxieties do indeed affect the child most vitally has been observed by Anna Freud and Dorothy Burlingham (1943) in their studies of displaced children in wartime. Their observations demonstrated that infants up to three years did not become anxious during the terror of the London Blitz unless *their mothers began to feel anxious*. The infants re-

---

[8] Short of prolonged observation of the mother-child couple throughout the first year of life, evidence of these anticipatory affective responses in infancy can best be conveyed via motion pictures.

mained *unaffected by external stimuli* until the meaning of these stimuli was transmitted *to them via their mothers' affective attitude.*

The operation of these processes is well illustrated in the case of the mother whom we watched one day feeding her infant with an expression of deep concern on her face. Manifestly she was pouring far too much at a time into his mouth. At the same time, swallowing movements of her throat showed that she was identifying with her child, so to say, encouraging him to swallow by performing the act herself. But it immediately became clear that her swallowing represented a desperate effort to overcome an overpowering nausea, which soon began to express itself in her face. The child of course was not experiencing nausea; it was only the mother who was nauseated, for neurotic reasons of her own, at the idea of swallowing milk. Consequently she was overdoing the pouring in, to get it over with quickly, and she succeeded in making the child regurgitate, to her own increased revulsion.

This is a drastic example, taken from the feeding situation in which a mother can most easily be observed and her conflicts detected. However, it should be realized that conflicts will interfere in all the relations of such a mother with her baby. Take that other mother who was diapering her child —the hesitancy, the extraordinary retardation of her movements suggested a slow-motion film. She placed the baby on the scale as if she were lifting a heavy weight, which she might drop at any moment. And while fixing the diaper with a safety pin which she had been handling as if it were a loaded gun, she succeeded in the end in drawing blood. Throughout this procedure, changing expressions alternated in her face. The benign look with which she approached the child quickly gave way to rigid effort when she was lifting him onto the scale, then changed to gloom, replaced by a forced smile while she was fumbling with the safety pin.

These isolated examples are in effect characteristic of the

totality of the emotional climate in which the eczema child is raised. He is all the time faced with affective signals coming from his mother, which ostensively *seem* to correspond to the given situation. But in the next moment her unconscious conflict reasserts itself, anxiety wells up, she suppresses all signals, only to shift into an overcompensation of the cause of her anxiety and to transmit signals contrary to her feelings; though on the next occasion she may just as well exaggerate the signals which are appropriate to her feelings.

In one word, what she transmits will be neither consistent with her inner attitude nor will it correspond to her actions in regard to the child. What she does cannot be taken as a signal in the usual sense of the term, for it is not related to the partner. What she expresses depends not on her conscious or even on her unconscious relations with her child but rather on the variable climate of her unconscious guilt feelings, ghosts from her past, provoking anxiety which does not permit her truly to identify with her child. And so she particularly avoids the most elementary form of identification, that of immediate, of affective physical contact.

In other words, her messages are not signals, but only signs or symptoms. To the adult, to the psychoanalyst, they might be meaningful. As road signs on the path of normal development they are meaningless for the child.

Accordingly, forming object relations in response to ambiguous and inconsistent signals becomes an uphill task for the child. Forming object relations, however, weaving the intricate net of exchanges between mother and child, is the basis of all subsequent affective learning, inseparably linked with identification. On our successive test charts the eczema child showed scores which are indicative of a deterioration of the social and of the learning sectors. This means that social relations on the one hand, memory and imitation on the other, are influenced. As was explained above, a selective lesion has been inflicted on both primary and secondary identification. This lesion is the direct result of interference with, and impairment of, the forming of the first object relations. This lesion is particularly striking in the area of human relations; it is less striking in regard to the child's relations to inanimate objects. Hence the lesion is noticeable in the nonappearance of the eight-month anxiety. As these infants have not formed normal object relations, they are unable to distinguish affectively the mother from the stranger, and therefore show no anxiety when approached by a stranger.

I have previously expressed some reluctance to adopt the concept of "somatization" for explanatory purposes. Yet two factors—Pavlov's experiments with ambiguous signals on the one hand, these children's congenital predisposition (their cutaneous excitability) on the other—make it plausible to assume that the cutaneous disease arose in response to conflicting signals. Of course, we do not know what particular processes in the child's psyche generate this cutaneous symptom. It is as if these children cathected the cutaneous covering (by which I mean its psychic representation) with increased libidinal quanta. We might ask ourselves whether this cutaneous reaction represents an adaptive effort, or alternatively, a defense. The child's reaction could be in the nature of a demand addressed to the mother to incite her to touch him more frequently. It could also be a form of narcissistic withdrawal, in the sense that through the eczema the child would be giving himself the stimuli in the somatic sphere which his mother denies him. We do not know.

CONCLUDING REMARKS ON INFANTILE ECZEMA

It is interesting to note that infantile eczema, just like the three-month colic, is limited to a certain developmental phase; a spontaneous cure occurs, usually after the end of the first year. Again, we may ask ourselves: why is this disturbance self-limiting? I believe that these limits are contingent upon the progress of maturation, just as in the three-month

colic. After the end of the first year, the child acquires locomotion; that makes him increasingly independent of the signals originating from the mother. He now becomes capable
of substituting normal object relations—of which the eczema-
afflicted child had been deprived—by stimuli which he can
obtain himself. He now can get on without so many contacts
with his mother; he can replace maternal stimuli by contacts
with things, with other persons whom he can seek out; for
he has left behind him passivity and progressed to directed
activity. It is to be expected that the interlude of eczema, during the first year of life, will leave permanent traces on the
psychic development of the child; what they are we can only
surmise.

Having published these findings and propositions in 1951,
I was interested to learn that they have been supported independently by dermatologists. In the same year Donald H.
Williams (1951) published a paper on atopic dermatitis in
53 children, 13 months old or more. Some of his statements
came close to my own propositions: "In 46 [out of 53] instances the atopic dermatitis first became evident during the
12 months following birth." Further on he stresses: "It appears that atopic dermatitis is in most instances associated
with *a child with a characteristic temperament* [italics mine]
and with a mother whose witting or, more frequently, un-
witting attitude to that child is one of rejection." And he
summarizes: "An atopic child with an inordinate hunger for
affection finds himself confronted with a mother who un-
wittingly is not satisfying this need." At the same time Williams explains the need repeatedly as "the daily acts of love
toward the child, such as the enfolding arms, the caress, and
soft words."

On the pediatric side, Rosenthal (1952, 1953) published
findings on a series of 26 infants who developed eczema
in the first year of life; he stresses as the outstanding psychological factor the mother's overt behavior of avoiding physical

contact with her child. The author comes to the same conclusion as I did: these infants were "predisposed," as he puts
it. Rosenthal is a clinician. My experimental findings on the
reflexes of such infants at birth bear out his assumptions.

Oscillation between Pampering and Hostility
(Rocking in Infants)

CLINICAL AND OTHER DATA

The very common motility disturbance known as rocking
behavior in infants is particularly frequent in the institutional
setting. In itself the behavior can hardly be called a pathological one, for practically every child engages in it at one
time or another. Before the age of six months, rocking is
rare, however, and when it occurs it is carried out in the
supine position. In general, children perform their rocking
activity after the first six months of life in the knee-elbow
position. After the tenth month, rocking—or its equivalent—
may be performed in the standing position.

When rocking in infancy takes a pathological turn, it becomes the principal activity of the children affected by this
condition and substitutes for most of the usual activities common at the same age level. This was quite conspicuous in the
children we observed systematically. Furthermore, we were
struck by the violence with which rocking was carried out and
which involved motor behavior and expenditure of energy far
in excess of that generally seen in children of the same age.

This syndrome was studied with the collaboration of Katherine M. Wolf, in a group of 170 children, in the institution
called "Nursery" (described in Chapter II). We were interested in establishing the incidence and significance of three
autoerotic activities in the first year of life, namely, rocking,
fecal play, and genital play.[9] In the course of this investiga-

---

[9] Our findings and conclusions were presented in the article "Autoerotism"
(Spitz and Wolf, 1949).

tion we found that of the 170 children observed by us in that institution, 87 were rocking at some time during the first year of life, while 83 did not show this behavior.

We therefore attempted to establish what made certain children indulge in rocking and others not. We looked for possible etiological factors and divided them into congenital, hereditary, and environmental ones.

We investigated the population for congenital differences. The results led us to believe that gross congenital dysfunctions were not present. As regards heredity, the information available on our population was not adequate. We felt, however, that with a 50:50 ratio, hereditary differences probably were not significant either, because the differences in the averages of the developmental quotients between the rocking and the nonrocking children were minimal.

This leaves us with the environmental factor as the decisive one. In the Nursery, certain variables were under institutional control and kept constant for all the subjects involved; these were food, housing, clothing, hygiene, cots, toys, and the daily routine.

There remains in this institution one environmental variable subject to change: the human element, which at this age of the child represents the highest emotional valency. As stated repeatedly, in the first year of life the human elements are provided by the mother, by the object relations. We therefore investigated in what way the maternal attitudes and behavior differed in the case of rocking and nonrocking children.

The relation between the rocking children and their mothers is a peculiar one. It certainly is not absent; but it is far from being a well-balanced, close relation. In general, the mothers of these children were extrovert personalities with a readiness to intensive, positive contact, and definitely alloplastic tendencies. They were mostly infantile personalities, with a lack of control over their aggressions, expressed in frequent outbursts of negative emotions and violent manifest hostility.

These mothers were victims of their own emotions, and, due to their infantile personality, they were unable to realize the consequences of their behavior and were unusually inconsistent in dealing with their environment. In the setting of the penal nursery, their babies were of necessity the main outlet for their labile emotions, so that these babies were exposed alternately to intense outbursts of fondling, of "love," and to equally intense outbursts of hostility and rage. In one word, there were rapid oscillations between pampering and hostility.

As for the personality of the rocking children, we were struck by a certain regularity in the developmental profiles of the group. As mentioned earlier, each child was tested at regular intervals; we discovered that rocking children have a characteristic developmental profile of their own, while the profiles of children who do not rock do not show much uniformity; indeed, they vary widely.

Regardless of the general level of their development, two thirds of the rocking children show characteristic low points in their developmental profile. These low points may represent an absolute retardation of a given sector in respect to the chronological norms of all sectors or a relative retardation, that is, performance in one sector lags behind that of the other sectors of the personality.

The two sectors in which rocking children are retarded are the sector of social adaptation and that of manipulative ability. The manipulative sector reflects the way in which the child handles and masters toys, tools, inanimate things in general. It measures the child's relation to "things." The sector of social relations, on the other hand, reflects the child's progress in human relations. Combined, the retardation in both sectors adds up to the incapacity of the rocking children to *relate* either to their living or to their inanimate surround, to their inability and lack of initiative in dealing with their environment.

How does the mother's behavior contribute to this developmental deficiency? The late Katherine Wolf advanced the proposition that only after relations to the libidinal object had been established, only after object constancy had been achieved, will the infant be able to relate to inanimate things.

Our assumption, then, is that in rocking children, the mother has stunted the establishment of the primal, of the libidinal object, and thereby made all later object relations difficult or impossible for the child. In other words, the mother's behavior, self-contradictory and inconsistent, leads her baby to store in his memory conflicting object presentations. This fund of memory traces does not lend itself to being amalgamated into a unified libidinal object through the fusion of the drives directed to the mother. Such experience impairs the formation of an object which can remain identical with itself in space and time. The object presentation genetically is not identical with itself, because of the vagaries, because of the ups and downs of the mother's emotional temperature. The original experience with the libidinal object-to-be creates, above all, an expectancy pattern. Where that is lacking, each single object presentation will have to be approached on a trial-and-error basis, as an experiment, as an adventure, as a peril.

DYNAMIC PROCESSES

Libidinization of the Body and Its Parts. These considerations shed some light on the dynamics which move these children to select rocking as their main activity. In normal development the infant would proceed through successive stages leading to the establishment of the libidinal object. This development is in part the result of exchanges with his mother; the experience so provided activates processes in the course of which various parts of the infant's body become libidinized. More precisely, it is the psychic representations of these body parts which become cathected. Some of these body regions, parts, or zones are undoubtedly biologically "predestined erotogenic zones" (Freud, 1905b); witness the fact that the fetus sometimes sucks his thumb already *in utero* (Hooker, 1939, 1952).

Accordingly I am inclined to advance the proposition that the libidinization of specific body parts as well as their localization has a biological basis or biological substratum: it is intimately connected with the chronology of myelination. The uterine manifestation of the thumb-sucking pattern is linked to the fact that among the earliest zones to be myelinized in the fetus are the zones of the stomach, mouth, and hand (Tilney and Casamajor, 1924). Hence these zones, mouth and hand—or rather their central representation—show affinity for each other. In this sense one could say that already in the course of evolution these zones have been privileged over the rest of the as yet nondifferentiated bulk of the body.

One might expect as a consequence of this prenatal hand-mouth coordination that the postnatal one described by Hoffer (1949)—and with it, at a later stage, finger sucking—will play a prominent role in the infant's autoerotic activities.

However, early myelinization is not the only way for a body part to become privileged. In fact, the infant selects a variety of organs for his oral attention, e.g., the big toe, the lips, the tongue, etc.—but only *after* they have become invested with cathexis through object relations. The hand as an active medium for autoerotic gratification goes through a similar evolution. We are familiar with the obviously autoerotic play of the hand with parts of the body, mostly with the ear; it may replace thumb sucking or be carried on simultaneously with it. For some reason, cathexes which usually belong to the representation of the oral zone have been diverted to the hand. Actually, the activity itself has innate components, for rhythmic manual activity can be observed already in the neonate during nursing and is probably phylogenetically related to the approach behavior of the nursing mammal. When, however, autoerotic manipulation becomes more important than the normal outlets of the other activities of the child (and here we also include thumb sucking), then we are in the presence of an individually acquired behavior. Furthermore, it is probably acquired in a particular kind of object relation. Ear pulling, and even hair pulling are relatively benign examples of such activities; face scratching, head rolling, head banging, less so.

From this brief enumeration it will be seen that even areas of the body which have no phylogenetic predisposition whatsoever are frequently erotized in the course of development. As Freud (1905b) remarked in respect to erotogeneity, "Any other part of the skin or mucous membrane can take over the functions of an erotogenic zone," and he elaborated that it was the quality of the stimulus which generates the pleasurable feeling, more than the nature of the part concerned. He stressed rhythmicity as one of the more conspicuous qualities of such stimuli. Although Freud explicitly called attention to the importance of rhythmicity nearly sixty years ago, it remained one of the most neglected aspects of infant activity in psychoanalytic research. One of the few analytic authors who devoted some thought to rhythmicity is Hermann (1936). Although I took up the subject in 1937, I must confess to negligence in not having followed it up sufficiently in my own observations on infants, partly because of the lack of suitable technical devices. With current perfection in recording apparatus, observers of children should have no difficulty in getting that important information which is contained in rhythmic activity. At this point I can record only some impressions; for instance, even in the neonatal stage the rhythms of sucking and hand movements seem coordinated, though they are not necessarily identical. How this coordination may relate to rhythms emerging at a later stage is as yet unexplored.

A Disturbance of Object Formation. If we now review the different forms of autoerotic activity available to the infant in his first year, such as thumb sucking, playing with the lips, with the ears, nose, hair, with certain privileged limbs, playing with the genital, etc., we realize that each of these forms of activity involves an "object" and necessitates the cathecting of an object representation. This is a secondary, narcissistic cathexis, and the activity it involves has autoerotic quality. That is due, among others, to the rhythmic nature of the stimulation, as a result of which this particular "object," this part of the body, becomes privileged and distinguished from the rest of the body.

The only autoerotic activity which does not require such a selection, such a singling out of a privileged "object," is rocking. For in rocking the whole body of the infant is subjected to the autoerotic stimulation. The activity is an objectless one —or rather the object activated is the object of the *primary* narcissistic drive. This is not in the nature of a regression; actually the rocking infants are retarded. They have been arrested in their development; they never had the opportunity to progress (and this needs stressing) beyond the primary narcissistic investment. They were not offered the opportunity of forming the memory traces of an object, constant in time and space, and consistent with itself. They were not afforded the opportunity to invest the representations of privileged parts of their own bodies in action, counteraction, interaction, with their mother's body. As object to be, the mother was so self-contradictory that she did not lend herself to become the model for the formation of the object identical with itself in space and time—and therefore the establishment of relations with other objects became likewise impossible. Or if not impossible, they became impaired through the inadequacy of the original experience. There is another aspect of rocking, which in a certain way corroborates these assumptions. It is one of the few autoerotic activities at this age in which the child frequently manifests something in the nature of an orgastic pleasure, a wild delight. No fractioning of the libidinal drive into different subordinate modes of discharge (such as one sees it in genital play and play activity of all kinds) occurs in rocking. The drive in its totality is directed toward the primary narcissistic object, to the child's own body. This is comparable to the establishment of genital primacy, when the partial drives derived from the erotogenic zones are concentrated on the genital. But in rocking there is no such reconcentration, for the drive has not yet been divided into partial drives. The partial drives at this age have not been allocated to their appropriate zones, and it is rather the undifferentiated drive with which the psychic representation of the own body will be narcissistically invested.

In summary, inconsistent, contradictory behavior of the mother makes the establishment of adequate object relations impossible, and arrests the child at the level of primary narcissism, so that he is limited to the discharge of his libidinal drive in the form of rocking.

CYCLICAL MOOD SWINGS OF THE MOTHER (FECAL PLAY AND COPROPHAGIA)

CLINICAL OBSERVATIONS

Coprophagia and fecal play are rarely seen in the first year of life. To the best of my knowledge, there are no published records of any systematic investigations of the phenomenon.

Among the relatively large number of infants (366) which we studied systematically for extensive periods during their first year, this behavior was observed in one setting only, namely, the Nursery. There we found 16 cases, that is about 10 per cent, of the infant population present. The coprophagic behavior was observed between the ninth and the fifteenth month of life.

To determine the conditions which bring about coprophagia, we began a systematic investigation of the entire population residing at that time in the Nursery, namely, 153 children and their mothers.

Fecal play was recorded in our population as early as eight months and three days of age. Most of our cases fall between the tenth and the fourteenth month of life. In 11 of the 16 cases, the fecal play culminated in coprophagia. We will therefore speak of coprophagia and fecal play interchangeably. Though the play with feces as such went on for long periods at a time, and showed many variations, the mouth movements accompanying it, the facial expressions, and the sequence of gestures indicated that all this playing was but a preliminary to the final act of putting the feces in the mouth and, in several cases, to swallowing them. When swallowing the feces was not observed, it may well have occurred during our absence. We therefore came to the conclusion that fecal play during the first year of life is intimately connected with oral ingestion.

It is a handicap of the written text that I cannot exhibit the motion pictures taken of the behavior. Instead I shall give as close a description as possible of the material contained in the condensed protocol of one of our cases. This account is a fair sample of the entire range of the behavior patterns observed in coprophagia (see Spitz, 1948b).

Case 3 (1; 1+26). In the standing position when approached by the observer, she offers her hands filled with feces, which she tries to put into the observer's mouth. She is not unfriendly, reciprocates the observer's advances and smiles.

When the observer withdraws to a distance, she sits down, an abstracted expression on her face. The expression is not depressive. She takes a pellet of feces, rolls it between her thumb and index fingers, then smears it over the sheet and over her legs. She takes another pellet, manipulates it, passes it from one hand to the other. She uses large walnut-sized gobs for manipulation. From these she forms pea-sized pellets which she puts into her mouth at rare intervals, chewing them. As she does not spit them out, they are probably swallowed. The abstracted facial expression deepens and she passes an audible fecal movement. She lifts her skirts, looks at the full diaper; her face lightens with pleasure while she listens to the flatus she is passing. Except when listening to the flatus, she vocalizes a lot. When the fecal provisions in her hand are exhausted, she begins to manipulate the full diaper with one hand, lifting her skirt with the other, and looking at her manipulations. Now she bends forward, seizes the full, wet diaper between her teeth and alternately chews and sucks the urine-soaked fecal mass through the diaper. From time to time she sticks two fingers sideways into the diaper, picks out some feces, forms a pellet, and slips it into her mouth.

This play was observed for one hour and twenty minutes. The observer's presence did not disturb the child; on the contrary, she related her play to him in a flirtatious, smiling, laughing, vocalizing, contact-creating manner, without any apprehension, from time to time offering feces to the observer.

This manner of contact-creating, of communicating, is also present, though not in the same way, when she is addressing herself to her diaper or to the feces. I mentioned her vocalizations. When she is not vocalizing but smearing the feces or considering in an absorbed manner the pellet she is holding in her hand, one notices mouth movements which presumably have something to do with ingesting.

This assumption is borne out by our observation of another child who did not relate to the observer but was deeply engrossed for long periods in handling the feces. This child would lift the pellets, look at them, making mouth movements, passing his tongue over his lips in manifest eating behavior followed by a swallowing movement. This boy put the feces into his mouth only after producing this behavior for a long time.

These protocols are presented for their completeness. However, not all these behavior patterns are present in every given coprophagic child; neither the offering of feces to the observer (seen in three instances), nor the contact-seeking, the smile and the laughter is present in each and every case. On the other hand, the forming of pellets and eating them are characteristic of the coprophagic child. Only one child, though smearing feces like the others, did not form pellets, but instead stuck large pieces of feces into his mouth. This child was mentally deficient.

Earlier findings have led us to expect that often a specific form of behavior disorder in the infant reflects and is indicative of a concomitant specific form of mother-child relation. This expectation was again confirmed in the mother-child relationship of the coprophagic child.

HIGHLIGHTS OF THE MOTHER'S PERSONALITY

We again begin with an account of the mother's personality. We had shown earlier that the personality of the mothers in the "Nursery" and the disturbance of their psychic structure vary over a wide range; psychosis and psychotic trends, however, were relatively rare. It came as a surprise to find that the bulk of psychoses in this setting was concentrated in the group of the mothers whose children manifested fecal play. Among these 16 mothers, 11 showed the clinical symptoms of depression; 2 of them were paranoiacs; of the remaining 3, 1 was homicidal, but no diagnosis was made; on 2 we have no information.

These figures become even more significant when we compare the incidence of depression among the mothers of children who engage in fecal play and coprophagia with mothers in the same institution whose children show no fecal play.

Table V shows that there is a significant positive correlation between depression in the mother and fecal play in the infant.[10]

[10] Significant beyond the .01 level of confidence utilizing chi-square and Yates's correction.

TABLE V
TABLE V

RELATION BETWEEN DEPRESSION IN MOTHERS AND FECAL
PLAY IN CHILDREN IN NURSERY

Mothers	Child	
	Fecal Play (N = 16)	*No Fecal Play* (N = 137)
Depression	69%	3%
No Depression	31%	97%
	100%	100%

MOTHER-CHILD RELATIONS

A closer study of the relation between the depressive mothers and their children reveals further meaningful details. In the first place we found that these mothers showed marked intermittent mood changes toward their children. The duration of a given mood ranged from two to six months. In some of the cases we recorded mood reversals up to four times in the course of one year. These moods varied from extreme hostility with rejection to extreme compensation of this hostility in the form of "oversolicitousness."

I have put the term "oversolicitousness" in quotes for a good reason. The protocols of many of the coprophagic cases contain remarks to the effect that the mother is tender or loving to her baby; but the remarks are qualified by the statement that this love has some exaggerated traits. We noted, for instance, a hungry, fascinated incapacity of the mother to tear herself away from her child. Or we found a mother saying, "I cannot look at other children, only at my own." Or such a mother may dislike the other children to the point where she not only neglects them but does them actual harm.

The rejecting or hostile behavior is, in its way, equally peculiar. Overt rejection in the mothers of noncoprophagic children usually took the form of a mother's declaring that she did not want her child, and she then offered him for adoption. However, such overt rejections are rare in our coprophagic cases. Equally infrequent are overt hostile statements of these mothers about their children. One such mother said, "I hate my child to be called 'darling.' " Whatever the overt manifestation of feeling, we found unconscious hostile behavior to their children in all 16 of the mothers.

A surprisingly large number of the coprophagic children (6) suffered injury at the hand of their own mothers. They suffered burns, they were scalded; one was dropped on his head, one was nearly drowned during bathing. We had the impression that, without the alert supervision of the staff, few of these children would have survived. In passing it is worth mentioning that the only two cases of actual genital seduction of children by their own mothers which have come to our notice in this study project were found among the group of depressive mothers.

While in 7 cases the mother's love is manifested during the first months of the baby's life, and the hostility comes later, in 5 cases the obverse is true. In 4 cases our records are incomplete in this respect.

THE AFFECTIVE STATE OF THE COPROPHAGIC CHILD

Turning now to a description of the children, we found that the personality of the coprophagic child shows conspicuous peculiarities besides the symptoms of coprophagia. To be sure, coprophagic children suffer from a psychiatric disturbance of a special kind, for which as yet we have no term, and so we speak of them as *coprophagic* children. Of the 16 coprophagic infants, 10 *looked* depressed. I am deliberately making a sharp distinction here between "suffering from a depression" and "looking depressed."

The coprophagic children show the *affective state* of depression. Besides those who look depressed, for instance, others at times showed a facial expression resembling that of paranoid suspicion; a third group looked as if they were in a catatonic daze. Therefore I consider this a clinical picture *sui generis,* which at an early level of infantile development appears to combine the characteristics of orality (hence the depressive looks of some of these children) with anality.

In view of these outward appearances I wish to caution the reader not to equate the appearance (or the behavior) of coprophagic children with the deeply depressed look present in children suffering from anaclitic depression, of which I shall speak in greater detail in Chapter XIV. There are many striking symptomatic differences between coprophagic children who *look* depressed and children suffering from anaclitic depression.

Coprophagic children present their oral symptoms even *while* showing the affect of depression. Children suffering from anaclitic depression present striking oral symptoms only *after* they have recovered from their depression. Furthermore, even when looking depressed, coprophagic children seem socially minded—in their own, odd way. For example, three of the coprophagic children tried to feed their feces to any person present, be that of the observer or another child. During this "socializing" they smiled at the observer.

It is perhaps of interest to note that, when a noncoprophagic child was being fed fecal pellets by a coprophagic child, he would accept them trustingly, but then spit them out and afterwards ward off further tidbits offered by the coprophagic child. In other words, the taste for feces is not a characteristic of infancy, but probably is peculiar to the coprophagic child.

DYNAMICS OF THE MOTHER-CHILD RELATIONSHIP
IN COPROPHAGIA

The mothers of our coprophagic children have a personality characterized by deep-seated ambivalence. Periodically when their superego has the upper hand, the hostile components are repressed, the picture is that of a self-sacrificing, self-debasing mother, who envelopes her child with love. During this period such mothers may, for instance, constantly pester the observer with worries about their child, particularly during the first month, when they often believe that the child is deaf or blind. Or, another example, one mother said, "My baby is so little [at the time he was one year old], I am afraid of hurting it." Or again in another case, an unsophisticated observer, a nurse, remarked about a mother: "She is defiant, like a lioness with her cub." These "love" periods lasted for an appreciable time, never less than two months; and would then be replaced by a swing to hostility. The hostile periods again lasted for an appreciable time.

The child is in effect confronted with a potential libidinal object which maintains a consistent attitude long enough to permit the forming of object relations. However, this period comes to an end; the second phase of the cycle begins, in which the potential object becomes its own opposite. Now this "new" object remains constant long enough so that the child can form a set of new object relations; but it also compels the child to establish a compensatory reaction to the loss of the first, the "original" object.

How does the inconsistency, the oscillation, of the mothers of the rocking children differ from the mood swings of the mothers with coprophagic children? Rocking children were exposed by their mothers alternately to intense but *brief* outbursts of love and equally intense and brief outbursts of rage. The mothers of these rocking children had an infantile personality which was incapable of a consistent attitude lasting for days, let alone months. Their tantrums alternated with kissing jags within the hour, and at no time could their behavior be anticipated by the child. His potential libidinal object alternates between opposite poles and passes so rapidly through every point of the compass of emotions that all attempts at forming an object relation must fail. But it would be an error to equate this picture with the *long-wave* periodicity observed in the mothers of the coprophagic children.

Both the rocking children and the coprophagic children encounter obstacles in object finding and object relations. It is therefore of particular interest to consider what they put in place of the libidinal object which the normal child establishes toward the end of the first year.

Rocking is an archaic activity, it is *preobjectal*. Its object is a primary narcissistic one; therefore, rocking appears in the normal child in the first eight months as a simple infantile form of autoerotic behavior without any pathology attached to it. It is pathological only when it becomes the main activity of the child and persists throughout the whole of the first year and later.

Fecal play, on the other hand, consists in the actual manipulation of an "object," or rather, a "thing." Therefore, fecal play presupposes object relations of a sort, even though these may be pathological. It is noteworthy that in 5 out of our 16 cases of fecal play, genital play was also observed, and that it appeared before the coprophagia developed. This suggests that relatively normal object relations had been achieved, but were later disturbed. One might say that here the subsequent fecal play indicates a derailment[11] of the original object relations.

However, this additional information does not yet provide us with a valid explanation of why fecal play, and particularly coprophagia, is chosen by these children. Such an explanation can, at present, only be offered in the form of a tentative working hypothesis.

In his study of melancholia, Freud (1917a) demonstrated that one of the most conspicuous aspects of the depressive syndrome is the oral incorporation of the lost object. This

---

11 For an extensive discussion of the concept of derailment of object relations (as seen in the clinical pictures of coprophagia, rocking, and eczema), see Spitz "The Derailment of Dialogue" (1964).

finding was elaborated by Abraham (1911, 1924), and since then its validity and usefulness have been attested by extensive therapeutic experience. In the depressed individual the oral incorporation is unconscious, though evident to the observer.

I have commented on the peculiar nature of love in the depressive mothers; on their hungry fascination with their child, which can go to the point of cunnilingus. In the original study I advanced the proposition that coprophagic children identify with the unconscious tendencies manifested in their mothers, and that this identification leads the child to oral incorporation.

"GOOD" AND "BAD" OBJECT: THE INDUCTION OF AFFECTIVE STATES IN THE CHILD BY THE MOTHER

In the fifteen years which have passed since, I have further studied processes, forms, and stages of identification; in particular I considered the circumstances under which it comes about in infants toward the end of the first year of life (1957). I reached the conclusion that the child can identify only with external characteristics of behavior on the one hand, and with certain global affective attitudes of the object on the other. These are the attitude "for" or the attitude "against." In view of the basic significance, at this early age, of "taking in" and of "spitting out," I feel inclined to advance the proposition that these incorporative and eliminative modalities also belong among the global affective attitudes sensed by the child. This proposition appears to find support in the symptoms of the coprophagic children which suggests that they identify with the mother's incorporative tendencies.

These considerations link up with a proposition recently introduced into psychoanalytic thinking by Anna Freud. In a series of four lectures on child analysis given in September, 1960, under the auspices of the New York Psychoanalytic Society, she discussed certain aspects of the child's relationship to a depressed mother. She remarked that the child's behavior does not reflect a process of simple identification. The mother's depressive mood generates in the child an inclination toward depressive tendencies. The depressed mother retreats from the child, and the child, in Anna Freud's words, "follows her into the depressive mood."

Anna Freud made it clear that she considers this phenomenon to be in the nature of "infection" and that it is not an imitation of the mother's gestures which produces this mood in the child. The child simply responds to the affective climate, not to the cause of the affect; he is thus infected by the affective climate.

It seems to me that in the symptoms of coprophagic children we have a working example of Anna Freud's proposition. Perhaps I should no longer speak, as I did in the past, of an identification of the coprophagic child with the unconscious tendencies of the mother, but of an "infection" of the child with the mother's devouring tendencies. Or, as I would say now: *the child follows the mother's attitude; but he follows it in global terms, which are the only ones he is as yet able to assimilate. These are the terms of "taking in" and "spitting out."* This would lead the coprophagic child to the oral incorporation of his object.

This conjecture provides a bridge between two independent propositions on the subject of depression. One of these propositions is Freud's finding that the most conspicuous aspect of the depressive syndrome is the oral incorporation of the lost object. The other is Anna Freud's proposition that the child follows the mother into depression without therefore necessarily being depressed himself.

Given the fact that the coprophagic syndrome arises in the wake of a radical change of the mother's attitude, which, for the child at this age, is tantamount to losing her, we can now discern three components in the clinical picture of coprophagia:

1. Depression leads to oral incorporation of the lost object.
2. The child follows the mother into depression.
3. The coprophagic child has suffered what amounts to the loss of the "good" object (eventually destined to fuse with the "bad" object into the libidinal object proper).

The "loss" of the mother going into depression is not a physical loss, like when the mother dies or disappears for some reason. It is an emotional loss; for the mother, in changing her emotional attitude, also radically changes the signals which identified her as good object for the child. Physically, she remains the same mother she was. Emotionally, the good mother, the libidinally invested object, is lost. This is a loss which can be experienced in this form only in the first year of life, at this developmental stage, in other words, it is stage specific. At any later stage, the change in the mother's mood would be experienced differently. For instance, the preschool child would react with "you are bad to me"; the school child, with "Why are you mad at me?" the adolescent, with "Why don't you like me any more?" and the adult, with "What happened to you?" But such mental operations are beyond the capacities of the coprophagic children, they are too immature. Only cathectic displacements with affective consequences are available to the child at this point, because at the time at which the emotional loss occurs, the fusion of good and bad object is not yet completed and the libidinal object is only *in statu nascendi*. As long as the libidinal object is not established, the object presentations of the infant are discrete presentations of good and of bad objects. The potential object is recognized not by its perceptual attributes—but in virtue of situational attributes which possess emotional valency. Accordingly, the good object remains separate from the bad object until the two are fused as a result of countless iterative action exchanges in the framework of object relations. Only after this fusion is completed successfully is the libidinal object proper formed through the confluence of the good with the bad object.

The depressive mother blocks this normal development when she withdraws from the child into her depression; the radical change of her emotional attitude transforms her into a bad object. While the good object invites the opportunities for action exchanges with the child, the mother who has withdrawn into her depression avoids and withholds them. The child is thus deprived of the opportunity to complete the fusion. In his need for action exchanges, he follows the mother into the depressive attitude and so acquires her global incorporative tendency, attempting to maintain what he had already achieved in the way of object relations.

THE ROLE OF STAGE SPECIFICITY

Another aspect in the picture of coprophagia is that in its symptoms it carries the hallmark of the developmental stage at which it arises. I have so far referred to this stage as the one in which the libidinal *object* is established. From the point of view of libido *development,* however, this stage, situated at the end of the first year of life, is also that of the transition from the oral to the anal phase.

In this connection, though in a different frame of reference, data from experimental child psychology contribute further information. Gesell (1954) observed that at this age level the child will fill small objects, gravel, pills, etc., into a narrow-necked bottle so reliably that he used this activity in one of his tests as a test item for measuring fine-finger coordination. Charlotte Bühler (1928) relates an even more pertinent observation: a child attempting to make a ring from plasticine did this by first making *pellets* from the material and then joining them together until a ring was formed. Bühler calls this approach "synthetic." True, her observations refer to a later age than that of our coprophagic children; but the tendency is there. I suspect that pellet formation is a tendency characteristic of the anal phase, in accordance with the zonal mode (Erikson, 1950a). Just as the mode of the oral zone is incorporative and combines with biting, that of the anal zone is the retentive-eliminative, pellet-forming one.

The stage specificity of the changes in the coprophagic children's object relations may also explain why, despite depressive mothers, some of the other children studied do not become coprophagic. In the noncoprophagic control group there were 5 children who had depressed mothers. I assume that in the case of these 5 the sequence "bad object *after* good object" may have been reversed, or the shift to the bad object may have occurred either before or after the critical age for coprophagia.

This pathology is by no means limited to the institutional setting. Institutions have no monopoly on maternal depression. It is not rare in private homes and occurs in all social strata.

The circumstance of stage specificity makes it more plausible that the coprophagic infant chooses feces for his incorporative behavior. To be sure, no material is as readily available to the child as his own feces. But over and beyond this, the inception of the anal phase directs the infant's attention to his bowel functions. In this phase, therefore, an "object" becomes available to a child who has just suffered an object loss: it is an affectively charged object, for it was part of the child's body. Furthermore, it is invested with affective charges belonging to the erotogenic zone from which it was eliminated. This object is the fecal object—but of course it becomes an object only when it is being eliminated.

COMMENTS

Before concluding the present chapter, I return once more to the topic of the depressive mother and how her child follows her into the depression. We wish to examine this process from the viewpoint of the dyadic relation and consider the difference between the infant's and the mother's role. From the structural viewpoint, during the earlier part of this relation the ego of the child has just begun its function of regulating drive discharge processes. Its regulating activity is still closer to the primary than to the secondary process.

For in the beginning the infant's ego is a rudimentary, exceedingly sketchy organization, with large gaps between the ego nuclei of which it is composed. Many ego apparatuses are still missing; the child can survive only because his mother serves as his external, as his auxiliary ego (Spitz, 1951) which rounds off his incomplete, inadequate psychic structure and provides the sensorimotor apparatus needed for adaptive and regulative functioning. The two together, mother and child, constitute the dyad, and most of the infant's actions are dependent on the linkage with, and on their continuation in, the mother's actions. The way in which these actions are carried out, lovingly facilitated in their completion, or unfeelingly blocked, is predicated on the mother's attitude, conscious or unconscious.

The infant's actions either originate in the actions of the mother and then are extending them; or the situation may be reversed: the infant's actions trigger the mother's actions, which will then continue and complete the infant's action. Within the first year, those of the infant's actions and attitudes which proceed independently from those of the mother are limited. Therefore, one has to conceive of the infant's actions within the dyad as forming, together with those of the mother, a continuity of which they are a part. This interlocking, which corresponds in part to Benedek's (1938) and Mahler's (1952) concept of symbiotic relations, begins as identity of infant and mother, that is, as primary identification. But even by the end of the first year, differentiation between child and mother is far from complete.

Saying that the infant's actions within the dyad are an extension of those of the mother and vice versa is but an attempt to explicate Anna Freud's felicitous formulation that "the child follows the mother into the depression." Similarly, when I stated in the past that the coprophagic child "enacts the unconscious attitude of his depressed mother," I was visualizing just such an extension (in the infant) of drive derivations and their aims, as expressed in the mother's actions.

To summarize: in the first year of life, coprophagia is co-variant with depression in the mother. Two elements in the mother's depressive picture provoke the child's pathology:

1. The periodical nature of her mood swings.
2. The unconscious oral-incorporative tendencies characteristic of depression.

In the child we found three factors relevant to coprophagia, which all serve and facilitate the child's striving to get back to the mother:

1. The facilitation provided by "following the mother's mood." This is a precursor of identification; identification proper is not available at this stage because of the ego's incompleteness.
2. A dynamic facilitation arising out of the child's reaction to the loss of the "good" object.
3. A phase facilitation through the child's having arrived at the transition from the oral to the anal phase.

The reader will note that, while in point 2, it is the "good" object which is lost, the object, according to point 1, which the child follows into depression is the "bad" object. However, as already mentioned, at this stage the object is the target for drive discharge. Therefore the "bad" object exerts a "pull" comparable in its way to that of the "good" object.

Maternal Hostility Consciously Compensated
(The Hyperthymic Child)

The clinical picture of the consequences of consciously compensated maternal hostility is one on which we have exceedingly scarce case material. The reason for this lack of observed cases is a simple one: this maternal attitude is rather inconspicuous and only apparent to the sophisticated psychiatric observer. The same goes for the response, and the condition develops in its full-blown form at an age beyond the scope of our present investigation. Accordingly, the confirmation that this is a circumscribed clinical picture will have to be derived from a longitudinal observation in which both the parents and the child are carefully followed. I have tentatively included the following short description to sensitize readers engaged in such work to this possibility, so that they can establish whether this proposition is valid or whether it requires modification.

Maternal behavior in these cases is the result of a conscious conflict. For such mothers the child serves as an outlet for narcissistic and exhibitionistic satisfaction—and not as a love object. However, such a mother is aware that her attitude toward her child is improper, she feels guilty, and therefore overcompensates consciously by a subacid, syrupy sweetness. This maternal attitude is primarily found in intellectual and professional circles.

The fathers in these cases turned out to be aggressive and quite successful in their jobs. This may be due to their capacity for overt expression of hostility. In their relations to the child, they are hearty, loud, somewhat exhibitionistic types, who do not know where to stop, and as often as not may frighten the child through rough and ready handling, over the concerned mother's protest.

The children themselves impress the observer by their manipulative proficiency. That is not particularly surprising;

I recall a few cases where as a rule the children were practically crowded out of their play pens by the mass of toys accumulated there by the overcompensating parents who were trying to buy off their guilt feelings. Naturally, the children were exceedingly familiar with inanimate objects, and clever in manipulating them. But in the social sector of their personality their developmental profile shows a conspicuous retardation, in line with the kind of human relations offered them by the parents. By the time they are in their second year, they are apt to be hyperactive, not very sociable, destructive with toys. On the other hand, they are uninterested in contact with human beings, and become hostile when approached. The catamnesis of the cases followed by us leads me to believe that their personality tends to develop in the direction of children described by John Bowlby (1946) under the name "aggressive hyperthymic."

CHAPTER XIV

Emotional Deficiency Diseases
of the Infant

In Chapter XII, I stated that a *quantitative* factor is primarily responsible for emotional deficiency diseases, whereas in psychotoxic diseases it is a *qualitative* one. Therefore in the psychotoxic disturbances it was the mother's individual personality which came under scrutiny.

In the etiology of emotional deficiency diseases, the mother's individual personality plays a minor role, for these conditions result, as a rule, from the mother's physical absence, through sickness, through death, because of her child's hospitalization, while at the same time the substitute provided for the mother is either inadequate or practically nonexistent.[1] It follows that the child is deprived of maternal care and of vital emotional supplies which he normally would receive through the interchanges with his mother.

As the nosogenic factor is a quantitative one, the damage suffered by the child deprived of his mother will be proportionate to the length of that deprivation. I have therefore distinguished two categories, that of *partial* affective depriva-

[1] This does not exclude the possibility of a mother, even where present, depriving her child of normal emotional supplies; nor does it exclude the possibility that the mother neglects her child by being occupied outside of the home, either for economic reasons or because of her insufficient interest in her child.

267

tion and that of total affective deprivation. The two syndromes resulting from affective deprivation are not sharply divided; there are transitions from one to the other.

PARTIAL EMOTIONAL DEPRIVATION (ANACLITIC DEPRESSION)

THE CLINICAL PICTURE AND ITS PROGRESSIVE NATURE

In the course of a long-term study of infant behavior we observed 123[2] unselected infants, the total population of that institution at that time, each for a period of twelve to eighteen months. In this institution, here referred to as the Nursery,[3] we encountered a striking syndrome.

TABLE VI

POPULATION

	White	Colored	Totals
Male	37	24	61
Female	40	22	62
Totals	77	46	123*

* See footnote 2.

On the whole, these infants in the Nursery had normal, good relations with their mothers during the first six months of their lives, and showed good progress. However, in the second half of the first year, some of them developed a weepy behavior which was in marked contrast to their previous happy outgoing behavior. After a time, this weepiness gave

[2] The figure 123, as well as the figures which will follow, in regard to this investigation of partial emotional deprivation, refer to my first publication on this subject, "Anaclitic Depression" (1946b). It should be noted that in a later publication (1951), the corresponding figure is 170 cases; this discrepancy arises because as time went on we were able to add 47 more infants to our population. The added subjects provided further confirmation of findings and statements made earlier.

[3] For a detailed description of the conditions prevailing in this institution, see Chapter II.

way to withdrawal. They would lie prone in their cots, face averted, refusing to take part in the life of their surroundings. When we approached them we were mostly ignored, though some of them would watch us with a searching expression. If we were insistent in our approach, weeping would ensue, and in some cases screaming. It made no difference whether the observer was male or female.

The weepy withdrawing behavior would persist for two or three months, during which some of these children lost weight instead of gaining. The nursing personnel reported that some suffered from insomnia; this was so disturbing that the child could not be left in the room with the other four children but had to be segregated. All showed an increased susceptibility to intercurrent colds. Their developmental quotient showed first a retardation of personality growth and then a gradual decline.

This behavior syndrome lasted approximately three months, getting progressively worse. Then the weepiness subsided. It was replaced by a sort of frozen rigidity of expression. Now these children would lie or sit with wide-open expressionless eyes, frozen immobile face, and a faraway look, as if in a daze, apparently not seeing what went on around them. Contact with children who had reached this stage became increasingly difficult and finally impossible. At best, screaming was elicited.

Among the 123 children observed during the whole of the first year of their lives, we found this clear-cut syndrome in 19 of our subjects. There were individual differences, for instance, weeping might dominate the picture for a few weeks; or in some cases there might be an attitude of complete withdrawal. In others, where we succeeded in overcoming the initial rejection of our approach, we found a desperate clinging to the adult. Apart from such individual differences, the clinical picture was so clear-cut that once we had called attention to it, it was easily recognized even by untrained observers. A typical case history follows:

Case 5 (female, colored) (Spitz, 1947b). Nothing unusual was noted during the first six months. She is a particularly friendly colored child, who smiles brilliantly at the approach of the observer. At the age of six and a half months we noticed that her radiant smiling behavior had ceased. During the following two weeks, she slept heavily throughout the twelve hours of our observation. Thereafter a change in her behavior took place which was recorded as follows: she lay immobile in her crib; when approached she did not lift her shoulders, barely her head, to look at the observer with an expression of profound suffering sometimes seen in sick animals. As soon as the observer started to speak to her or to touch her, she began to weep. This was unlike the usual crying of babies, which is accompanied by a certain amount of unpleasure vocalization, and sometimes screaming. Instead she wept soundlessly, tears running down her face. Speaking to her in soft comforting tones only resulted in more intense weeping, intermingled with moans and sobs, shaking her whole body.

This reaction deepened in the ensuing two months. It was more and more difficult to make contact with the child. In our protocols there is a note seven weeks later to the effect that it took us almost an hour to establish contact with her. During this period she lost weight and developed a serious eating disturbance; she had difficulty in taking food and in keeping it down.

This is a fairly typical picture of the syndrome. Individual differences may include a clinging to the observer and a weeping in his arms, or the already-mentioned insomnia and agitation.

I shall now review the average progress of this syndrome, month by month, as observed in the 19 children in this first study plus another 15 children subsequently studied.

First Month: The children become weepy, demanding, and tend to cling to the observer when he succeeds in making contact with them.

Second Month: The weeping often changes into wails. Weight loss sets in. There is an arrest of the developmental quotient.

Third Month: The children refuse contact. They lie prone in their cots most of the time, a pathognomonic sign (see Fig. 14). Insomnia sets in; loss of weight continues. There is a tendency to contract intercurrent diseases; motor retardation becomes generalized. Inception of facial rigidity (see Fig. 15).

After the third month: facial rigidity becomes firmly established. Weeping ceases and is replaced by whimpering. Motor retardation increases and is replaced by lethargy. The developmental quotient begins to decrease.

THE ETIOLOGICAL FACTORS

We discovered that *all* children in our sample population who developed this syndrome had one experience in common: at some point between the sixth and eighth month of life all of them were deprived of the mother for a practically unbroken period of three months. This separation took place for unavoidable external administrative reasons. Before the separation the mother had the full care of her infant. Due to the special circumstances obtaining in this institution, she spent more time with her child than she would, had she been living in the family setting. After separation from their mothers, each of these children developed the syndrome described above. No child developed this syndrome whose mother had not been removed.

The symptomatology and facial expression of these children was strongly reminiscent of that found in adults suffering from depression. In view of the infant's incomplete psychic apparatus, in view of the specific etiological factors which produce this syndrome, it was mandatory to distinguish it clearly from the nosological concept of depression in adults. I therefore have called this syndrome "anaclitic depression" (1946b).[4]

The disturbance presents other noteworthy peculiarities. One is that when the child suffering from anaclitic depression remains deprived of his mother without his being provided with an acceptable substitute for a period lasting longer than three to five months, then further deterioration of the child's condition sets in. I have found that, after three months of separation, there is a transitional period of about two months, during which all the symptoms already mentioned become more marked and are consolidated. Conversely, if during this transitional period the mother returns, most of the children recover. It is doubtful if the recovery is complete; I would assume that the disturbance will leave scars which will show in later years; conclusive evidence of this is still lacking.

However, when the separation exceeds five months, the whole symptomatology changes radically and appears to merge into the prognostically poor syndrome of what I have described as "Hospitalism" (1945a), of which more later.

The progressive course of anaclitic depression is well illustrated by the children's developmental curve. Figure 16 shows the difference between the average developmental quotients of children who were separated and those who were not separated from their mothers.

Even more impressive than this comparison of the D.Q.s of the two groups of children is Table VII, which refers only to separated children.

[4] Recently Bowlby (1960) emphasized the need to distinguish "depression as a nosological concept" from the term "depression" as an affective state. I fully concur with him; the term "depression" has frequently been applied loosely, both to conditions observed in adults and to disturbances seen in infants (see Spitz, 1960a). In my work I have used the term "depression" as a nosological concept in speaking of the clinical entity which I have called *anaclitic depression*. This clinical entity will be discussed later from the point of view of structure and dynamics.

ENVIRONMENTAL DIFFERENCES IN DEVELOPMENT

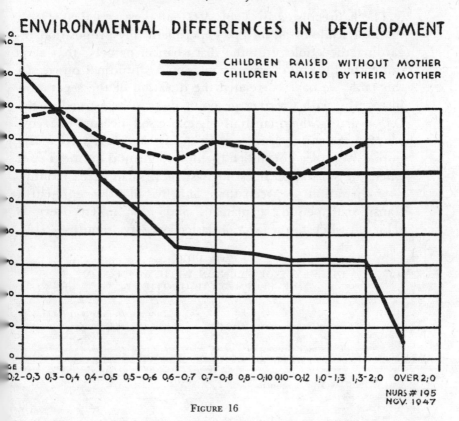

FIGURE 16

TABLE VII

INFLUENCE OF LENGTH OF SEPARATION FROM MOTHER
ON LEVEL OF DEVELOPMENTAL QUOTIENT

Duration of Separation in Months	*Average Decrease of Points of D.Q.**
Under 3 months	12.5
3 to 4 months	— 14
4 to 5 months	— 14
Over 5 months	— 25

* As already mentioned in Part I of this book, we do not consider the developmental quotients an adequate yardstick of infant development, either as a whole or in the various sectors. They are a convenient device for the crude comparison of different *groups* of infants; as such they may serve as supportive evidence, an illustration as it were, of the clinical data and record.

The figures listed in Table VIII support, practically with the exactitude of an *ad hoc* experiment, my proposition regarding the etiology of the disturbance, namely, that it is caused by the child's separation from his libidinal object. In this table we have correlated the duration of the separation in months, with the average point increase registered in the D.Q.—that is, the quantitatively expressed measure of recovery after the child's reunion with the mother. It is particularly impressive to see how much the developmental quotient rises when the separation does not last more than three months, how separations between three and five months represent a transitional period, a plateau, and how no recovery is achieved when the separation lasted over five months.

TABLE VIII
INFLUENCE OF REUNION WITH MOTHER ON
DEVELOPMENTAL QUOTIENT

Duration of Separation in Months	Increase in Points of D.Q. After Reunion
Under 3 months	+ 25
3 to 4 months	+ 13
4 to 5 months	+ 12
Over 5 months	− 4

The symptomatology of the children separated from their mothers is strikingly similar to the symptoms with which we are familiar in adult depression. Furthermore, in the etiology of the disturbance, the loss of the love object is prominent both in the adult and in the infant, so much so that one is inclined to consider it a determining factor.

However, from the point of view of structure and dynamics, depression in the adult and depression in the infant are not comparable; they are completely different psychiatric entities. The dynamics in adult depression are predicated upon the presence of a sadistically cruel superego under whose relentless persecution the ego breaks down.

Nothing comparable exists in the infant, where at this stage even the precursors of the superego cannot be discerned. Therefore, what we observe here is only a similarity in the superficial nosological picture. The symptoms are similar, but the underlying process is basically different. For this very reason I introduced a new psychiatric category, that of *anaclitic*[5] depression to designate the infantile disturbance described above. It has to be set off clearly from adult depression, from Melanie Klein's concept of the "depressive position,"[6] and from Bowlby's concept of mourning.

A necessary condition for the development of anaclitic depression is that prior to separation the infant should have been in *good* relations with his mother. It is striking that when *bad* mother-child relations existed prior to separation, the infants separated from their mothers presented disturbances of a different nature. I first classified these cases under the category of "mild depression" (1946b). Being most impressed at the time by the conspicuous symptoms of severe depressive behavior in the infants, I believed that what I called mild depression were simply deviant cases.

In view of the fairly relevant number of such deviant cases, I proceeded to explore our entire available data on the mother-child relation of this population, and correlated them with the severity of the disturbances of the individual children.

The results of this correlation are illustrated in Figure 17. The figures speak for themselves. It is evidently more difficult to replace a satisfactory love object than an unsatisfactory one.

---

[5] Anaclitic = leaning up against. "The first autoerotic satisfactions are experienced in connection with vital functions which serve the purpose of self-preservation" (Freud, 1914b). "The anaclitic choice of object is determined by the original dependence of the infant on the person who feeds, protects and mothers him. Freud states that in the beginning the drive unfolds anaclitically, that is, by leaning onto a need gratification essential for survival" (Spitz, 1957).

[6] For a discussion of Melanie Klein's concept of the "Depressive Position," see Waelder (1936) and Glover (1945).

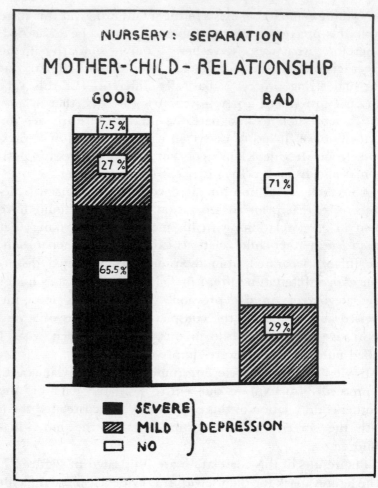

NURSERY: SEPARATION

MOTHER-CHILD-RELATIONSHIP

GOOD   BAD

7.5 %

27 %

71 %

65.5 %

29 %

■ SEVERE
▨ MILD   } DEPRESSION
☐ NO

FIGURE 17

Accordingly, anaclitic depression is much more frequent and much more severe in the cases of separation following good mother-child relations. We did not see a single case of anaclitic depression in infants with manifestly bad mother-child relations. In these cases it would seem that any substitute was at least as good as the unsatifactory biological mother.

In the course of our later investigations it turned out that these "mild depression" cases concealed a variety of psychotoxic disturbances. Such psychotoxic disturbances were not due to the loss of the object but developed as a result of the relationship which preceded separation from the mother.

TOTAL EMOTIONAL DEPRIVATION (HOSPITALISM)

In anaclitic depression, recovery is prompt when the love object is returned to the child within a period of three to five months. If there are any emotional disturbances of lasting consequence, these are not readily apparent at the time.

In total deprivation matters are quite different. If one deprives children during their first year of all object relations for periods lasting longer than five months, they will show the symptoms of increasingly serious deterioration, which appears to be, in part at least, irreversible. The nature of the mother-child relation (if any) existing prior to the deprivation appears to have little influence on the course of the disease.

We observed total deprivation and its consequences in a Foundling Home situated outside of the United States, housing 91 infants (Spitz, 1945a, 1946a). In this institution the children were breast-fed during their first three months by their own mothers, or by one of the other mothers, if the child's own mother was not available. During these three months the infants had the appearance (and tested out at the developmental level) of average normal children of the same city.

After the third month mother and child were separated. The infants remained in the Foundling Home, where they were adequately cared for in every bodily respect. Food, hygiene, medical care and medication, etc., were as good as, or even superior to, that of any other institutions we have observed.

But, as one single nurse had to care for eight children

(officially: actually up to twelve children would devolve to the care of one nurse), they were emotionally starved. To put it drastically, they got approximately one tenth of the normal affective supplies provided in the usual mother-child relationship.

After separation from their mothers, these children went through the stages of progressive deterioration characteristic for partial deprivation described before. The symptoms of anaclitic depression followed one another in rapid succession and soon, after the relatively brief period of three months, a new clinical picture appeared: motor retardation became fully evident; the children became completely passive; they lay supine in their cots. They did not achieve the stage of motor control necessary to turn into the prone position. The face became vacuous, eye coordination defective, the expression often imbecile. When motility reappeared after a while, it took the form of spasmus nutans in some of the children; others showed bizarre finger movements reminiscent of decerebrate or athetotic movements (Spitz, 1945a).

In our tests these children showed a progressive decline of the developmental quotient. By the end of the second year, the average of their developmental quotients stands at 45 per cent of the normal. This would be the level of the idiot. We continued to observe these children at longer intervals up to the age of four years (Spitz, 1946a). Figure 18 shows that by that time, with a few exceptions, these children cannot sit, stand, walk, or talk.

These mortality figures stand out even more shockingly when compared with those of other institutions. In the Nursery, for example, we observed an average of 55 children per year. Over a four-year period we therefore followed 220 children, of which 186 were observed for more than six months, beginning with birth, and of these in turn more than half beyond the first year of life. Among all these children, we recorded two deaths through intercurrent disease. Of the

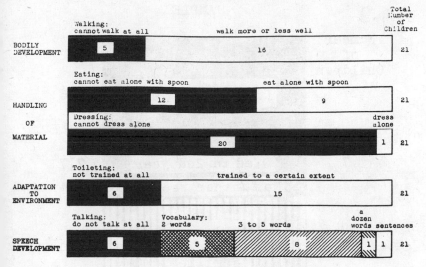

FIGURE 18

The progressive deterioration and the increased infection liability of these children led in a distressingly high percentage to marasmus and death (see Figs. 19 and 20).

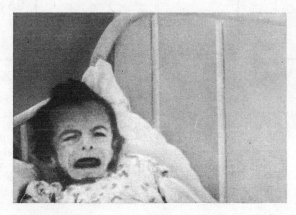

FIGURE 19

Marasmus.

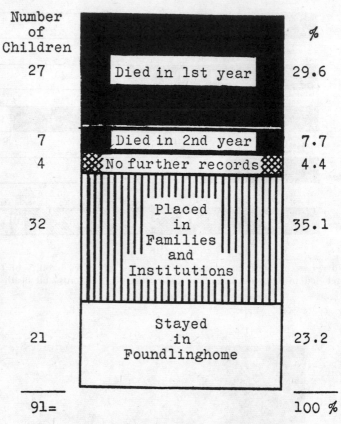

FIGURE 20

Of the 91 children originally observed in the Foundling Home, 34 had died by the end of the second year; 57 survived. On the fate of 4 of these we could get no information; 32 of them were placed in private families and institutions—on these we could not get any information either. It is therefore possible—we should rather say probable—that the total mortality percentage was much higher. As it is, even without this assumption, this is a shockingly high mortality.

Nursery children whom we could follow up within six months after they had left the institution two more children died. This shows convincingly that institutionalization itself does not generate high mortality rates in infants, but that a specific factor within the institution is responsible. There is one major difference between the Nursery and the Foundling Home: in the Nursery the infants had mothering, in the Foundling Home they did not.

I have outlined in previous Chapters that mothering provides the baby with the opportunity for affectively significant actions in the framework of object relations. Absence of mothering equals emotional starvation. We have seen that this leads to a progressive deterioration engulfing the child's whole person. Such deterioration is manifested first in an arrest of the child's psychological development; then psychological dysfunctions set in, paralleled by somatic changes. In the next stage this leads to increased infection liability and eventually, when the emotional deprivation continues into the second year of life, to a spectacularly increased rate of mortality.

I have advanced the proposition that the succession of symptoms of the hospitalism syndrome parallels closely the sequence of symptoms described by Selye (1950) following prolonged exposure to stress (Spitz, 1954, 1956b). Table IX illustrates these parallels.

Starting out with physical stressor agents, Selye soon recognized that emotional stress is a particularly potent activator of the pituitary, adrenocorticotrophic function. I consider prolonged emotional deprivation such a stressor agent.

In conclusion, I call the reader's attention to the terms I have used in dealing with this subject. I have spoken advisedly of *affective* (emotional) deprivation. In recent years a great deal of illuminating and interesting work has been done with animals and humans on the effects of sensory deprivation (Hebb, 1949; Bexton, Heron, and Scott, 1954; Heron, Bexton,

TABLE IX

PARALLELS BETWEEN THE GENERAL ADAPTATION
SYNDROME AND THE EMOTIONAL DEPRIVATION
SYNDROME

General Adaptation Syndrome (Selye)	Emotional Deprivation Syndrome (Spitz)
Tension	Weepiness
Excitement	Demanding Attitude
Loss of Appetite	Loss of Appetite
	Loss of Weight
Resistance to Evocative Stimulus Increases	Social Sector Increases
Adaptability to Other Agents Diminishes	Arrest and Regression of D.Q.
Libido Subnormal	Absence of Autoerotic Activity
Depression of Nervous System	Withdrawal
	Insomnia
	Decreased Motility
Adaptation Stops	Regression of D.Q. Irreversible
Resistance Ceases	Infection Liability
Arteriosclerosis of Brain Vessels	Facial Rigidity
	Atypical Finger Movements
Breakdown	Morbidity Increases
Death	Spectacular Mortality

and Hebb, 1956; Azima and Cramer-Azima, 1956a,b; Lilly, 1956; Harlow, 1958; Solomon, 1961). It should be realized that sensory deprivation and emotional deprivation are not interchangeable concepts. Granted, in the present state of the art, it is practically impossible to inflict the one without involving the other. An enormous number of experiments has lately been performed on a variety of animal species in the field of *sensory* deprivation. Attentive scrutiny of these experiments shows that the higher the place of the species on the evolutionary scale, the more severe the consequences. The conclusion is inescapable that the severity of the damage inflicted by sensory deprivation increases in direct ratio to the level of ego development characteristic for the species and to the quantity of object relations.

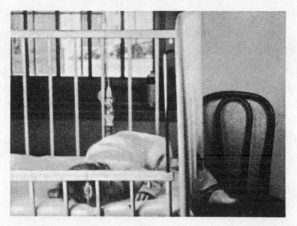

FIGURE 14
Pathognomonic Position.

Accordingly, in birds like ducks, recovery after prolonged sensory deprivation is rapid and easy. Already in greylag geese the effects are difficult to reverse. The picture is similar in lower mammals. But when we get to Harlow's rhesus mon-

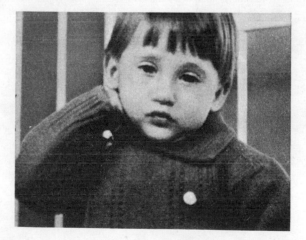

FIGURE 15
Anaclitic Depression.

keys, the consequences of emotional deprivation become completely irreversible. Harlow states that such consequences are expressed primarily in a disturbance of the animal's emotional functioning, of his responses and of his social relations.[7]

Accordingly, I believe that further experimentation and study will be required before we can delineate the nature of the two forms of deprivation and isolate their effects from each other. In recent papers I have made a first attempt in this direction (1962, 1963b, c, 1964).

[7] Personal communication, 1961.

CHAPTER XV

The Effects of Object Loss: Psychological Considerations

Anaclitic depression and hospitalism demonstrate that a gross deficiency in object relations leads to an arrest in the development of all sectors of the personality.[1] These two disturbances highlight the cardinal role of object relations in the infant's development.

More specifically, the catamnesis of our subjects affected by these two disturbances suggests a revision of our assumptions about the role of the aggressive drive in infantile development. The manifestations of aggression[2] common in the normal child after the eighth month, such as hitting, biting, chewing, etc., are conspicuously absent in the children suffering from either anaclitic depression or hospitalism. I have posited earlier in this study that the development of the drives, both libidinal and aggressive, is closely linked to the

[1] In a paper on the development of a blind-born child Fraiberg and Freedman (1963) extensively confirmed this proposition and illustrated it with impressive motion pictures.

[2] My usage of the terms "aggression" and "aggressive drive" has nothing to do with the popular meaning of the word "aggressive." The aggressive drive, "aggression" for short, designates one of the two fundamental instinctual drives operating in the psyche, as postulated by Freud (1920) (and referred to by some authors as "aggressive instinct"). Accordingly, when I speak of "aggression," I do not imply hostility or destructiveness; although at times these also may be among the manifestations of the drive.

285

infant's relation to his libidinal object. The infant's relation
with the love object provides an outlet for his aggressive drive
in the activities provoked by the object. At the stage of infantile ambivalence (that is, in the second half of the first
year) the normal infant makes no difference between the
discharge of the aggressive or the libidinal drives; they are
manifested simultaneously, concomitantly, or alternately in
response to one and the same object, namely, the libidinal
object. In the absence of the libidinal object, both drives are
deprived of their target. This is what happened to the infants
affected with anaclitic depression.

Now the drives hang in mid-air, so to speak. If we follow
the fate of the aggressive drive, we find the infant turning aggression back onto himself, onto the only object remaining.
Clinically, these infants become incapable of assimilating
food; they become insomniac; later these infants may actively
attack themselves, banging their heads against the side of the
cot, hitting their heads with their fists, tearing their hair out
by the fistful. If the deprivation becomes total, the condition
turns into hospitalism; deterioration progresses inexorably,
leading to marasmus and death.

As long as the infants were deprived of their libidinal object, they became increasingly unable to direct outward, not
only libido, but *also* aggression. The vicissitudes of the instinctual drives are, of course, not accessible to direct observation. But one may infer from the symptomatology of anaclitic
depression that the pressure (impetus, Freud, 1915b) of the
aggressive drive is the carrier, as it were, not only of itself, but
also of the libidinal drive. If we assume that in the normal
child of that age (that is, the second half of the first year) the
two drives are being fused, we may also postulate that in the
deprived infant a defusion of drives occurs.

How does this come about? When the separated infant cannot find a target for the discharge of its drive, he first becomes
weepy, demanding, and clings to everybody who approaches

him: it looks as though these infants are trying to regain the lost object with the help of their aggressive drive. Somewhat later, visible manifestations of aggression begin to decrease; after two months of uninterrupted separation the first definite somatic symptoms appear in the infant. They consist of sleeplessness, loss of appetite, and loss of weight. I have made an attempt to explain in detail each of these symptoms (1953a).

In anaclitic depression, when the pathological process due to deprivation is halted by the return of the love object, the obverse of the defusion of the two drives can be inferred. At that time we witness what seems to be the effect of a partial refusion of the drives in the rapidly returning activity of these children. When the mother is returned following a separation of less than three to five months, these infants appear completely transformed. They become gay and lively; they are happy with their mothers and with grownups in general, and they enjoy active games and play with other children. They also become more aggressive against others, for a while at least, than any normal infant of the same age. They may become actively destructive of objects, clothes, bed clothes, toys, etc. But this destructiveness is not comparable to the contactless, objectless destructiveness of the toddler and the preschool child who survived despite prolonged deprivation of emotional supplies.

It is also among the infants whose mothers have been returned to them after a few months of absence that we found the biting children and those who tear out other children's hair—not their own. I filmed one such infant who systematically tore a piece of skin off another child's instep, leaving a bleeding lesion.

What is the fate of the libidinal drive after the two drives have been defused from each other? Our observations on the autoerotic activities of infants in the first year of life provide us with some hints in this respect. We find that in infants subjected to a prolonged deprivation of affective supplies all autoerotic activities of any kind stop, including thumb sucking. Theoretically speaking it is as if the infant had returned to a form of existence which obtained during the stage of primary narcissism; he is unable to take as an object even his own body, as he would at the stage of secondary narcissism. One gets the impression that in these marasmic infants the only task that still devolves upon the libidinal drive is to insure survival, to maintain the flickering flame of life as long as possible.

The infants suffering from marasmus had been deprived of the opportunity to form object relations. Consequently they had not been able to direct the libidinal drive and the aggressive drive onto one and the same object—the indispensable prerequisite toward achieving the fusion of the two drives. Deprived of an object in the external world, the unfused drives were turned against their own person, which they took as object. The consequence of turning nonfused aggression against the own person becomes manifest in the destructive effects of deterioration of the infant, in the form of marasmus. The return of the equally unfused libidinal drive onto the self counteracts this destruction; operating on lines similar to primary narcissism, the libidinal drive spends itself in the effort to insure survival.

In my opinion, in the normal state of fusion of the two drives, aggression plays a role which is comparable to that of a carrier wave. In this way the impetus of aggression makes it possible to direct both drives toward the surround. But if the aggressive and the libidinal drives do not achieve fusion, or, alternatively, if a defusion has taken place, then aggression is returned against the own person; and in this case libido also can no longer be directed toward the outside.[3]

[3] One might ask what happens to the two drives during the period of deprivation, why they became defused, why it appears as if the aggressive drive had been subjected to a fate different from that of the libidinal drive. At this stage of our knowledge these are purely academic questions. However, I believe that Freud's proposition regarding the affinity of the libidinal drive

Neutralization. We can also examine the vicissitudes of the drives following object loss in the light of Hartmann's concept of neutralization (Hartmann, 1952, 1953, 1955; Kris, 1955; Hartmann, Kris, and Loewenstein, 1949), according to which instinctual energy can be transformed into neutralized energy. Neutralization can indeed obviate the pernicious consequence of defusion. However, neutralization presupposes a certain level of organization of the ego which the infant does not achieve before the last quarter of his first year, if then.

That is the stage at which we can speak of the infant having achieved a first level of true ego organization, the first integrated ego structure, which is quite unlike the rudimentary, not quite unified ego we have postulated for the third month of life. We have spoken of these two levels of ego development as the first and the second organizers of the psyche. The first major step in the integration of the ego takes place in the transitional months which separate the two. Certain conditions have to be fulfilled to enable the infant to pass successfully through the complex and difficult processes of this first major stage of transition, that is, to proceed on the path leading to the second organizer of the psyche (Spitz, 1959).

Prominent among these conditions is the atmosphere of

---

to the internal organs (Freud, 1905b) sheds light on these problems. Freud spoke later, particularly in "The Economic Problem of Masochism" (1924c), of the muscular apparatus as the channel of discharge for the aggressive drive. Organ systems are considerably slower in the function of discharge than is skeletal musculature. It is even to be assumed that the former have the capacity of holding energy in a bound state (Breuer and Freud, 1895). This is not true of the skeletal musculature which discharges energy rapidly, and in bursts of brief duration.

We might speculate about the existence of an organic, a physiological basis, which in the case of pathological inhibition of discharge would produce the defusion of the two drives when the pathology inhibits their discharge. Once the libidinal drive becomes separated from the aggressive drive, through defusion, the difference between the rhythm of discharge in the internal organs from that prevailing in the skeletal musculature could perpetuate the cleavage and lead eventually to a different fate for each of the drives. Perhaps some of the propositions of Cannon (1932) might find application in this context. Any such statement can only indicate one of the possible directions of our thinking.

security, which is provided by stable and consistent object relations. A continuous access to free discharge must be available to the infant, in the form of affect directed to the libidinal object, leading to interaction between infant and object.[4]

After the establishment of the ego, around the end of the first year of life, the precursors of defense mechanisms will be increasingly elaborated. The personality of the child begins to unfold and character traits become conspicuous. In the course of this development the drives (which had been fused in establishing the libidinal object) will be subjected to many further vicissitudes, among which are neutralization as well as the channeling of greater or smaller quantities of each drive into the psychic representation of one or the other organ, of this or that activity, reflecting the particular zonal mode (Erikson, 1950a) which happens to be in ascendance.

The outcome of this extensive experimentation with the drives is a gamut of drive mixtures, the composition of which varies both qualitatively and quantitatively. Of course, when I speak of experimentation with drive mixtures, I imply also that many of these experiments will be unsuccessful in accomplishing their aim, be that achieving gratification[5] or avoiding unpleasure. Unsuccessful experiments are abandoned; the normal child will give them up with relative ease, for the security and the consistency of his object relations make the costs of such a sacrifice acceptable. The secure affective climate permits him to compensate disappointments and frustrations in another sector of object relations, or through new experiments, or both.

This is where neutralization comes in. For neutralization

[4] Independently, Erikson (1950a) expresses this view in somewhat different form and calls it "the first stage of basic trust (about first year)," while Therese Benedek (1938) speaks of it as "confidence."

[5] It is hardly necessary to remind the psychoanalytically alert reader that I use the term "gratification" to cover the consequences of a wide spectrum of psychological experiences, including masochistic ones.

is predicated on the establishment of the dominance of the reality principle; the individual must be able to realize that his immediate goal may be either unobtainable or may entail too much unpleasure. This insight itself demands mental operations from the child, which require a level of ego integration at which gratification can be delayed and the instinctual drive held in suspense.[6] A further prerequisite for the ability to neutralize the drives is the above-mentioned climate of emotional security which can be afforded only when the libidinal object proper has been established (toward the end of the first year of life).

One is reminded of the manner in which motor patterns and motor behavior are acquired in the first months of life when one observes the eight-month-old child's repetitive trials and attempts: the way he directs and redirects instinctual drives; how partial drives are differentiated from them, reintegrated and utilized. Just like in the first months of life unsuccessful *movements* are relinquished, the eight-month-old relinquishes unsuccessful *behavior;* just like successful movements are integrated into the inventory of the three-month-old, successful sets of behavior sequences become routine items in the child's approach to the world toward the end of the first year. Among the random movements those which led to the goal were selected; among the various behavior sequences and emotional responses those are retained which bring returns.

A favorable affective climate will facilitate experimentation through actions and relations and attempts to achieve goals on a higher level. At this level *immediate* need gratification is no longer the exclusive goal. Maintenance of gratification in terms of object relations on the one hand, of developmental

---

[6] Expressed in Piaget's terms, this corresponds to a relatively advanced level of reversibility, which is achieved at the fourth stage, when the infant is able to retrieve the hidden toy behind two successive hiding places. (But see Appendix.)

progress and autonomy on the other, acquires an increasing importance. Goals which are not consonant with these aims will be abandoned. Perhaps one might say that motor patterns in the first months of life have *goals;* but drive manipulation after the establishment of the ego has *aims.*

When a goal is abandoned, the energy invested in its attainment seeks for an outlet, remains undischarged, and will have to be dealt with. Random excitation and uncoordinated activity (the original mode of discharge in the first weeks of life) is no longer quite ego syntonic for the one-year-old, particularly when the continuation of good and consistent object relations offers the greatest amount of gratification. True, the reign of the ego is not so firmly established that it would exclude temper tantrums. But the fact is that temper tantrums are rare in the child with good and gratifying object relations. Instead, new devices to deal with undischarged energy will evolve. On the conscious level, compensation will be accepted. In the unconscious sector of the ego, defense mechanisms will be developed and neutralization of the drive becomes possible.

In the light of these considerations I submit that *neutralization has a role in the sector of drives comparable to that played by the reality principle in the sector of action.* Before neutralization becomes available, defused instinctual drives will lead to destruction, to the destruction of the object or of the subject, or both. But when it can be neutralized, the drive energy will be held in suspense, pending a more favorable opportunity to use the neutralized energy for achieving an ego-syntonic aim. Neutralization of the drive thus represents, just like the reality principle, a detour function.

If we may generalize from the "normal" populations we observed, neutralization of the drive serves the function of defense. Thus neutralization can be added to the list of the mechanisms of defense; the reality principle as detour function and adaptive device would be its precursor.

CHAPTER XVI

Conclusion

In this study I have attempted to present a rounded picture of my work on the genesis of the first object relations, and of their component elements; on their successive stages found in normal development, and also on some of their disturbances in the course of the first year of life. This picture is but an outline, incomplete in many respects. Future research will be conducted with more subtle instruments, and indubitably expand, correct, and modify my findings; it may arrive at sharper definitions and at a new set of concepts. What I offer, therefore, is a first approximation, which sheds some light, at times unexpectedly, on a whole series of phenomena.

I have indicated that unimpeded progress in the establishment of object relations is a prerequisite of normal development and functioning of the psyche—a necessary, but not a sufficient condition. I have discussed deviations in the establishment of object relations and the disturbance of the infant's psychic development frequently associated with such deviations. Some of these disturbances of early infancy, be they psychogenic affections or psychosomatic conditions, bear a striking resemblance to disturbances with which we are familiar also in the adult. I have stated that these resemblances do not make the two, the disturbance in the infant and the psychiatric disease in the adult, either homologous or even analogous. On the contrary, I have stressed that the pathological conditions seen in infancy are independent clinical pictures *sui generis,* because they affect an organism having a psychic structure quite different from that of the adult. However, when disturbances as serious as some I have described occur during the formative period of the psyche, they are bound to leave scars on the psychic structure and function. Such scars are likely to constitute a *locus minoris resistentiae,* on which disturbances occurring at a later age can find a foothold. The disease appearing later may belong to a completely different nosological category or it may not; these are questions which await investigation. However, I believe that it is highly probable that early infantile psychogenic disturbance creates a predisposition for the subsequent development of pathology.

At the present state of our knowledge, this is a hypothesis; clinical and experimental studies as well as observations of Anna Freud (1958), of John Bowlby (1953), of Putnam et al. (1948), of Margaret Mahler (1960), of Berta Bornstein (1953) and of many others appear to support it (see also Lebovici and McDougall, 1960). Conclusive proof, confirmation or invalidation of my hypothesis will be forthcoming when the findings of an adequate number of longitudinal studies, beginning with birth, become available.

Meanwhile even such a tentative working hypothesis opens up vistas both in the field of prevention and in the area of the therapy of some of the disturbances in child and adult. I have advanced some ideas on prevention in my paper "Psychiatric Therapy in Infancy" (1950a).

In the area of therapy, attempts have already been made under the name of *anaclitic* therapy (Margolin, 1953, 1954). Since the disturbances, both in child and adult, appear to be linked to psychic scars traceable to early pathogenic object relations, it is logical that appropriate therapeutic procedures must reach back to the preverbal period, which precedes both the oedipal and pregenital phases (Spitz, 1959).

What we have uncovered in the present study suggests that disturbances in the formation of earliest object relations probably result in a serious impairment in the adolescent's and the adult's capacity to establish transference in the therapeutic situation. Margaret Mahler (1952) has traced two forerunners of such deviant development in the toddler, which she calls the autistic and the symbiotic child. The adult counterpart of the autistic child shows lack of contact, withdrawal, and in extreme cases, catatonia. The symbiotic child, on the other hand, finds his counterpart in the adult who shows certain forms of pathological infatuation, extremes of dependency with strong suicidal tendencies.

I believe that the predominance of good object relations during the first year of life is the prerequisite of the capacity to establish transference. That is why the phenomenon of transference was first discovered in the psychoanalytic therapy of *neurotics*. The initial conflict in neurosis takes place years after the object is established, which suggests that the earliest object relations of neurotics were relatively satisfactory.

By contrast, we used to consider some of our patients too narcissistic to be amenable to psychoanalytic treatment. Until recently they were believed to be unable to establish transference. Today we know that this is not so; but the handling of such atypical transferences is exceedingly difficult and involves technical modifications of therapy. These modifications may perhaps be inferred from the process which leads to the capacity for transference, namely, from the history of the development of object relations; specifically, from the individual disturbance of object relations of the given patient. In other words, what has been lacking in the patient's object relations should be provided by the therapist. The diagnosing of such a lack is made easier by the phenomenon of stage specificity: the particular emotional injuries suffered by the patient can be traced with the help of his specific fixation points (Spitz, 1959).

This study raises a number of other questions which I have either barely touched upon or completely ignored. One of these questions is the sociological significance of these findings. In the opening paragraphs of this book I mentioned that object relations are fundamentally social relations. I cannot conclude this book without a brief comment on the earliest object relations from the sociological and historical perspective.

What is the significance of the first object relations for social structure? Freud outlined the answer in his book *Group Psychology and the Analysis of the Ego* (1921). Basing himself on the phenomena of hypnosis and love, Freud formulated the concept of a "mass of two" whose origin he traced to the mother-child relation. He made it evident that the transient relation between hypnotizer and hypnotized is the prototype of the relation of the group to its leader.

All later human relations with object quality, the love relation, the hypnotic relation, the relation of the group to its leader, and ultimately all interpersonal relations have their first origin in the mother-child relation. Our investigation therefore provides a starting point for the understanding of the forces and conditions which make a social being out of man. Affect and affective interchanges are of central significance in this constellation of forces and conditions. The ability of the human being to establish social relations is acquired in the mother-child relation. It is through this relationship that the channeling of the fused drives onto the libidinal object is accomplished and the template for all later human relations laid down.

The investigations of cultural anthropologists, such as Margaret Mead (1928, 1935), Ruth Benedict (1934), Kardiner (1939, 1945), Redfield (1930), Montagu (1950), and many others, demonstrated that a close link exists between the mother-child relations in a given culture on the one hand, and the forms of cultural institutions of that society. However, this close link is not to be interpreted in terms of simple cause and effect in either direction. I pointed out (1935) that the manner of rearing children in a given society does not of itself determine the nature of that society's cultural institutions or the form of the relations between its adult members. Conversely, it is not only the cultural institutions of a given society which determine the form and scope of the mother-child relations prevailing there. Reciprocally influencing each other in a historical progression, the two are inextricably interwoven in an ongoing process. They represent the precipitate of historical, traditional, and environmental forces of the given society.

The nature of cultural institutions sets the limits within which object relations can operate. Kardiner (1945) in his study of the tribe of Alor provides a good example. In Alor society the role of the woman is to work in the field, while the husband goes after his business.

The females work in the field, while the husbands dun for debts. The mother feeds the child in the early morning, does not take the infant with her, but lets it fend for itself or leaves it in the care of some reluctant older sibling, who has no interest in the job and no love for the infant. Toddlers screaming after their mothers, begging to be taken along, are an everyday sight in this community; every Alorese complains that his mother abandoned him in childhood.

... There is no period in the life of a child when it enjoys a tenderness and parental solicitude. As soon as the children grow up a bit, especially the females, they are pressed into the service of helping their mothers. . . .

What do we find in these people? They have no attachment to their parents; . . . they have a low order of conscience, only guilty fear. The relations between the sexes are abominable and all forms of human relatedness are . . . very seriously impaired.

... The Alorese are suspicious, distrustful of themselves and everyone else. They are guarded and defensive, timid, insecure and with a feeling of being constantly threatened. . . .

. . . Their capacity for cooperation is very low . . . they have no idea of what goes on in the other person's mind. Such cooperation as does exist, is on the utilitarian basis and unreliable. In the exchange of favors everyone cheats everyone.

There is no creativity. Their art is crude and careless. They tolerate dilapidation and decay, live only for the moment and have no capacity for planning. Their folklore is pervaded with the constant motive of hatred of parents. . . . They have no concept of virtue and have no concept of reward for good behavior.

Of the three reasons which Kardiner gives for the survival of this society, the following two are relevant to our subject: "this society has never had to face an external danger by conquest or famine . . . their aggression is markedly undeveloped: that is to say that the emotional tone of the aggression is very strong, but their ability to implement it is exceedingly weak."

Mores and traditions of the Alor force the mother to abandon her child, to work in the fields, and the father to be absent. Therefore this society imposes a dearth of object relations on the infant, just as was the case in the infants deprived of affective supplies which I described in Chapter XIV. This dearth of affective relations prevents the individual from initiating or sustaining interpersonal relations, beyond the limits of immediate economic profit, with other adults in his own society. In their turn, the miserable adult relations in this tribe determine the nature of the cultural institutions and attitudes which regulate all and any interpersonal relations, including the mother-child relation. Hence, a vicious circle is established.

This constellation of factors ensures immutable cultural forms over the centuries in the rigidly traditional preliterate society. By contrast, our occidental society undergoes relatively sudden changes of societal conditions as a result of economic, ideological, technologic, and other transformations. Such arbitrarily and often suddenly imposed transformations modify, among others, the framework of mother-child relations. In the course of the last three centuries, we have been subjected to at least two major transformations of this kind:

1. The progressive decay of the patriarchal authority as a consequence of the introduction of Protestantism (Spitz, 1952).

2. The rapid deterioration of the mother-child relation starting about a century ago which set in with the advent of the industrialization of production. The corresponding change in ideology opened the way for drafting the mother into factory work, so that she was removed from her family and her household as effectively as in Alor.

These two, the decay of the patriarchal authority and the mother's absenteeism, have combined and set the stage for a rapid disintegration of the traditional form of the family in our Western society. The consequences are revealed in the increasingly serious problems of juvenile delinquency and in the growing number of neuroses and psychoses in Western adult society. These developments have called forth new solutions; cultural institutions, unknown up to then, emerged. I am referring to foster homes, adoption services, child guidance clinics, social workers, baby sitters, for a time also the ever-increasing number of insane asylums, both for adults and children, and the ubiquitous call for the training of astronomical numbers of psychiatrists to treat the disturbances caused by our civilization itself. These solutions, however, are only palliative measures. It is becoming imperative to go to the source of the evil itself. This evil is the rapid deterioration of those conditions which are indispensable for the normal development of earliest object relations. If we wish to safeguard our existing civilization from this peril, we have to create a preventive social psychiatry. That is a task which goes beyond the competence of the psychiatrist. Like all preventive medicine, it is a task for society. All the psychiatrist can do is to publish his findings and urge society to apply them.

From the societal aspect, disturbed object relations in the first year of life, be they deviant, improper, or insufficient, have consequences which imperil the very foundation of society. Without a template, the victims of disturbed object relations subsequently will themselves lack the capacity to relate. They are not equipped for the more advanced, more complex forms of personal and social interchange without which we as a species would be unable to survive. They cannot adapt to society. They are emotional cripples; more than a century ago jurisprudence coined the now obsolescent term "moral insanity" for these individuals. Their capacity for normal human and social relations is deficient; they were never given the opportunity to experience libidinal relations and to achieve the anaclitic love object. Even their capacity for transference is impaired, so that they are handicapped in profiting from therapy.

Such individuals will be unable to understand, much less discover and join the intricate and many-hued bonds of the relations which they have never had. The relations they are able to form barely reach the level of identification and hardly go beyond, because they have never been able to achieve the earliest, the most elementary one, the anaclitic relation with their mother. The misery of these infants will be translated into the bleakness of the adolescent's social relations. Deprived of the affective nourishment to which they were entitled, their only resource is violence. The only path which remains open to them is the destruction of a social order of which they are the victims. Infants without love, they will end as adults full of hate.

Appendix:
The Geneva School of Genetic Psychology and Psychoanalysis: Parallels and Counterparts

W. Godfrey Cobliner

In our accounts and comments on the infant's behavior we had occasion to refer, more than once, to the work of Jean Piaget and his associates. This was not because of an academic interest or a mere accident. Piaget's *psychologie génétique* is, besides psychoanalysis, the only developmental psychology that has succeeded in constructing a coherent network of propositions which accounts for psychological unfolding and explains behavior.

It is concerned with how behavior as an *entity* evolves and not with that of isolated functions, organs, or abilities. It claims that this unfolding passes through distinct stages leading to ever more complex behavior; thus ontogenesis is both continuous when it passes through a stage and discontinuous when it traverses from one stage to the next higher one. It follows that the effect of past life experience lingers on so that it determines both present and future.

Like psychoanalysis, the Geneva school is among other topics also concerned with the mechanics of adaptation. Both

Instructor in the Department of Psychiatry, Division of Behavioral Science, New Jersey College of Medicine and Dentistry.

301

schools assert that psychological unfolding is predicated upon the balanced interplay between intrinsic (maturational) factors and experiential factors; this interplay provides incentives for adaptive performance. Psychoanalytic theory stresses an additional internal factor to which it ascribes great significance in mental development. It is the intrapsychic conflict that is generated by a clash between various opposing intrinsic forces; it sets in motion the differentiation and structuralization of the psyche.

In his work Piaget has dealt only with a well circumscribed area of development, chiefly with the study of how cognition (perception, memory, problem solving) evolves from motor action. His attention has been centered on what he calls psychological *structures* rather than on psychological functioning. He visualizes psychological structures as the *constituent elements* of mental functions. Conflict of forces is not envisaged so that dynamics are virtually absent from his system. Precisely because of this emphasis, Piaget's work and that of the Geneva school has yielded data which complement findings by psychoanalysts on child development.

Psychoanalysts have been well aware all these years of the importance of the contributions made by the Geneva school; but, having been fully occupied with the study of the dynamics of mental processes in disturbed people and with the laws governing unconscious processes, they could neither fully appreciate the value of Piaget's findings and propositions nor apply them in their own investigations. Added to this is the undeniable fact that the psychoanalytic setting and its principal device of investigation—the relative immobilization of the subject in a reclined position resulting in a relative regression—is hardly conducive to a systematic study of cognition and of its development, or to an exploration of perceptual processes and their vicissitudes. Thus it happened that Piaget's contribution was neglected until a fresh impetus was generated by psychoanalysts engaged in direct infant observation or in child therapy. The neglect is now being remedied as has been done, for instance, in the preceding chapters and in the work of Anthony, Leitch, Escalona, Gouin Décarie, Erikson, Kris, Rapaport, Wolff, and others.

The delay by psychoanalysts and other psychoanalytically oriented scientists in the study of Piaget's work is also due in part to the difficulties inherent in his exposition, which he has fully and frequently acknowledged (see, for example, Piaget, 1945, Preface), and to a rather unique, often intricate terminology; thus, for instance, the individual items of his terminology are loosely defined or their meaning changes in different contexts; in addition, the dividing lines between percept, memory, image, and representation are not always drawn as sharply as one would wish it to be.

Piaget's difficult style reflects perhaps the fact that he is a reluctant psychologist and by temperament more an epistemologist. His interest in child development was aroused after he had accepted a position calling for psychological testing of children (Flavell, 1962). Once in contact with children he turned his attention to the exploration of cognitive development, and ever since his goal has been to lay a foundation for a genetic epistemology based on scientific and on developmental data rather than on philosophy. His orientation is directed toward abstraction, general laws. The findings on children merely supply the means for the attainment of this end.

Freud, by contrast, was more interested in the individual, in the human being, his way of functioning. Freud centered his attention on affective and conative elements and processes. It would appear that Freud's propositions on thought, its origin, role, and impact on the individual and on human relations, although they profoundly influenced Piaget, were, so to say, mere by-products of the mainstream of his thinking. It would be a fascinating, challenging, and most useful study to explore the many analogies and parallels between propositions stated by Piaget and those worked out by Freud's disciples. In the last analysis the two groups of propositions will turn out to be essentially based on Freud's original formulations. There is little doubt that the influence up to now has been in one direction only, from psychoanalysis toward the Geneva school, but this may change in the future. Many factual data assembled by Piaget and his associates support psychoanalytic propositions, which often antedate Piaget's empirical work on the subject as was shown here in previous chapters.

In the light of these considerations it seems useful and timely to include between these covers an exposition, however brief and incomplete, of the principal findings and ideas of Piaget on cognitive development and on the constitution of the permanent object. This will be a very modest contribution to the subject, being limited to the first eighteen months or so of the infant's life.

Most of the other of Piaget's basic contributions on the construction of reality—such as space, time, and causality—will be left out and so will be his important contribution to the knowledge of imitation, which in its conclusions differs radically from psychoanalytic explanations; above all, no exposition will be made of his impressive work on symbolic and language development.

This task could have been accomplished in two other ways: first, by footnotes on the preceding pages accompanying each relevant psychoanalytic account of a given event or behavioral item; second, by referring the reader in each such instance to a specific passage in the scholarly, systematic exposition of Piaget by Anthony, Gouin Décarie, Rapaport, Wolff, and others. Both procedures, it seems, would have placed an undue burden on the patience and efforts of our readers. We have instead chosen to offer a cohesive presentation which, we hope, will accomplish these tasks: point up certain salient convergences between psychoanalytic findings and postulates and those of Piaget concerning the life span covered in the foregoing chapters; show how psychoanalysis and the Geneva school explain phenomena from different perspectives that complement one another; acquaint those among our readers who are still unfamiliar with Piaget's contributions with his central ideas in at least a rudimentary fashion so that they can, encouraged, take up their own study of the material.

Some Basic Assumptions of Piaget and His Concept of the Psyche

Over the years Piaget has claimed that the principal task of the psyche is that of securing the individual's adaptation. Psychological adaptation, he says, differs from organic or biological adaptation by its versatility and efficiency. In organic adaptation the individual is limited to changes within his system to restore equilibrium which has been disturbed in the process of his interaction with the environment. Restoring equilibrium through the mechanism of homeostasis has the compelling feature of immediacy; it takes place in the *hic et nunc*—the here and now. By contrast, psychological adaptation (because it makes use of perception and memory) allows the individual to interpose space and time for the act of equilibration, be it in the form of preventive action, delay, or change of locale. In this way the individual, thanks to psychological operations, is freed from the shackles of the *hic et nunc,* can expand his radius of action, and is no longer at the mercy of somatic processes.

The psychoanalytic model of the psyche deals with similar problems; where in Piaget's concept adaptation is the principal task of the psyche, the psychoanalytic model assigns this task to one of the psyche's agencies, to the ego.

There is, however, evidence that at one time Piaget envisaged a larger model of the psyche in which he attempted to account also for the way the organism harnesses inner forces, the energies of the psyche. In a paper written twenty years ago (Piaget, 1942) which has since been ignored by Piaget, by his associates, and even by his critics, he has outlined the steps by which the psyche achieves successively a growing control over inner forces and places them in the service of rational action; fragments of this model are repeatedly alluded to in many of his subsequent papers, but because of their contextual isolation their meaning escapes the average reader (Piaget, 1947, 1954, 1956).

In the 1942 paper Piaget suggests that three fundamental structures of *mechanisms,*[1] as he calls them in one passage, govern psychic performance and enable the individual to assume an increasing measure of control over his actions: they are *rhythm, regulation,* and *grouping.*

In the first weeks of life the infant's movements seem to be chaotic. On the surface one cannot discern any order, any patterning in the individual movements, but in fact, Piaget asserts, the activity as a whole is not random.

When the infant has extended his arm he has thereby stretched a given set of muscles; he must return the arm, contract the set of muscles, bring both back to their initial position or condition; likewise, after he has put his finger into his mouth, he must eventually take it out again, etc. Now Piaget claims that the infant's motor activity is held in bounds by psychophysiological tendencies which are not in the nature of *montages héréditaires* (inherited functional panels, or layouts). The infant's movements, he claims, are held in check by a *temporal* element. This temporal element is crystallized through the performance of activities in conjunction with needs and reflexes. Through the practice of reflexes (responding to needs and external stimulation) the infant gradually acquires new activities and patterns of activi-

---

[1] The term mechanism in the context of Piaget's system bears little resemblance to the psychoanalytic (defense) mechanisms.

ties. These new activities are distinguished by four features: (a) they are repetitive, be they simple or complex; (b) they have two successive phases, one ascending or positive, the other descending or negative (as, for example, in muscles that are first stretched and then contracted); (c) the interval between the phases is more or less regular when the inner and outer conditions remain the same; (d) the movements proceed in one direction only, they are irreversible. Because these formal features are commonly found in rhythmic patterns Piaget called this mechanism of control "rhythm."

Piaget elaborates on his thesis and explains the operation of the rhythm. The following sequence is said to take place: first, a tendency arises in the baby which makes him carry out a given motion; that motion upsets the existing equilibrium, resulting in a temporary disorganization; now a second tendency of equal strength arises which makes the baby carry out motions diametrically opposite to the original one, that of the first phase. Gradually the baby's body then reverts to the initial state, equilibrium is restored, and the cycle is completed. Because of the time lapse, because of the transient disorganization, the control mechanism represented by "rhythm" is evidently primitive. The baby is fully occupied with "managing" his own body, is incapable of acting upon the environment. One might say the inefficiency of the "rhythm" control is due to its *phasic* or *serial* character, it is synchronized with and centered upon the subject's body.

Piaget does not cite data, observational, experimental, or mensural from his own work or that of others, to support his thesis that rhythm is indeed the principal element of this mechanism in the neonate. Rhythm is widespread in the cosmos, in mechanical motion of the inanimate and the living alike. In fact, there are countless activities of man, for example, those connected with physical effort or those associated with recreation like music and dance, in which rhythm plays a central role (see Spitz, 1937).[2] This being so it seems somewhat risky, without adequate documentation, to attribute to a particular motion sequence in the neonate rhythmic quality; second, to claim at the same time that this very rhythmic quality constitutes a fundamental psychological mechanism governing action and serving the maintenance of equilibrium. However, the foregoing does not dispute the validity of Piaget's general thesis on the existence of psychological controls in the neonate.

According to Piaget, two opposing tendencies act successively in the stage governed by rhythm, and through this very serial arrangement the baby manages to attain a primitive sort of equilibrium.

As the baby grows, so do his resources. His activities widen and proliferate. The two opposing tendencies now appear simultaneously; they are pitted against one another and thereby create in the given areas of the psyche a static equilibrium. This equilibrium contrasts with the labile, amorphous one attained by rhythm. The previous lability, though, should not be mistaken for a flexible mobility. Examples of the static, rigid equilibrium are found in primitive perception (not subject to correction by intellectual faculties) and are operative in the Mueller-Lyer Illusion, in the Phenomenon of Delboeuf, and in others described by the Gestaltists. Piaget comments that in these phenomena a given tendency produces a sensory deformation of the image which would continue unchecked unless it is halted by the appearance of an inverse countertendency. Tendency and countertendency

[2] Rhythmic patterns are observable very early in the baby. An example was cited above in a previous chapter. In the nursing situation—that is, the dyadic constellation—the baby while nursing contracts and moves his hands rhythmically on his mother's body. The cycle of these motions may be the same as that governing his swallowing or that of other phenomena in progress inside his organism, or again may be the same as that of motions originating in the mother. Further detailed observation is needed to establish the nature and dependence of this phenomenon (see Chapter III).

meeting together now produce a rigid, static equilibrium exemplified in the deformed image characteristic of the phenomena. The rigidity of the equilibrium is revealed when it becomes upset: the image simply "breaks," it cannot be reconstituted; the balance of the constellation shifts and a new equilibrium is established elsewhere in a novel constellation. This type of achieving equilibrium Piaget calls "regulation." To repeat, the two opposing tendencies present in the phase of rhythm have become *synchronous* in the phase of regulation; by virtue of this fact the tendencies are transformed into *structural components* within the edifice of a static equilibrium.

Piaget has not demonstrated the ubiquity of regulation as a psychic mechanism except for a few examples cited above. Yet he claims that regulation as a mechanism is fundamental, just as rhythm is in a previous stage.

As maturation and development proceed further, a host of organic and psychic tendencies emerge, ever more complex in nature, interdependent in operation. The child no longer deals with a few tendencies and countertendencies but with whole clusters of them. They are fitted into series, into networks and systems, and the resulting organization is subject to the laws of composition. The psychic control over this constellation of forces Piaget calls "grouping," a term borrowed from mathematics. Thanks to grouping, the child can marshal his inner tendencies in the service of (volitional) action. His action and mental operations become *reversible*. Because of this *reversibility—the capacity to invert an operation in the mind* (or in action), *the ability to examine a task from two opposite viewpoints*—the equilibrium which the child achieves is flexible and highly mobile. Again, to emphasize the point, this sophisticated equilibrium is quite unlike the flowing amorphous one of the rhythmic stage; the child can now distribute his forces, he can direct them, regulate their strength for a given purpose. Hence he is able to time his action, he can coordinate means with ends. In short, his action becomes *rational* instead of *impulsive*. It is obvious that grouping governs a good deal of action in the grownup and is indeed fairly ubiquitous in human endeavor. Piaget does not suggest that grouping is acquired volitionally, it just comes about as if prefigured in the organism.

As pointed out earlier, Piaget is chiefly concerned with the cognitive area of the psyche and its developmental sequences, yet he emphasizes that the three fundamental structures of the psyche whose existence he successively traces in motor action, perception, and rational action, are also operating in the realm of affective unfolding (1942, 1947, 1954, 1956).

Thus he states that in the adualistic or psychophysiological phase, affects and somatic excitation are closely interwoven and both are held in equilibrium by rhythm.

Later on, when emotions emerge and integrate, they become the regulators of affective life. Following Janet, Piaget states that emotions direct individual action by acceleration, deceleration, or by the process of energizing.

The simultaneous appearance of two antagonistic emotions produces a static equilibrium in the affective economy, just as two opposing sensory tendencies achieved it in the cognitive area. Hence regulation is achieved by pitting two opposite emotions against each other. The highest form of control, corresponding to grouping, in the cognitive area, is the harnessing of psychic energies through the influence of *values and sentiments*. Action is fully reversible only when values are crystallized and become operative (Piaget, 1947).

Piaget's concept of the psyche, outlined in the successive installation of these three structures or mechanisms, exhibits unmistakable parallels with certain aspects of the psychoanalytic model which deserve further discussion.

First is the general idea of psychic energy. As pointed out earlier, Piaget has been essentially concerned with structures, conceived as components of psychic functioning (1956), and he holds that energy flow is controlled by the psyche itself rather than by physical agents inside or outside the individual's organism.

Second, Piaget's idea of the regulation of psychic energies is paralleled by Freud's propositions relating to the pain-pleasure principle and the reality principle. These principles are concepts that account for harnessing of psychic energies and for the course of human action in general. When the pain-pleasure principle governs psychic life, immediate discharge of instinctual drives and their derivatives (manifested as impulsive action) influences individual behavior; when the reality principle exercises its control the discharge of drive and drive derivatives can be delayed and detoured and thus put into the service of rational action. This rational action marks the individual's commerce with the environment.

Third, the checking of impulses through values is a phenomenon which, in the psychoanalytic model, is said to derive from the superego.

The salient difference between Piaget's *structures* and Freud's *principles* is their respective closeness to the animate. Piaget's structures in spite of their progressive flexibility remain physicalistic, mechanistic. While they make full provision for shifts in equilibrium, they disregard the transformation of energy. Freud's principles fit far better into a biological universe; they are conceived to account for the individual's progressive adaptation to life indicated by his elasticity and flexibility in his give and take with the environment; they also fully consider the play of forces that secure an optimum of continuity in the *milieu interne*.

Although Piaget's formulations on the central role of rhythm in life are open to challenge, the phenomenon of rhythm deserves more attention by psychologists and psychoanalysts than it has received until now. It is well known that rhythm enhances efficiency of performance and, subjectively, imparts pleasure to the very expenditure of effort. While this seemingly self-evident fact is quite accessible to exploration, rhythm is nowhere systematically explored in the psychoanalytic literature as a fundamental mechanism.[3] The dictionary definition of rhythm mentions "movement marked by regular recurrence of, or regular alternation in elements, etc., hence periodicity." There is a scarcely noted remark by Freud in *Beyond the Pleasure Principle* (1920) and again in his paper "The Economic Problem of Masochism" (1924c) to the effect that the pleasure one experiences from tension mounting and tension decrease may be due to the rate of change occurring *within a given time unit.* While Freud did not use the term "rhythm," the reference to the temporal element unmistakably points to rhythmic phenomena. Since periodic increase and decrease of tension marks all discharge phenomena, Erikson's (1950a) propositions on zonal modes and their alternation take on added meaning in this context. It follows that Freud's, Piaget's, and Erikson's isolated statements on the subject of temporal elements, whether they do or do not refer to rhythm, invite the immediate study of new areas of psychic activity. Promising, for example, is the systematic tracing, recording, and measuring of modes of discharge in different processes, zonal or purely psychological ones, such as emotions; beyond that is an inquiry of how temporal elements influence various cognitive and conative processes at different developmental stages; an exploration of whether these temporal elements are subject to changes; lastly whether and how temporal elements govern the operation of drive-restraining functions such as defenses, etc.[4]

The foregoing considerations suggest that one encounters two principal elements in the phenomenon of rhythm. One is that of order, harmony, organization, structuring, all of

[3] However, see Spitz (1937) and more recently Jacobson (1953) and the discussion remarks of Greenacre (1954) and A. Freud (1954b).

[4] Aspects of these phenomena are now being explored under the direction of J. Kestenberg (personal communication).

which are endowed with rational qualities. The other is clearly of more subjective make-up. It is exciting, pleasure-imparting, irrational, and somewhat demonical in quality. Both elements, it would seem, are contained to some extent in musical works and perhaps also in artistic creations appealing to other than auditory modalities. The musically receptive reader will have no difficulty in recognizing that a given piece of music leans toward one or the other rhythmic element under consideration. Indeed, it is hard to dismiss the impression that entire schools of music or even musical works of specific ethnic groups incline toward an emphasis of one or the other rhythmic element. Finally, this conjectured one-sided stress may be a characteristic feature of a given composer suggesting a high specialization (or again a limited versatility), provided his creative activity was not suddenly cut short.

Returning to the second basic mechanism, regulation of psychic energies, the salient difference between the notions advanced by psychoanalysis in the concept of the reality principle and those stressed by Piaget, lies in the discontinuity of Piaget's mechanisms. Piaget assumes that with the advent of regulation, rhythm disappears as a mechanism channeling psychic energies; in turn, regulation vanishes when grouping (control of affective life, exemplified in the hegemony of values and sentiments) is established.

Psychoanalytic theory, on the other hand, insists that the pleasure principle, though dislodged from its supremacy by the reality principle, remains operative *throughout* life, and governs side by side with the reality principle. Indeed, because of this very assumption, psychoanalysis can and does account for many aspects of human behavior such as the absence of reason in matters pertaining to drive gratification, to ideals, to beliefs and even to that of political action. The same cannot be said of Piaget's model.

There is no need to pursue the parallel between Piaget's

general model of the psyche and that of psychoanalysis any
further. This is so because Piaget's account of the affective
development and its vicissitudes remains sketchy and somewhat dated. It suffers from a certain dearth of research data
(of which Piaget elsewhere abounds) supporting his conclusions; essentially the bulk of the documentation is derived
from the contributions made early in the century by such
illustrious psychologists as Claparède and Janet as well as
others relatively unknown to contemporary students (Piaget,
1954).

The Concept of Stages in Ontogenesis

Piaget's long-term study of children made him conclude
that psychic unfolding is neither an even, continuous process,
a strictly discontinuous process marked by sudden achievements, nor one that is chaotic. He noted that in the child
there is a strict order in the acquisitions of new abilities,
invariable in *all* children, no matter what their background,
their previous experience, their motivation, and their endowment. Thus he arrived at the concept of stages of psychic
development, a term which denotes these uniformities (Piaget,
1955, 1956):

A. A stage is marked by dominant characteristics which
are interdependent and form a *totality*, a structural whole.

B. Stages are set off by breaks in the unfolding of the
psyche. There is a *sudden* acquisition at its beginning; this
gain is consolidated, integrated with previous acquisitions.
Later on a new acquisition is being prepared. Accordingly,
the passage from an inferior to a superior stage is an integration—hence the notion that psychic growth is both continuous and discontinuous.

C. The date of an acquisition of psychic faculties, skills,
or mechanisms characteristic for the particular stage varies
considerably from population to population and, within that

population, from individual to individual; such variation is determined both by a set of external and intrinsic factors and by previous individual life experience. These circumstances can advance, retard, or impede the acquisitions.

D. However, the serial order of the acquisitions remains *constant;* it is the same for all populations, it is universal.

Piaget stresses that the elements of a given stage are *invariably integrated into the next higher one;* this is indeed the hub of his concept of stages. This very proposition gives his psychological system the genetic quality that one misses in most other conceptual accounts of psychic development.

Piaget holds that progress in stages governs all areas of psychic unfolding, of becoming, though he has worked out details for only one area, that of intelligence. He stresses that specific details valid for intelligence do not apply, for example, to the area of perception (1956). In the area of intelligence Piaget distinguishes three main *periods:*

1. Sensorimotor intelligence (0-24 months).
2. Period of conceptual intelligence: concrete operations (2-10/11 years).
3. Period of conceptual intelligence: formal operations (11/12-13/14 years).

These periods are then divided into subperiods and finally into stages.

Piaget's concept of stages, his sharp division of psychic unfolding into distinct episodes, finds no corresponding parallel in classical psychoanalytic theory. While the concept of libidinal phases accounts for psychosexual development, these phases are not true steps like those envisaged in Piaget's system. Thus, oral elements may be conspicuous in the child's anal phase; anal and genital tendencies may overlap in the normal adult. Erikson's (1950a) stages, too, lack a sharp demarcation.

The undeniable fact of sudden mental achievements in

childhood years has recently been worked out on a conceptual level in an expansion of classical psychoanalytic theory. It has been suggested that the nature of unfolding, of maturation of developments, proceeds in such a fashion that different lines of development[5] converge at certain periods to form nodal points or *organizers of the psyche* (Spitz, 1954, 1957, 1959; and earlier chapters in this study). The corollary of this set of propositions, namely, the thesis of dependent development, truly parallels Piaget's notion of stages both as regards formal aspects (break in an otherwise continuous process) as well as in its substantive aspects (cognitive and affective areas). It is remarkable that in a way Spitz's set of propositions accounts for a wider spectrum of phenomena than Piaget's.

Spitz's propositions cover sequential cumulative effects of given achievements; they consider dyssynchronization of achievements in the diverse lines of development resulting in *developmental imbalance*. Finally, Spitz makes conceptual provisions for arrest, retardation, and faulty unfolding; these three are virtually absent in Piaget's conceptual scheme.

Piaget assumes that the progress from stage to stage and within stages is determined, in addition to the three classical factors—heredity (maturation), physical (external or internal) environment, social influence—by a fourth element, namely, equilibration. The latter is said to be a tendency inherent in the organism striving to establish an ever more mobile and stable[6] equilibrium of forces within the organism and the psyche. The concept of equilibrium is fashioned after the tenets of the second law of thermodynamics (though with an inverse direction of vectors, namely, increase in dif-

---

[5] This term, introduced by Anna Freud (1963b) designates a serial progress in distinct psychic sectors and stresses their continuity and cumulative character.

[6] Stability and mobility of equilibrium are compatible with each other; in fact, the greater the mobility the steadier is the equilibrium. The opposite of stable, to be sure, is unstable, labile, not mobile.

ferentiation) and is also akin to Cannon's concept of *homeo-stasis* and Bertalanffy's *steady state*.

Piaget believes that the trend toward greater complexity, toward differentiation and integration, exemplified in stages is immutable, teleologic, a finalistic phenomenon. The trend is best rendered by the term "active and dynamic equilibrium characteristic of life" (1956).

Psychoanalysis contains the seeds of a notion similar to equilibration as far as the human species is concerned. It is to be found in the long-term aims of instinctual drives. Freud and classical psychoanalytic theory holds that Eros, the sexual instinctual drive, quite apart from its specific function in mating and reproduction, is behind that tendency in human life which builds, integrates, organizes, binds, and synthes-izes. It is evident in object (social) relations, in thought proc-esses, in creative endeavors, even in communal life. However, there is no psychoanalytic proposition accounting for the for-ward tendency of ontogenic processes in the individual; the periodic rise of tension in the organism gives rise to a need for its discharge through various outlets, and such discharge insures stability and equilibrium. But psychoanalytic theory does not, explicitly, show how this cycle influences develop-ment. It is conceived as a self-limiting episode.

Piaget's notion of equilibration, of the trend toward ever more stable equilibrium, is closely linked to his notion of reversibility, which has a key role in his accounts of develop-ment. The concept of reversibility is anchored in Piaget's approach to psychic phenomena, which he prefers to express in mathematical terms. Equilibrium is exemplified in the equation of Le Châtelier where it accounts for the course of events in a chemical mixture in the stage of transition. In Le Châtelier's equation the equilibrium is linked to its re-versibility, like the behavior of the arms of a scale. Piaget believes that in similar fashion reversibility governs all higher mental and intellectual processes. He cites various forms of reversibility—the ability to invert mental operation—and each of them marks the inception of a given developmental stage.[7]

Piaget suggests that equilibration processes govern all spheres of the personality both cognitive and affective; and the three fundamental structures of the psyche—rhythm, regulation, grouping—all serve the equilibration tendencies. Ultimately, of course, equilibration is an aspect of adaptation, but one that is, so to speak, anchored in Anlage.

PIAGET'S METHOD

Piaget's Method of gathering facts is a unique blending of the experimental and the clinical approach. At first he relied exclusively on verbal methods, but following incisive and constructive criticism from various quarters and notably that coming from American colleagues (Anthony, 1957) he switched to experimentation and made his subjects manipulate various materials. As far as the preverbal stage is concerned, one can recognize these principal features (Inhelder, 1962):

A. The child is given material to which he responds or which he manipulates.

B. One then observes how he behaves vis-à-vis obstacles and conflicts (decisions relating to choice) deriving from this activity and the nature of the material.

C. The experimenter establishes the child's performance not merely by noting a given result as is customary in the (standardized) experimental method, but by introducing variations and an essentially exploratory approach, so that the consistency and the range of the child's production are apprehended.

[7] Psychoanalytic readers will not be surprised by Piaget's analogic thinking, and be reminded that a large segment of the psychoanalytic model of the psyche, especially that accounting for dynamic processes, is based on analogy, on concepts borrowed from hydraulics.

Where possible and practical, one follows up with probing, which adds the clinical dimension. Claparède described the method in his introduction to one of Piaget's earlier works (1923) as follows:

> The clinical method, . . . the art of questioning, does not confine itself to superficial observations, but aims at capturing what is hidden behind the immediate appearance of things. It analyses down to its ultimate constituents the least little remark made by the young subjects. It does not give up the struggle when the child gives incomprehensible or contradictory answers, but only follows closer in chase of the ever-receding thought, drives it from cover, pursues and tracks it down till it can seize it, dissect it and lay bare the secret of its composition.

The analysis of the material so gathered consists in a classification of the different types of cognitive activity (reasoning); in an analysis in terms of logical models; an analysis of the frequency of response and dispersion by ages; that is to say, a given child is offered the same material more than once at different ages, so that the time of initial successful performance is noted (after previous total or partial failures), as well as the successive refinements by the child as he develops and matures. Finally, the data are interpreted by means of ordinal scales.

It is this general method that led Piaget to the amassing of a formidable amount of developmental facts. It also allowed him to order the data in a most admirable way which he capped by the construction of a scientific system of interlocking and interdependent propositions. The system is capable of accounting for a wide spectrum of sensory and thought patterns and their development, a system never equaled by any other school of psychology except psychoanalysis. The explanatory and heuristic value of many of Piaget's propositions has yet to be recognized; they suggest experiments that promise to open up unchartered areas of mental life.

Developmental Mechanisms in Piaget's System

The propelling forces advancing psychic unfolding and integration stem from a variety of elements inside and outside the organism. Among the innate forces the most outstanding is the ubiquitous tendency toward equilibrium.

These propelling forces are progressively channeled into certain directions and exert their impact through the twin mechanisms—or processes—of *assimilation* and *accommodation*. According to Piaget, these two mechanisms are actually the prime devices of the adaptive tendency. A third mechanism serving to integrate developmental energies in the Piaget system is the *schema*.

A schema in Piaget's concept is a mental structure (i.e., an action or thought pattern laid down as a mnemonic trace) which the individual acquires through the practice of movements triggered by reflex mechanisms; subsequently these patterns are applied in situations similar to that in which they were first acquired. The schema is a psychic element of the generic class of representations that arises from interoceptive or proprioceptive stimuli of a global, concrete nature and emerges before the mental image, the idea, and the abstract representation.[8]

For example, the newborn, at birth, is equipped with the rooting and sucking reflexes which are primed and when properly triggered are set in operation. After the child has practiced rooting and sucking, both are laid down as action

---

[8] It is noteworthy that the schema, being the precipitate of the subject's motor action, lends itself very *easily to the re-enactment of that which it represents*. This feature distinguishes it sharply from other representations which because of their external source can merely re-enact in conscious life the sensation accompanying the experience not the stimuli themselves. Genetically the schema should therefore rather be referred to as a borderline element between the motoric and the psychic, in analogy to the concept of the instinctual drive which is a borderline concept between the somatic and psychic.

patterns in the form of mnemic traces. This mnemic trace constitutes a motor *schema*. Subsequently when the child's sucking lips encounter his finger and he begins to suck it, this constitutes a generalization. An assimilation has taken place, an existing schema has been used to cope with a modified stimulus. The sucking pattern at birth was a *reflex schema*. But as soon as the finger is sucked volitionally, the schema has acquired *psychic content;* it has become a schema *proper*. The child has effected an incorporation; the schema has been generalized, while its make-up is unchanged.

Accommodation is a mental activity which serves to change an initial *schema* so that it becomes adapted to a new situation. This happens in two circumstances: (a) the initial schema no longer serves its purpose because of some progress in the child's maturation (expansion of the scope of his activity); the child has outgrown its usefulness just as clothing of a given size no longer fits after a while; (b) the external situation is so novel that the initial schema cannot deal with it.

Assimilation is a mental activity of the child whereby an external situation is so *perceived or handled* that it can be dealt with by an existing schema. For example, when the child has learned to move a rattle suspended on a hook, and then applies his motor action to a suspended doll, this *generalization* is an act of assimilation.

Although Piaget is well aware of the fluid character of the developmental process, the propelling forces press in one direction only—forward. The possibility of an arrest of the movement, its retardation, its regression, its derailment never enters the picture. This contingency is tacitly assumed to be a problem of differential psychology.

However, Piaget's system, unlike most other psychological schools, makes full provision for the historical continuity of the psyche. He emphasizes that thought and intellectual un-

folding evolve not only in content but also in make-up, and
it is the schema which serves as the key link in this expansion.
The schema has a role analogous to standing type in the
printing of recurrent items in a periodical. It insures the
continuity of the individual's psychic make-up so that past
experience governs behavior and adaptation. "The development of thinking," Piaget (1919) states, "manifests certain
distinct systems or 'schemas,' whose genesis and history can
be traced and which correspond to the psychoanalytic 'complexes.' "

Accommodation and assimilation are, in effect, psychic
mechanisms which are instrumental in the modification and
growth of the psyche; they are vehicles of learning and serve
the individual in his mastery of the surround; they are instrumental in mobilizing resources such as action or thought
patterns (schemas) acquired earlier; finally, they fashion new
patterns where and when needed.

Thus Piaget, admittedly, was influenced by the psychoanalytic "complexes" in forming the concept of schema, and
also by the concept of instinctual drive (see footnote 8 above).
There is no exact counterpart in the psychoanalytic model
for the mechanisms of assimilation and accommodation since
problems of adaptation remained on the periphery of psychoanalytic theorizing until a decade or so after the emergence
of ego psychology (Hartmann, 1939). However, the concept
of *autoplastic* and *alloplastic* changes coined by Freud (1924a)
and Ferenczi (1919) are closest to assimilation and accommodation, and these terms suggest that even much earlier
psychoanalysts had been aware of the importance of the
problem.

The profound influence exerted by psychoanalysis on
Piaget's system is prominent in his ideas on thought and its
evolvement and by extension on that of the object. It is best
to trace this influence in a presentation along historical lines.

PIAGET'S CONTACT WITH PSYCHOANALYSIS

Early in his career Piaget came under the influence of psychoanalysis through comprehensive reading of the literature and personal exchanges with analysts, and this influence is evident in his early publications (1919, 1923, 1933). In 1922, for instance, at the International Psychoanalytical Congress in Berlin, he presented a paper entitled, "Symbolic Thought and the Thought of the Child," in which, as he put it, "Freud had been interested." Therein Piaget suggested that children's thought appears "to be the intermediate between symbolic thought and rational thought" (1945, p. 170).

This topic was to become the seed for many of his later ideas and empirical work. It is ubiquitous in his notions concerning the child's construction of reality, space and time, the object, and the development of language which, in that context, is the child's communication with the outer world and the objects. So powerful and lasting was the impact of psychoanalysis that it prompted him to write, one year after the Congress, in the Foreword to his first book (1923):

"It will . . . be apparent how much I owe to psycho-analysis, which in my opinion has revolutionized the psychology of primitive thought" (p. 21). In this text, he states: "Janet, Freud, Ferenczi, Jones, Spielrein, etc., have brought forward various theories on the language of savages, imbeciles, and young children, all of which are of the utmost significance for an investigation such as we propose to make of the child mind from the age of six" (p. 26f.).

The propositions formulated on the basis of this experimental work bear the hallmark of psychoanalytic influence, referring as they do to qualities of the primary and secondary processes. "Psycho-analysts have been led to distinguish two fundamentally different modes of thinking: *directed* or *intelligent thought,* and *undirected* or, as Bleuler proposes to call it, *autistic* thought. . . . Now these two forms of thought

... differ chiefly as to their origin, the one being ... guided by the increasing adaptation of individuals one to another, whereas the other remains individual and uncommunicated" (Piaget, 1923, p. 63f.).

Continuing, he takes up a related topic, that on the link between thoughts, images, and words in the realm of representation: "Intelligence, just because it undergoes a gradual process of socialization, is enabled through the bond established by language between thoughts and words to make an increasing use of concepts; whereas autism, just because it remains individual, is still tied to imagery, to organic activity, and even to organic movements. The mere fact, then, of telling one's thought, of telling it to others, or of keeping silence and telling it only to oneself must be of enormous importance ..." (p. 64).

It is not immediately apparent whether this grouping of ideas, reminiscent of similar notions advanced by Freud earlier and also in his then latest book (1923), was solely the fruit of Piaget's current work with his group of children or whether it was equally inspired by his past contact with psychoanalysis. The question in no way diminishes the originality and creativity of Piaget's contributions. It merely suggests the likelihood of psychoanalytic influence and, quite apart from it, points up the fact that Piaget with his entirely different orientation, with a different approach, with different subjects, with different procedures arrived at propositions closely parallel to those advanced by psychoanalysis.

This convergence of findings and propositions, their mutual confirmation, greatly enhances their scientific value; because they are obtained by way of different approaches and from different perspectives they gain increased objectivity.

Piaget's notions on the period of childhood preceding the consolidation of the permanent object are contained in the following passage:

"Mme. Spielrein . . . has tried to prove that the baby syllables, *mama,* uttered in so many tongues to call the mother, are formed by the labial sounds which indicate nothing more than a prolongation of the act of sucking. 'Mama' would therefore be a cry of desire, and then a command given to the only being capable of satisfying this desire. But on the other hand, the mere cry 'mama' has in it a soothing element; in so far as it is a continuation of the act of sucking, it produces a kind of hallucinatory satisfaction. Command and immediate satisfaction are in this case therefore almost indistinguishable" (1923, p. 27).

The reader will recognize that, while paraphrasing Spielrein, Piaget makes use of Freud's hypotheses that the infant hallucinates the gratification when he is unable to get it in reality. This proposition and others closely linked to it (omnipotence, etc.) undoubtedly influenced Piaget in his formulation of his concept of the child's egocentricity.

Piaget acknowledges in these passages his debt to psychoanalysis. Because he gradually moves away from psychoanalysis after 1933 he is no longer informed of its further progress. Whenever from then on he criticizes psychoanalysis he refers to the trends and the emphasis prevailing in the early 1930s. Thus, for example, he argues some twenty years later, in his lectures at the Sorbonne (1954, p. 65), that psychoanalysis overlooks the scope of the child's achievement in overcoming his narcissism. There is more to it, he says, than a simple shift in the distribution of cathexis as suggested by Freud. He is unaware of psychoanalytic findings in the realm of ego psychology which invalidate his criticism!

It is indeed a great loss to the progress of psychology that the contact between psychoanalysis and the Geneva school was severed some thirty years ago. The loss can be remedied now by an intensive study of Piaget's contributions; this is the more imperative in view of the fact that some of Piaget's findings actually corroborate propositions of ego psychology and complement them in many instances.

THE THREE CONCEPTS OF OBJECT IN CONTEMPORARY PSYCHOLOGY

The comment on the passing of narcissism provides the natural bridge to the discussion of the final topic in this chapter, that of the object and object formation in Piaget's system and in psychoanalytic theory.

Three object concepts figure in contemporary psychological literature. The object of academic psychology, the permanent object of Piaget, and the libidinal object of psychoanalysis. Some of the differences between the last and the first concept were briefly outlined in an earlier chapter (see Chapter III); a more comprehensive description of all three follows now.

The object of academic psychology as it appears in the countless laboratory projects of experimental psychology is delimited by the coordinates of space and time. Existential in nature, it can be recorded by the simplest devices and undeniably is devoid of any psychological content. It is an ahistoric "fixture" more fitting into a physicalistic model than into human behavior.

Piaget's permanent object goes a step further. It has a history, a sensorimotor history. Piaget posits that it is built up gradually in the individual's mind; it is the product of cumulative sensorimotor experiences rather than the result of the mere maturation of the baby's somatic or psychic functions. In the setting of normal somatic functioning and of a relatively stable environment (both tacitly implied by Piaget) object attainment is inextricably tied to experience, specifically to motor action which makes for the accretion of ontogenetic elements in the psyche in the form of memory. This acquisition and accumulation of experiential elements is conceived by Piaget as a build-up of schemata. A plurality of schemata arise simultaneously and are instrumental in orienting the child in the four basic categories of reality—space, time, object, and causality. The formation and consolidation of the object category are closely interlocked with the crystallization of the other fundamental "categories." Once established, though, the permanent object is no longer tied to its history; it does not bear the traces of *previous* interaction of the individual with his environment, with that particular object or objects in general. The schema and the dimension of causality are inseparable from the permanent object and they distinguish it from the object of academic psychology. Piaget mentions occasionally that the permanent object, naturally, has an affective component and in some instances uses this fact to explain behavior; however, so far he has not made any conceptual provision in his system to spell out the implications.

The libidinal object contains elements of both the academic object and the permanent object of Piaget. In fact, it will be shown later that its consolidation is predicated upon the baby's prior attainment of certain aspects of Piaget's permanent object. This being so, a wide gulf nevertheless separates the notion of the libidinal object from that of the other aforesaid object concepts.

The libidinal object, unlike the "academic" and Piaget's permanent object, derives from the infant's percepts that originate in his recurrent interaction with the human partner, that is, with his mother or her substitute. The libidinal object is therefore from the start endowed with dynamic features. This is so because the foremost, significant quality of the human partner is his ability to respond appropriately and timely, his ability to *attune* to the infant's vital needs. Progressively the mother synchronizes her ministrations with the infant's needs, a "dialogue" (Spitz, 1963a, b, c, 1964) is established between the infant and his object-to-be (mother). A flux of concerted interactions results that soon will take place in recurrent temporal intervals progressively anticipated by the infant. These exchanges activate step by step emerging functions and capacities in the infant. Concurrently, the frequent and recurrent interaction serves to build up in the infant's nascent mind images that are precipitates of interactive, interoceptive and proprioceptive stimuli. For example, stimuli that reach its rudimentary awareness in activities of grasping, in skin and lip contacts, in activities of sucking and swallowing, in experiences that increase tension or those that relieve it.

Later fragmentary images of the human partner emerge, are built up, and crystallize in the infant's mind. They reach his memory through kinesthetic, dermal, auditory, and other pathways, but gradually the visual impressions prevail. These fragmentary images owe their very existence to the close contact between the infant and the object-to-be. In this close contact, by the nature of the situation, the human partner expresses his affects which in turn "induces" similar affective states in the infant. They are associated with the experience of powerful somatic changes that cannot fail to leave impressions in the infant's memory having traveled there along proprioceptive and interoceptive pathways.

It follows that the initial image of the human partner of the object-to-be is shaky unless it is fortified by concomitant internal images of experienced affects. Out of this multitude of interoceptive, proprioceptive, and exteroceptive stimuli a global image of the human partner, of the libidinal object-to-be, emerges which is progressively differentiated and crystallized. It is suggested that the first image of the object derives from exteroceptively mediated sensory impressions *whose permanence and intensity are due to a set of contemporary and complemental mnemic traces of interoceptive and proprioceptive origin.*

The matrix of the libidinal object is thus shaped by remembered fragments of interaction with the human partner in his first period of life—the mother or her substitue. It is an image built up in experiences in which sensory input, motor, and later symbolic elements jointly leave compound memory traces.

Whereas the "academic" object and the permanent object are primarily of cognitive nature, the libidinal object owes its distinction to its affective nature. It is firmly linked to the individual's image of his affective experiences that were generated in his encounters with the first human being ministering to him, assuaging his bodily, emotional, and other needs.

Because of all these considerations, the libidinal object, unlike the "academic" and the permanent objects defies one of the laws of classical logic: it does not remain identical with itself. In line with the changing emotional needs of the individual, in line with the incessant growth and alteration of his images of affective experiences, the libidinal object changes in the life course of the individual.

In a simplified manner one could say that the libidinal object is a representation that arises from, and throughout life remains closely linked to, individual needs, instinctual drives, and their derivatives. The conditions governing the gratification (or frustration) of these needs, etc., undergo changes as life proceeds and these changes accordingly transform the nature of the libidinal object. This setting occasions its marked subjective quality as well as the fact that it does not remain identical with itself over time. The libidinal object can therefore be defined solely in reference to the subject; it is designated by the subject's drive constellation directed toward it, by his cathectic investment in it. This constellation is quite complex and fluctuating; so much so that it defies adequate programming on current computer devices.

The comparison of the three "objects" is not an invidious one. It cannot be repeated too often that the emergence of the libidinal object is inconceivable without the concomitant attainment of certain aspects of the permanent object. It is therefore naïve to claim that the concept of the libidinal object transcends or is "superior" to the permanent object as a conceptual tool accounting and explaining human behavior. The two objects complement each other. Psychoanalysis has, until recently, neglected to concern itself with cognitive dimensions, and its current concept of the libidinal object is something of a dead weight in rigorous theorizing. To do justice to its scientific heritage psychoanalytic theory must fill this gap in its conceptual framework.

It seems fitting therefore to give now a brief account of the successive steps that lead to Piaget's permanent object on the one hand, to the attainment of the libidinal object on the other. Since knowledge is still incomplete regarding the precise time in the infant's life at which he reaches the individual landmarks in this development, chronological references will be few and confined to major events.

THE DISCOVERY OF THE NON-I

By innumerable experiments, by his many observations of children, Piaget has contributed substantially to the store of facts and data on how the infant builds up, step by step, his notions of the outside world. But before the infant can do that, he must become aware of his own responses, according to Piaget. His ideas are based on a reconstructive assumption and on intuition.[9]

In the beginning, he says, the infant does not "see," "hear," "feel," etc., anything external to himself. His outside world is made up of a series of moving "sensory displays,"[10] centered around his own activity. They lack stability, they come and go, form and dissolve; they lack permanence, they have no objective space, and there is, naturally, no causality (Piaget,

[9] Piaget follows here the tradition established by Freud and Ferenczi. These propositions by Piaget received a measure of empirical support only when Spitz (1957) interpreted the material gathered by von Senden (1932).

[10] The term "sensory displays" is used here to render Piaget's expression *tableaux sensoriels*. In the literature this expression is mostly translated as "sensory pictures" which is a misnomer and misleading.

1954). The picture comes pretty close to some facets of the psychoanalytic concept of undifferentiation or nondifferentiation.

The child lives in the sensorimotor stage: he senses and apprehends the world by means of his own motor activity and as it expands and becomes organized so does his impression of the world around him. Right after birth the infant moves, stretches, displaces his limbs, and then returns to the initial position; he stretches and contracts his muscles, he exercises his reflexes. Primitive perception is derived from this kind of motor action, Piaget asserts. Gradually, with increasing experience, the movements are synchronized; different movements are fitted into a series to reach a given objective. Seriated movements are coordinated into a system which serves to explore new territory.

The infant begins to reach for the sensory displays with his fingers, his hands, touches them. Now he becomes aware that the sensory displays emanating from the "something out there" coincide with impressions conveyed by his own muscle (or motor) action on the "something." The two fuse more and more frequently; they leave a mnemic impression of some sort. These impressions combine with others derived from different sensory modalities. The process culminates in the formation of the permanent object.

Piaget's observation indicates that before the child's recognition of "things," long before he has a notion of the permanent object, he responds to stimuli, and he obviously "remembers" them. And yet he does so in the absence of any recognition. Piaget explains: the neonate and infant can "relate" to an external "object" without recognition and what he remembers are not exteroceptive stimuli or a set of exteroceptive stimuli but rather a cluster of proprioceptive and interoceptive stimuli. In this context Piaget asserts that the infant learns to "relate" to his own finger; this happens after he accidentally had placed the finger into his mouth when

332   *Appendix*

hungry and, in a reflexive manner, begins sucking. To be sure, the infant does not yet recognize the finger as part of his own body. He only senses it as something that can be moved. Likewise, when the infant turns his head into the nursing position (in the first few weeks of life), this again is not a recognition of a perceptual display but a mere "relating" to the mother.[11] His explanation of these phenomena is of the greatest importance:

> Let us examine . . . the way in which the child rediscovers the nipple. Ever since the third day (Obs. 3), Laurent seems to distinguish the nipple from the surrounding teguments; he tries to nurse and not merely to suck. . . . Of course there could be no question . . . of the recognition of an "object" for the obvious reason that there is nothing in the states of the consciousness of a newborn child which could enable him to contrast an external universe with an internal universe. . . . Neither could there be a question of purely perceptive recognition or recognition of sensorial images [displays] presented by the external world. . . . To the newborn child, on the contrary, there can only exist awareness of attitudes, of emotions, or sensations of hunger and of satisfaction. Neither sight nor hearing yet gives rise to perceptions independent of these general reactions. . . . When the nursling differentiates between the nipple and the rest of the breast, fingers, or other objects, he does not recognize either an object or a sensorial picture [display] but simply rediscovers a sensorimotor and particular postural complex (sucking and swallowing combined) among several analogous complexes which constitute his universe and reveal a total lack of differentiation between subject and object [Piaget, 1936, p. 36f.].

This "relating" of the infant to the nipple, then to the finger, gradually brings out a *sensing* of his own responses, through the practice of reflexes and stimulated by inner needs

---

11 Spitz (1955b) is more specific: he points out that the phenomenon of "turning toward" in the infant derives from sensations in the organs of the inner ear that react to any gravitational changes.

and by interaction with the environment. In the beginning many of the infant's functions such as sucking, the rotation of the head, linked to the reflexes are *primed* (a felicitous term recently suggested by Wolff, 1963). As needs become pressing (for instance, thirst and hunger), sucking is triggered off by an appropriate stimulation of the lips. The repeated experience of this cycle slowly produces an awareness in the infant of his changing states, so that new activities become self-stimulating.

After the awareness of his own responses is established the infant can begin to sense, to apprehend, and finally to recognize the existence of a "non-I" apparently by noting that changes in his inner states coincide with the presence or absence of his mother. Piaget (1954) concedes, and here the influence of his psychoanalytic contact becomes once more apparent, that the outstanding "item" in the "non-I" is the person who takes care of him, the mother or her substitute. On her body the infant acquires the first notions of space and she is the first object, a detail in his "non-I."

In the first chapter of his book, *The Construction of Reality in the Child* (1937), Piaget shows how the child acquires the notion of a detail in the "non-I," that of the object or that of *things that are permanent, have substance and constant dimensions.* (Piaget argues that in the infant the evolution of his notion of the permanent object is inseparable from the parallel evolution of the other three *categories of reality,* namely, those of *space, time, and causality.* This exposition will not deal with these latter categories.)

In Piaget's concept the permanent object is constructed "little by little" during six developmental stages (0-18 mos.) as follows:

In the first two stages (those of reflexes and of the earliest habits), the infant's world is made up of moving and disappearing sensory displays that can be recognized but have no substantial permanence of spatial organization.

In the third stage (that of secondary circular reactions), the sensory displays are invested with some notion of permanence which, as Piaget argues, is reflected in the infant's prolongation of movements (of grasping, etc.) when the display has vanished. These movements have a clearly passive character.

In the fourth stage of this developmental sequence (application of known means to new situations), the infant actively searches for things that have disappeared from his visual field; this search has become systematic but is still unrelated to the place of their disappearance which the infant has just witnessed. He rather searches for the thing in a special place, for instance, where he found it hidden the last time.

During the fifth stage, the infant directs his search for the things to the very location where he saw them disappear. However, he does not take account of their displacement outside his visual field.

Finally, in the sixth stage, the search for the thing is undertaken by the infant regardless of the displacement, visible or invisible. Piaget (1954) concludes that "there is an image of absent 'things' and their displacement." The permanent object is established, which Piaget explains as follows: "It is a polysensorial complex which one can see, hear, touch, etc., and which from the subject's viewpoint persists in the absence of all perceptual contact."

The sequence of steps outlined by Piaget which culminate in the child's attainment of the permanent object has the stamp of an orderly, structural emergence akin to the rise of a building according to a detailed blueprint. The mere stability and endurance of the building indicate that due consideration has been given to the force of gravity, to tension and stress tolerance, to the wear and tear generated by environmental forces and the elements. Since there are no moving parts in the building that interact, there is also no force flux within its structural parts. This analogy of the finished building roughly conveys Piaget's concept of the child's cognitive functions and how they become activated. His preference for the precise, the categorical, the mathematical makes of the human mind a mere edifice of structural elements.

It is, however, established that cognition without affective participation is an artifact, as we have seen in previous chapters. Cognition and cognitive processes are triggered and interlocked with affective processes and experiences. These internal psychic forces powerfully influence cognition, are instrumental in its unfolding, and, in general, propel ontogenetic development as much as do external influences.

Piaget does not ignore the importance of affective "aspects" of the permanent object. Time and again when discussing object formation on a concrete level he has acknowledged that affective elements contribute to the emergence of the object, and he has implied that the notion of the permanent object is linked to relations with a person in a privileged manner. Thus he states in one of his regular lectures at the Sorbonne in 1954:

> The other person is an affective object of the highest order, but it is at the same time the most interesting cognitive object . . . and I emphasize, the most instructive at this level, the source of perception. . . . Therefore, the other person is an object which brings about a multitude of exchanges into which enter both cognitive and affective factors. . . .

Nowhere else does Piaget speak so clearly about the affective elements of the object and the formative influences of the exchanges with the human partner.

It is therefore the more surprising to note that Piaget has not made provision for this privileged role of the human partner in any of his crucial experiments exploring the attainment of the permanent object but has confined them to the infant's manipulation of "things." In so doing Piaget has ignored his own premises on the equality of the affective and cognitive sphere and their synchronous development.

OBJECT FORMATION AND OBJECT RELATIONS

Piaget's theory of object formation deals with the child's progressive recognition of the environment which is conceived as an aspect of adaptation. Piaget, one recalls, distinguishes between the lower form of biological adaptation (homeostasis) and the advanced form of psychological adaptation—intelligence.[12]

Object formation constitutes a significant milestone in this rise of intelligence, according to Piaget. He puts the reader, as it were, into the shoes of the infant, allowing him to advance step by step on the road leading to the formation of the permanent object.

Inevitably the impression is created that this movement proceeds independently from environmental influences. Does the permanent object-to-be, for example, the human partner, play any role, however insignificant, in this unfolding? Piaget does not concern himself with this problem. But it simply cannot be that the permanent object is a prefabricated item, a *deus ex machina,* which is suddenly put into the infant's universe and at once takes control over his commerce with the surroundings.

The trouble is that the permanent object is a general category fitting well into Piaget's logical system of objective elements, instead of being the natural specific item that is part and parcel of the infant's subjective experience.

What are the psychoanalytic propositions regarding object formation? How is the interaction between subject and future object (object-to-be) formulated?

---

[12] Intelligence "is the most highly developed form of mental adaptation . . . the indispensable instrument for interaction between the subject and the universe when the scope of interaction goes beyond immediate and momentary contacts to achieve far-reaching and stable relations . . . its origins are indistinguishable from those of sensorimotor adaptation in general or even from those of biological adaptation itself" (Piaget, 1947, p. 7).

Psychoanalytic propositions relating to the rise of the libidinal object derive from the concept of psychosexual stages and the vicissitudes of the distribution of cathexis. With the advent of ego psychology and the concomitant emphasis on object relations these propositions were later considerably expanded. Piaget, being unaware of this development which started in the 1930s, claimed in his lectures at the Sorbonne (1954) that the psychoanalytic concept of object relations is narrow and incomplete, being linked to the evolution of instinctual drives and that of psychosexual stages.[13]

Piaget's critique has been dated for some time. Indeed, a considerable portion of psychoanalytic ego psychology is specifically concerned with the individual's adaptation to the environment and its repercussion on his mental development. Object relations—relations with people, with society—figure prominently in this inquiry. Object relations are regarded both as inducers of adaptation and as its product. The reciprocity between adaptation and object relations was demonstrated when on the basis of studies with larger groups of children a deficiency or a malfunction in their object relations turned out to impair both their physical and mental unfolding (Ainsworth et al., 1962).

Expanded classical psychoanalytic theory takes into consideration the exchanges that take place between the infant and the human partner which are at first on the level of biological interchange. According to these propositions, this biological interaction is progressively invested with psychological content, so that the sheer biological interchange is gradually transformed into a psychological interaction (Spitz, 1957).

In shifting the emphasis from the biophysiological level (psychosexual stages) to the psychosocial level (object relations) psychoanalytic ego psychology has gone beyond Piaget's conceptual framework. As was stated earlier, Piaget is not

---

13 These lectures have been given in the same form in the last couple of years.

concerned with the environmental impact on the child's mental growth; he rather considers the cognition of the environment by the individual as an index of mental growth and excludes the possibility that its arrest or derailment could be due to the nature of his interindividual relations.

It is true, though, that the contributions of ego psychology regarding the child's development have concentrated on affective development and the advances in knowledge on cognitive development are, with few exceptions, mostly made in the realm of theory and inference.

It remains now to present side by side the conclusions of Piaget and those of psychoanalytic inquiries concerning a specific area of the child's achievements, namely, that of his crystallization of the "object." This choice recommended itself because of the massive observations that are available and because among individual researchers there is relative agreement on their significance.

INDICATORS OF OBJECT FORMATION

An attempt has been made in the foregoing pages to sketch the central role of the object in mental performance and human behavior. Seldom, though, does one come across a statement in the scientific literature admitting that all our knowledge of the external world, that our picture of the universe, despite our advanced methods of uncovering and perfected mensuration, is ultimately anchored in the cognition of objects. The notion of the object is indeed a cornerstone of all scientific endeavor, no matter whether one engages in the "exact" or "hard" sciences or in the behavioral sciences.

Piaget has shown how the mechanical facets of this cognition of the object emerge; what stages it passes before it becomes fully operative. Since he was essentially concerned with formal thinking and the rational sphere, he tended to overlook or to minimize the subjective, the human element in this phenomenon.

Psychoanalytic inquiries into object formation centered on the dynamic aspects of this process. They were undertaken to uncover the forces behind the infant's effort to seek contact with the surrounding; to detect the psychic factors that lead to the formation of the object; and, finally, to explore the play of psychic elements within that goes on when the child engages in interchange with objects, be that in the form of action, communication, or mere ideation.

These two different orientations or approaches to object formation are complemental in nature, Piaget being mainly concerned with the "target," psychoanalytic research mainly with the psychic forces directed toward the "target." Accordingly, each of the approaches concentrated on specific aspects of this developmental episode.

Piaget mapped out the progress of the infant's cognitive performance that culminates in the achievement of representation. Referring to the child, Piaget holds that representation comes to pass *when a "thing" persists in his mind while it is no longer present in his senses.*

Psychoanalytic researchers worked on determining the behavioral counterparts of the *spreading of cathexis in a centrifugal direction from the subject to the percept, to the image of the nascent libidinal object.* They also explored the concurrent progressive crystallization of the libidinal object. In their view this development is linked to the changing character of the infant's relation to his principal caretaker.

Empirical work—observation of and experiments with children—made it possible to map the course of object formation and its major landmarks. This work was undertaken by Piaget and his associates, by child psychologists and teachers, and by psychoanalytically oriented researchers. The choice procedure was to protocol the behavior of an appropriate sample of children in two specific situations: (1) the recognition by the infant of sensory displays that engage his attention when they impinge on his perceptual system; (2) his response, particularly his anticipatory behavior, when these displays vanish while his attention is directed toward them.

Despite the intensive research work there is still insufficient knowledge on the precise chronological moment at which "the infant" reaches a given developmental landmark. Accordingly chronological information will only be cited here in reference to major events.[14]

Speaking of the infant Piaget states that during the first two stages "recognition [of an outside "thing"] does not necessitate any evocation of a mental image . . . it is enough that the attitude previously adopted to the thing be again set in motion . . . the subject recognizes his own reaction before he recognizes the object as such" (1937, p. 6). Thus toward the tenth day the infant after sucking momentarily on the quilt searches "for something more substantial," the breast. Piaget explains that the child merely sensed his own relief when he had encountered the nipple and when he now encounters the quilt he notes the absence of the remembered relief (1936, p. 36f.).

Psychoanalytic observers have noticed details in this situation not stressed by Piaget: the infant does not always search for something more substantial, his "recognition" is still tenuous; it depends on need pressures in the infant (see Chapter III). This phenomenon is beautifully described by Anna Freud (1946):

> When it [the infant] is under pressure of urgent bodily needs, as for instance hunger, it periodically establishes connections with the environment which are withdrawn again after the needs have been satisfied and the tension is relieved. These occasions are the child's first introduction to experiences of wish fulfillment and pleasure. They

[14] Piaget's experiments testing infantile behavior in response to a vanishing object during the period 1-18 months have recently been repeated and their scope considerably expanded in a scholarly study by Gouin Décarie (1962). The author could confirm by and large Piaget's results in the order in which the several achievements of the infant appear.

establish centers of interest to which libidinal energy becomes attached. An infant who feeds successfully "loves" the experience of feeding (narcissistic love) [p. 124].

[Nine years later the same author phrases her interpretation conceptually:] The libidinal cathexis at this time is shown to be attached, not to the image of the object, but to the blissful experience of satisfaction [1954a, p. 12].

Step by step the infant's cognition expands as he grows older. He begins to notice things on the "outside," first those connected with the experience of gratification (see Chapter IV). For example, in the beginning of the third month when the infant's line of vision encounters a human face, he follows its movement with concentrated attention. "No other 'thing' can elicit this behavior in the infant at this age level" (Chapter III; see also Figure 3). Spitz (1955b) explains that this interest is generated by the frequent affective experiences of the baby in the presence of the human face.

This advance toward object formation reaches a landmark in the smiling response (see Chapter V; Spitz 1948a; 1954; Spitz and Wolf, 1946). Spitz submits that this phenomenon ushers in the *preobjectal stage*. The baby does not yet recognize the human person or the human face but only the sign Gestalt of forehead, eyes, and nose in motion. According to Spitz, when the face is turned into profile many infants seem to search for the reappearance of the Gestalt in the vicinity of the ear.

Commenting on the same phenomenon (vanishing display) Piaget states that at first the infant merely looks hurt. Later on he also engages in active search (motor action) for the vanished display. Piaget makes the *absence of active search for the vanished "thing"* an indicator of a stage. It is not a permanent object yet, he states. Even later when toward the fourth month the child begins to cry when the face vanishes, he does not yet conceive of it as an object: the sensory display lacks *objective* permanence, it has merely been endowed with subjective or affective permanence:

> . . . it suffices, for the child to hope for the return of the interesting image (of his mother, etc.), that he attribute to it a sort of affective or subjective permanence without localization or substantiation; the vanished image remains, so to speak, "at disposal" without being found anywhere from a spatial point of view [1937, p. 13].

Piaget here makes a distinction between affective and cognitive permanence (i.e., mnemic performance) which raises three major problems that call for a brief discussion.

1. In general, Piaget implies that acquisition of perception and memory build-up go hand in hand; the moment the infant can "see" (i.e., adequately take in some distinctive features of a "thing") he can also remember what he has seen. There is no evidence to confirm Piaget's assumption. Experiments on the smiling response (Kaila, 1932; Spitz and Wolf, 1946; Ahrens, 1954; Polak, Emde, Spitz, 1964a) suggest that there is a gradual acquisition of perception in the infant which, in a simplified manner, proceeds on a course akin to the erection of a building by conventional methods: first a scaffolding goes up which serves to establish the outer structure into which other parts are then progressively fitted in. To verify that in perception this is really what happens we still rely on recognition in the infant (memory in the form of aided recall). But this need not imply that there is simultaneous emergence of perception and memory. It is by no means established that the gradual build-up of the percept is matched by a concurrent or identical sequence in the mnemic sector. All the more does it seem questionable to assume, as Piaget does, that there is memory (permanence) *before* there is a consolidated percept.

2. This latter assumption of Piaget is, remarkably enough, the current explanation of choice with subliminal visual ex-

periments in the adult, where it is explained in terms of defense mechanisms (Klein, 1959). In the infant's case, obviously, there is no defense (repression) at work to account for his incomplete cognition.

3. Piaget's definition of the term "object," linking it to "representation" as he does, is unfortunate and gives rise to misunderstanding (see his definition above). It is now understood that the first mnemic trace is in the form of a memory image, a simple replication of a sensory impression. Representation, in the conventional sense of the term, on the other hand, implies a conceptual achievement. The child is then already able, for example, to separate, to abstract salient features from a number of faces, and join them in a quasi-"objective" record—a representation "face" in his mnemic system, which is a categorical unit, a higher form of memory storage.

Piaget's general theoretical explanation of why the infant searches for the vanished thing is twofold: (1) the self-stimulating activity initiated by the practice of reflexes; (2) the tendency toward restoring equilibrium which has been upset by interaction with the environment. In this particular case, such an explanation seemed inadequate to him—specifically, why should an equilibrium be upset by an insufficiently apprehended stimulus? Affective permanence was therefore invoked as the cause of the behavior.

Current psychoanalytic propositions explain the infant's behavior more simply. They hold that a certain configurational percept (a Gestalt) formed by eye, nose, forehead—in motion—comes to be associated by the infant with an experience of gratification, i.e., relief from tension centered in the mouth (Spitz, 1955b; and Chapter III). In other words, the vanishing face of the mother acts merely as a trigger; the infant's crying is released when the memory image of a proprioceptive experience becomes activated. The influence of the vanishing face upon the infant's behavior is therefore indirect; it lacks the quality of a causal agent.

The psychoanalytic explanation does not stop there. It adds that the proprioceptive experience (relief from tension) can leave a distinct memory trace because the infant had invested it with libidinal cathexis. The same is not true of the exteroceptive stimulus (mother's face). The lack of cathexis still makes the face appear as a global configuration that is said to be part of the infant's congenital equipment (see Chapter III). Because it is not an item acquired in experience it has no corresponding memory trace, at least not in the current usage of the term, which ties it to learning (English and English, 1958).

The psychoanalytic propositions explain further how it happens that some time later the mother's face becomes a percept and then leaves a corresponding memory trace in the infant's mind. Gradually cathexis has been transferred from the experience of satisfaction to the provider of that satisfaction (food that relieves hunger and reduces oral tension). The provider is the mother or her substitute (A. Freud, 1946, p. 124). Some years later A. Freud explains this progress in conceptual terms in these words: "Libidinal cathexis shifts gradually from the experience of satisfaction to the image of the object without whom satisfaction would not have come about" (A. Freud, 1954a, p. 13). "I should imagine that it occurs towards the middle of the first year, and that it happens gradually" (1954b, p. 59).

Psychoanalytic theory therefore considers two concurrent lines of progress in the infant—a shift from proprioceptive perception to contact, and finally to distance perception; a concomitant shift of libidinal cathexis (the striving for, the interest in, the urge to be close, to relate) away from his own body to that of the human partner. Thus it may be said that the theory notes that *cognition travels centrifugally from awareness of inner sensation via the periphery (buccal zone, skin surface) to the apprehension of the surrounding,* beginning with the cognition of the human partner. The progress is initiated by cathectic transposition.

With the gradual acquisition of sensorimotor coordination the infant engages in a more active search for an "object"[15] that vanishes before his eyes. The details of this progress are known to us thanks to the meticulous studies undertaken by Piaget and his associates. It appears from these observations that at first the infant will search for the "object" only if the search constitutes an extension of his current sensorimotor activity: (1) he will search for the vanished "object" if he just has held it in his hand; (2) he will look for it within the radius of his hand movement; (3) he will look for an "object" which he had seen for some time uninterruptedly till the moment of its disappearance; (4) later on he will also look for an "object" which he had seen only a moment before it vanished.

The search for the vanished "object" progresses from searching at a familiar location (where the "object" was before) to the location within the radius of vision. This entire development has its counterpart in the expansion of the crib space (mentioned earlier in Chapter X). According to Piaget, the recognition of the object goes hand in hand with that of relating it to the space.

Piaget (1937) comments on the first series of experiments probing the infant's search for the vanished object, the displacement of which he has seen before his eyes.

> [These experiments] show us that the beginnings of permanence attributed to images [sensory displays] perceived arise from the child's action in movements of accommodation . . . the child no longer seeks the object only where he has recently seen it but hunts for it in a new place. He anticipates the perception of successive positions of the moving object and in a sense makes allowance for its displacement. [He continues, stressing the scope of this search:]

[15] "Object" denotes the permanent object-to-be.

He is limited to pursuing . . . with his eyes or with his hand the trajectory delineated by the movements of accommodation [p. 18]. . . . the displacement attributed to the object depends essentially on the child's action (movements of accommodation which are extended by looking) and that permanence itself remains related to that very action [p. 19].

The two developmental psychologies, psychoanalysis and the Geneva school, thus link the origin of external perception to proprioceptively perceived experiences. Psychoanalytic theory holds that cognition of the human partner "leans on" drive dynamics manifested as affective processes with concomitant cathexis resulting in attention. Piaget and the Geneva school point out that cognition "leans on" proprioceptive sensing of one's own motor activity.

The later progress toward the constitution of the permanent object is explored by Piaget in further experiments that culminate in displacements of the "object" behind one and later two screens, that is, in its invisible displacement.

In line with his hypothesis (not explicitly so formulated by Piaget) that the intellectual performance "leans on" the sensorimotor activity just under way, the child begins with the ability to recover an "object" that is only partially hidden before his eyes; later he becomes able to recover it when it is wholly hidden behind the screen. It is this particular example, the search for the vanished toy, which illustrates dramatically how the psychoanalytic model and the theoretical system of the *École de Psychologie génétique* complement each other in explaining the infant's behavior.

Psychoanalytic theory holds that the search for the toy by the child is activated by a wish (an interest), but this wish is sustained by the positive cathexis with which the toy, or rather the endopsychic (mental) image of the toy, has been invested.

A tacit, but nonetheless critical assumption underlies this

explanation of the infant's impulse to search for the missing toy. It is the logical inference rarely made explicit in current psychoanalytic literature: that *the emergence of the memory image is founded on the consolidation, on the constancy, of its corresponding percept.* This inference is valid also for the libidinal object, a fact which has important theoretical implications to be taken up later.

Two other points, however, raised by psychoanalytic theory deserve immediate attention. By the nature of things, the infant's search for the toy will often be futile, at least in the very beginning. If he continues the search despite such momentary setbacks, the strength of the positive cathexis alone, while being a necessary condition, is not sufficient. Met with such failure, and other things being equal, the infant would soon give up his search unless he has already acquired through experience and maturation the *capacity to tolerate the momentary frustration* which he has suffered in his current effort. In other words, he must have learned to endure a sudden rise of tension.

His effort to search is also dependent on the acquisition of the rudiments of *anticipation.* The anticipation of the success of an impending gratification gives impetus to this search and to many other activities (Kris, 1951, p. 97).

Current psychoanalytic propositions thus link cognition and conation (action) with intrapsychic processes which is nowhere provided by the Geneva school. It is precisely this assumed capacity to wait that enables the infant to exert some control over his instinctual drive. This drive restraint enables him to delay the satisfaction of his needs. Thus liberated, his scanning of the environment, his recognition of "things" in the external world, is no longer constantly interfered with by the pressure of his needs. He is no longer at the mercy of homeostatic mechanisms of the *hic et nunc* discussed earlier. When this happens, the infant begins to discern details in the appearance and in the actions of the privileged human partner who is the dispenser of both gratification and frustration. "In an increasing way," writes A. Freud (1954b, p. 59) "the mother is recognized as the source of pleasure and unpleasure and cathected as such."

Psychoanalytic theory assumes that because of this need-anchored primitive perception, the infant goes through a period during which he builds up two images of his mother. The mother who gratifies (the good object) and the one who frustrates (the bad object). The infant invests the image of the good object with libidinal cathexis which sustains his wish to be close to mother, to approach her; the image of the bad object is invested with this aggressive cathexis which sustains the wish to remove the mother (to push her, to hit her) to interfere with whatever she does that is frustrating; or conversely, the image of the bad object also arises when mother frustrates by inattention. These impulses as yet internally unrestrained prevent the formation in the infant of stable memory images. The memory image of the good object is instantly dissolved when sensory impressions spelling frustration are noted by the infant: the same goes, conversely, for the bad object.

Experience and concurrent maturation in the sensorimotor sector and progress in other spheres fuse the two memory images and prepare the way for the formation of the libidinal object. When this happens between the eighth and tenth month a redistribution of cathexis has taken place. As a result the infant's memory image of the libidinal object *transcends the momentary sensory impression, it is no longer dissolved by the current percept.* If this is true, then it follows that the libidinal object is predicated upon the prior consolidation of the mother's percept. *In other words, constancy of the libidinal object must be preceded by the formation of the corresponding permanent object* (that is, mother's image must persist in the child's mind when she is absent).

As the child matures he will be able to attach his libidinal cathexis to objects that are absent at progressively longer periods (A. Freud, 1952, p. 44f.). The libidinal object has been established, and it is predicated, as we have seen, on memory image and the capacity to tolerate frustration, to anticipate gratification.

This thesis, that the infant must first crystallize the permanent object before it can attain the libidinal object, can easily mislead the experimenter, whose orientation is solely guided by academic psychology or the conceptual system of Piaget. The fact that in the mother's case the permanent object has already been achieved does not, by the same token, mean that the infant has, in general, reached the stage of the permanent object. Psychoanalytic theory claims, and Piaget goes along in part with this assumption, that the human partner serves as a trail breaker in the child's mental development. It may well be, therefore, that the infant has not attained the permanent object for many "things" around the eighth to tenth month especially those that fail to interact with him when he subjects them to manipulation.

Once the permanent object is established and the infant has attained the libidinal object, he can freely engage in mental operation and thinking. He is now capable of manipulating things (permanent objects) not only with his hands but also in his mind. His progress can be assessed in a series of experiments involving once more the vanishing "object."[16]

1. Between six to nine months of age the child's behavior indicates that he is capable of reconstituting in his mind an "object" that is only partly visible. For example, if in his presence one gradually moves his favorite toy under a pillow, then stops just in time to leave it partly exposed, the child will retrieve the toy with ease. If, at that time, one goes on, however, until the toy completely vanishes before the infant's eyes, his face takes on an expression of utter bewilderment as

[16] It should be noted that the vanishing "object" already served Freud (1920) in his formulations on the child's psychic development.

though the toy had ceased to exist and he makes no attempt to move the pillow. The child's universe is still made up of pictures, Piaget (1937, p. 13) submits, emerging from nothingness at the moment of action, to return to nothingness when the action comes to an end.

2. Some time after the eighth month the child will retrieve the toy even if it is completely covered provided he has witnessed, as he did in the previous episode, the experimenter's maneuver. The child's initiative, though, is a matter of extending an action already in progress. This is borne out by the fact that if the experimenter at that time first wraps the toy into a towel and then places the towel under a second cover, the child will not engage in any search for the toy (Piaget, 1937, p. 50).

3. He becomes capable of just that (recovering the "object" behind two screens) in the fifth stage, around the eleventh month, provided the maneuver takes place in his presence. At this period the "object" has in the child's mind already been invested with an existence of its own, Piaget submits; it has acquired permanent substance. However, the child does not search for the toy (or another favorite "object") at that period, even though he seems to be aware of the nature of the experimenter's activity, unless he has witnessed the details of the act of hiding.

Piaget (1937) holds that at this stage the child searches within the context of a previously *observed* action; hence his search is no longer a mere extension of an action still in progress (p. 77). Obviously some degree of internalization has occurred.

4. During the last, the sixth stage (after the seventeenth month of life), the child becomes able to search for the "object" regardless of the displacement, visible or invisible, behind one or two screens. The "object" has now become a system of perceptual images endowed with a constant spatial form throughout its sequential displacement and constitutes

an item which can be isolated in the causal series unfolding in time (pp. 72, 93).

In Piaget's system, this performance—the recovery of the toy under these complex circumstances—signals the advent of reversibility. To carry it out, so he argues, the child has a memory image of the toy. He can perform a mental operation that lets him remove (in his mind) the screens that conceal the toy. In other words, he can invert the previous action as it were. The toy is simply made to reappear in his imagination, and this very accomplishment enables him to engage in the search which he could not undertake sometime before. It is not, to be sure, an act of mere learning or experience.[17]

Piaget asserts that the child's search for the vanishing toy can be explained simply by the emergence and increasing stability of his memory image which he links successively to motor action, to the child's growing grasp of space, and, finally, to the rise of his causal reasoning. There is no room in Piaget's notion for a separate element of motivation. Can one simply assume that whatever it is which prompts the child to want the toy exists from the beginning and is merely expressed when the sensorimotor coordination permits it? Is it not more likely that volition, just like other sectors of the mind, shows some growth, some proliferation? And if this is so, what are the specific stages and psychic processes connected with such a development?

This area is emphasized in psychoanalytic propositions which have been formulated by Spitz (1953a, 1960b, 1963a). Psychoanalytic theorizing is concerned with the dynamics of

---

[17] Piaget (1957) has recently made a distinction between *"renversabilité"* (simple inverting) and "reversibility" (to undo, reverse action in the mind, considering space, time, causality, and complex relations between them, implying operating with concepts) which is achieved around twelve to fourteen months of life. The former is said to refer to a simple inverting of an action without the child being aware of it that he is doing so. In this sense the child who around eighteen months removes the second pillow has only achieved *renversabilité*.

the infant's nascent intrapsychic forces which energize his search for the missing toy. It notes, first, that the disappearance of the toy causes a frustration in the child, indicated by the expression of bewilderment in his face. Unless the child can learn to master this momentary frustration, he is the victim of temporary disorganization and he can hardly take advantage of sensorimotor coordination at his disposal and channel it into goal-oriented action. To act under these circumstances (frustration), therefore, it is not enough to have a memory image (a target in the mind when it is no longer a percept), as Piaget suggests; the child must also have the capacity to "pull" it, as it were, into the area of awareness. Plainly, the existence of the memory image and its quality of being within the sphere of awareness are not the same, as many experiments have shown. The psychic process which accomplishes the transposition of an existing memory image to the threshold of awareness is linked to shifts of cathexes. It follows that the child can pursue his search of the toy only when he can cathect the "presentation" or image of the object.

Cathexis, it will be recalled, is conceived in analogy to an electric charge with which an image is infused or invested (Freud, 1926a). The energy of the charge flows from the instinctual drives, but it is somewhat harnessed. Libidinal cathexis (the urge to be close, to approach an object) flows from the sexual instinctual drive and is desexualized; aggressive cathexis (the urge to seize, to remove, to destroy an object) flowing from the aggressive drive is neutralized and can well serve a person in many constructive tasks (notably in those calling for autonomy and self-assertion).

Spitz (1953a) has postulated that at birth the two drives are undifferentiated, intermixed. It is therefore logical that in the beginning the child cannot, for example, evoke a memory image of the toy because he has no specific libidinal cathexis at his command even if at that time the percept of the toy had achieved constancy. The two lines of development must be synchronized.

Once the two drives segregate, the respective cathectic charges do not become automatically available to the infant. He has first to achieve a certain measure of frustration tolerance. In the first experiment the child showed bewilderment but could not act appropriately. He could not restrain his urge (to have the toy right now—*hic et nunc*); he became angry and therefore was not composed enough to *wait* until the libidinal cathexis could flow toward the image of the toy. *His frustration tolerance and his capacity to anticipate were inadequate.*

Some time later he can do both and then the memory image of the vanished toy is retrieved by libidinal cathexis from the "library of his mind" (Cobliner, 1955). When this happens the "target in his mind" sustains his search for the hidden toy.

When the infant is faced with two screens—that is, when the toy before his eyes is first wrapped into, lets say, a beret, and the beret in turn is put behind a pillow—a more complex performance is demanded of him. At that time one could assume that the image of the toy is invested with positive cathexis and the beret with negative cathexis. In the child's mind the two cathexes are still linked together. When the beret is now placed under the pillow, this in turn is invested with negative cathexis. At this juncture the child of a certain age gives up the search.

What the child needs to proceed is explained by Spitz in his unpublished paper (1960b). The child must first split the positive cathexis invested in the toy into two parts; one stays with the toy, the other part must be detached and reinvested in the memory image of the beret which, as was shown, is already invested with some measure of negative cathexis: In other words, the search can only be continued by an infant who can tolerate and maintain positive and negative cathexes, side by side, in the same memory image.

The splitting of the cathexes and the ability to maintain opposite, conflicting cathectic charges in the same image— *tolerance of ambiguity*—is therefore the prerequisite for the infant's solution of the complex task of recovering the toy behind two screens of diverse appearance. This ability not only marks the formation of the permanent object; it is also a great step forward in the recognition of the world as it is: a world that is not only good and bad, white and black, but one that has many in-between features, many gray shadings. The importance of this milestone in the child's life can hardly be overestimated.

This discussion of the psychic development examined in this book is now completed. The Geneva school of psychology is not concerned with abnormalities in thinking, cognition, etc.; but it is already clear from what has been said before that it would be rather easy to link them to the limitations prevailing at different developmental stages suggested by Piaget. The role of stage specificity as an aid in diagnosis and therapy has been pointed out elsewhere (Spitz, 1959).

The comparison of the theories of Piaget and Freud pertaining to the first two years or so of life disclosed their different viewpoints regarding human life. Piaget links the origin of mental functioning to the displacement of the individual in the objective environment. Freud holds that psychic functioning owes its rise to interindividual relations on the one hand and to derivatives of internal processes on the other.

The two system builders encompass within their theories the scaffolding of all other schools of psychology, and the scope of their panoramic view of psychic functioning and development remains unsurpassed to this day. Freud's system is more comprehensive, including as it does psychic spheres beyond the frontiers of the conscious and those outside normal functioning.

CONCLUSION

Anthony (1957) suggested that Freud and Piaget are perhaps the last two theorists who have dominated Western thought. In our democratic and egalitarian era scientists harbor a strong aversion to the dominance by a genius, perhaps because for many centuries authority worship was indeed the bane of scientific progress. The aversion is particularly forceful in the United States where it is embedded in tradition and political thinking.

The aversion to authority does not apply to Piaget, since it alone does not explain why there was until recently a complete absence of a balanced interest in his scientific contributions. But it applied to Freud and he has not fared any better. Popular and superficially known to the bulk of the educated public, his alleged teachings are a favored topic of afterdinner conversations. He is rarely studied in the original, even though his style and comprehensibility easily outrank those of his interpreters; he is attacked by some for his rigidity, by others for his changing viewpoints; by a third group he is termed obsolete, and a fourth chides him for his ignorance of cultural influence, and a fifth group reproaches him for his exaggeration of the role of determinism. The examples can be continued *ad infinitum*. The fact is that he is rarely read without prejudice by those who claim scientific objectivity.

It is perhaps a welcome development that authority worship has been eliminated from the scientific arena; but the pendulum has swung too far in the other direction, it would seem. The turning away from authorities should have led to a blossoming of a spirit of creative independence, to the individual pursuit of excellence with a minimum of duplication. Alas this has not come to pass.

Instead we have been witnessing for some time a narrowing of horizons in scientific exploration. Talent and time are concentrated on a few topics that are enjoying fad or fashion and these are researched *ad nauseam;* a premium is put on ferreting out piddling details with the expectation that they will lead to the disclosure of great truths. Yet it remains a fact that despite this aligning of multiple talents in the examination of a limited number of phenomena, despite a massive concentration of time and equipment, no brilliant insights have been gained and no broad principles have been formulated. No gates have been opened that promise a sudden ascent to higher perspectives. We seem to live on principles enounced in the past, and all we have done is to fit some perishable fabric around structures that have been there for more than a generation. It is perhaps no exaggeration to say that current psychological efforts are drowned in an ocean of data. These are interpreted elegantly, lucidly in terms of *ad hoc* formulations. It illustrates T. S. Eliot's remark, "Where is the knowledge that got lost in information and where is the wisdom that got lost in knowledge?" There is no lack of talent, to be sure, perhaps what is missing is character. From the worship of authority we have shifted to the worship of the collectivity. Instead of acquiring diversity we have drifted into conformity.

One way to stem this tide is perhaps a balanced return to the study of the system makers, with the avowed purpose thereby to revive the natural scientific urge to synthesize data instead of merely collecting them. It is a long way; system building promises no immediate awards or gains and rarely gratifies its creator with instant or popular recognition. We must learn to rebuild our frustration tolerance as scientists.

More than a century ago Alexis de Tocqueville made a remark in his book *Democracy in America* which with an obvious qualification reflects the present situation: "A false notion," he wrote, "that is clear and precise will have more power than a true principle which is obscure and involved."

This chapter is dedicated to the struggle for a temporary suspension of this rule.

Bibliography

Abraham, K. (1911), Notes on the Psycho-analytical Investigation and Treatment of Manic-Depressive Insanity and Allied Conditions. *Selected Papers on Psycho-Analysis.* London: Hogarth Press, 1927.
—— (1916), The First Pregenital Stage of the Libido. *Selected Papers on Psycho-Analysis.* London: Hogarth Press, 1927.
—— (1924), A Short Study of the Development of the Libido, Viewed in the Light of Mental Disorders. *Selected Papers on Psycho-Analysis.* London: Hogarth Press, 1927.
Ahrens, R. (1954), Beitrag zur Entwicklung des Physiognomie- und Mimikerkennens. *Z. exp. angew. Psychol.,* 2.
Ainsworth, M. D. et al. (1962), *Deprivation of Maternal Care: A Reassessment of Its Effects.* Public Health Papers, 14. Geneva: World Health Organization.
Ajuriaguerra, J., Diatkine, R., & Badaracco, G. (1956), Psychanalyse et neurobiologie. In: *Psychanalyse d'Aujourdhui.* Paris: Presses Universitaires de France.
Alarcon, A. G. (1929), *Dyspepsie des Nourrissons.* Paris: Baillière.
—— (1943), Conceptos Nuevos sobre Dietetica Infantil. *Pediatricas de las Americas,* 1.
Anthony, E. J. (1956), Six Applications de la Théorie Génétique de Piaget à la Théorie et à la Pratique Psycho-dynamique. *Rev. Suisse Psychol. Pure Appliquée,* 15.
—— (1957), The System Makers: Piaget and Freud. Symposium on the Contribution of Current Theories to an Understanding of Child Development. *Brit. J. Med. Psychol.,* 30.
Appell, G. & David, M. (1961), Case Notes on Monique. In: *Determinants of Infant Behavior,* ed. B. M. Foss. London: Methuen.
Ausubel, D. (1950), Negativism as a Phase of Ego Development. *Amer. J. Orthopsychiat.,* 20.
Azima, H. & Cramer-Azima, F. J. (1956a), Effects of Decrease in Sensory Variability on Body Scheme. *Canad. Psychiat. Assn. J.,* 1.
—— —— (1956b), Effects of Partial Perceptual Isolation in Mentally Disturbed Individuals. *Dis. Nerv. Syst.,* 17.

357

Baerends, G. P. (1950), Specializations in Organs and Movements with a Releasing Function. *Symp. Soc. Exp. Biol.*, 4. Cambridge: University Press.

Bakwin, H. (1938), Pure Maternal Overprotection. *J. Ped.*, 33.

Baldwin, J. M. (1940), *Dictionary of Philosophy and Psychology*. New York: Peter Smith.

Balint, A. (1954), *The Early Years of Life*. New York: Basic Books.

Balint, M. (1937), Early Developmental States of the Ego: Primary Object-Love. *Int. J. Psycho-Anal.*, 30, 1949.

—— (1948), Individual Differences of Behavior in Early Infancy, and an Objective Method for Recording Them. I. Approach and the Method for Recording. II. Results and Conclusions. *J. Genet. Psychol.*, 73.

Bateson, G., Jackson, D. D., Haley, J., & Weakland, J. (1956), Toward a Theory of Schizophrenia. *Behav. Sci.*, 1.

Beaumont, H. & Hetzer, H. (1929), Das Schauen und Greifen des Kindes: Untersuchungen über spontanen Funktionswandel und Reizauslese in der Entwicklung. *Z. Psychol.*, 113.

Bell, C. (1833), The Hand: Its Mechanism and Vital Endowments as Evincing Design. *The Bridgewater Treatises on the Power, Wisdom and Goodness of God as Manifested in the Creation.* Philadelphia: Carcy, Lea & Blanchard.

Bender, M. B. (1952), *Disorders in Perception*. Springfield: Thomas.

Benedek, T. (1938), Adaptation to Reality in Early Infancy. *Psychoanal. Quart.*, 7.

—— (1949), The Psychosomatic Implication of the Primary Unit: Mother-Child. *Amer. J. Orthopsychiat.*, 19.

—— (1952), *Psychosexual Functions in Women*. New York: Ronald Press.

—— (1956), Psychobiological Aspects of Mothering. *Amer. J. Orthopsychiat.*, 26.

Benedict, R. (1934), *Patterns of Culture*. Boston: Houghton, Mifflin.

Benjamin, J. D. (1959), Prediction and Psychopathological Theory. In: *Dynamic Psychopathology in Childhood*, ed. L. Jessner & E. Pavenstedt. New York: Grune & Stratton.

—— (1961), Some Developmental Observations Relating to the Theory of Anxiety. *J. Amer. Psychoanal. Assn.*, 9.

Bergman, P. & Escalona, S. (1949), Unusual Sensitivities in Very Young Children. *The Psychoanalytic Study of the Child*, 3/4.*

Bernfeld, S. (1925), *The Psychology of the Infant*. New York: Brentano, 1929.

—— (1935), The Psychoanalytic Psychology of the Young Child. *Psychoanal. Quart.*, 4.

Bernstein, L. (1957), The Effects of Variations in Handling upon Learning and Retention. *J. Comp. Physiol. Psychol.*, 50.

Bexton, W. H., Heron, W., & Scott, T. H. (1954), Effects of Decreased Variation in the Sensory Environment. *Canad. J. Psychol.*, 8.

Bibring, E. (1947), The So-called English School of Psychoanalysis. *Psychoanal. Quart.*, 16.

* *The Psychoanalytic Study of the Child,* currently 19 Vols., ed. R. S. Eissler, A. Freud, H. Hartmann, M. Kris. New York: International Universities Press, 1945-1964.

Bibring, G. L., et al. (1961), A Study of the Psychological Processes in Pregnancy and of the Earliest Mother-Child Relationship. *The Psychoanalytic Study of the Child*, 16.

Bierens de Haan, J. A. (1929), Animal Language in Its Relation to That of Man. *Proceedings of the Cambridge Philosophical Society*. Cambridge: University Press.

Bornstein, B. (1953), Fragment of an Analysis of an Obsessional Child. *The Psychoanalytic Study of the Child*, 8.

Bowlby, J. (1946), *Forty-Four Juvenile Thieves*. London: Baillière, Tindall & Cox.

——— (1951), *Maternal Care and Mental Health*. Geneva: World Health Organization, 2.

——— (1953), Critical Phases in the Development of Social Responses in Man. *New Biology*, 14. London: Penguin Books.

——— (1960), Grief and Mourning in Infancy. *The Psychoanalytic Study of the Child*, 15.

Brazelton, T. B. (1962), Observations of the Neonate. *J. Amer. Acad. Child Psychiat.*, 1.

Breuer, J. & Freud, S. (1895), Studies on Hysteria. *Standard Edition*, 2.*

Bridger, W. N. & Reiser, M. F. (1959), Psychophysiological Studies of the Neonate. *Psychosom. Med.*, 21.

Bridges, C. M. B. (1932), Emotional Development in Early Infancy. *Child Development*, 3.

——— (1936), The Development of the Primary Drives in Infancy. *Child Development*, 7.

Brody, S. (1956), *Patterns of Mothering*. New York: International Universities Press.

——— (1960), Self-Rocking in Infancy. *J. Amer. Psychoanal. Assn.*, 8.

Bruner, J. S. & Goodman, C. C. (1947), Value and Need as Organizing Factors in Perception. *J. Abn. Soc. Psychol.*, 42.

Bühler, C. (1928), *Kindheit und Jugend*. Leipzig: Hirzel.

——— (1937), *The First Year of Life*. London: Kegan, Paul.

——— & Hetzer, H. (1932), *Kleinkindertest*. Leipzig: Barth.

——— ——— (1935), *Testing Children's Development from Birth to School Age*. New York: Farrar & Rinehart.

Bühler, K. (1934), *Sprachtheorie*. Jena: Fischer.

Bychowski, G. (1956), The Ego and the Introjects. *Psychoanal. Quart.*, 25.

Calhoun, J. B. (1962), Population Density and Social Pathology. *Sci. American*, 206.

Cannon, W. B. (1929), *Bodily Changes in Pain, Hunger, Fear, and Rage*. New York: Appleton.

——— (1932), *The Wisdom of the Body*. New York: Norton.

——— (1936), The Role of Emotion in Disease. *Ann. Int. Med.*, 9.

Caplan, G., ed. (1955), *Emotional Problems of Early Childhood*. New York: Basic Books.

* *The Standard Edition of the Complete Psychological Works of Sigmund Freud*, 24 Vols., translated and edited by James Strachey. London: Hogarth Press and the Institute of Psycho-Analysis, 1953-

Cappon, D. (1961), Perceptual Organization in Infancy and Childhood. *Canad. Psychiat. Assn. J.*, 6.

Christoffel, H. (1939), Einige fötale und frühkindliche Verhaltungsweisen. *Int. Z. Psychoanal.*, 24.

Cobliner, W. G. (1955), Intracommunication and Attitude: A Methodological Note. *J. Psychol.*, 39.

Coleman, R. W., Kris, E., & Provence, S. (1953), The Study of Variations of Early Parental Attitudes. *The Psychoanalytic Study of the Child*, 8.

Craig, W. (1918), Appetites and Aversions as Constituents of Instinct. *Biol. Bull.*, 34.

——— (1922), A Note on Darwin's Work. *The Expression of the Emotions in Man and Animals. J. Abn. Soc. Psychol.*, 16.

Darwin, C. (1873a), *The Expression of the Emotions in Man and Animals.* New York: Philosophical Library, 1955.

——— (1873b), A Biographical Sketch of an Infant, *Mind*, 2.

David, M. & Appell, G. (1962), Étude des Facteurs de Carence Affective dans une Pouponnière. *Psychiat. Enfant.*, 4.

Dearborn, G. V. N. (1910), *Motor Sensory Development: Observations on the First Three Years of a Child.* Baltimore: Warwick & York.

Deutsch, F. (1947), Analysis of Postural Behavior. *Psychoanal. Quart.*, 16.

——— (1949), Thus Speaks the Body. I. An Analysis of Postural Behavior. *Trans. N.Y. Acad. Sci.*, Series 2, XII, No. 2.

——— (1952), Analytic Posturology. *Psychoanal. Quart.*, 21.

Engel, G., Reichsman, F., & Segal, H. (1956), A Study of an Infant with a Gastric Fistula. *Psychosom. Med.*, 18.

English, H. B. & English, A. C. (1958), *A Comprehensive Dictionary of Psychological and Psychoanalytical Terms.* New York: Longmans, Green.

Erikson, E. H. (1950a), *Childhood and Society.* New York: Norton.

——— (1950b), Growth and Crises of the Healthy Personality. In: *Identity and the Life Cycle* [*Psychological Issues*, Monogr. 1]. New York: International Universities Press, 1959.

Escalona, S. (1947), A Commentary upon Some Recent Changes in Child-Rearing Practices. *Child Development*, 20.

——— (1953), Emotional Development in the First Year of Life. In: *Problems of Infancy and Childhood*, ed. M. J. E. Senn. New York: Josiah Macy, Jr. Foundation.

——— (1962), The Study of Individual Differences and the Problem of State. *J. Amer. Acad. Child Psychiat.*, 1.

Fantz, R. L. (1957), Form Preferences in Newly Hatched Chicks. *J. Comp. Physiol. Psychol.*, 50.

——— (1958a), Depth Discrimination in Dark-Hatched Chicks. *Percept. Motor Skills*, 8.

——— (1958b), Pattern Vision in Young Infants. *Psychol. Rec.*, 8.

——— (1961), The Origins of Form Perception. *Sci. American*, 205.

Fenichel, O. (1945), *The Psychoanalytic Theory of Neurosis.* New York: Norton.

Ferenczi, S. (1916), Stages in the Development of the Sense of Reality. In: *Sex in Psychoanalysis.* New York: Basic Books, 1950.

———— (1919), The Phenomena of Hysterical Materialization. In: *Further Contributions to the Theory and Technique of Psycho-Analysis.* London: Hogarth Press, 1950.

Finkelstein, H. (1938), *Säuglingskrankheiten.* Amsterdam: Elsevier.

Fischer, L. K. (1952), Hospitalism in Six-Month-Old Infants. *Amer. J. Orthopsychiat.,* 22.

Flach, A. (1928), Die Psychologie der Ausdrucksbewegungen. *Arch. f. d. ges. Psychol.,* 65.

Flavell, J. H. (1962), Historical and Bibliographical Note. In: *Thought in the Young Child.* Monographs of the Society for Research in Child Development.

Fowler, W. (1962), Cognitive Learning in Infancy and Childhood. *Psychol. Bull.,* 59.

Fraiberg, S. H. & Freedman, D. A. (1963), Observations on the Development of a Congenitally Blind Child: A Contribution to the Study of Ego Formation. Paper presented at the Annual Meeting of the American Psychoanalytic Association, St. Louis.

Freedman, D. A. (1961), The Infant's Fear of Strangers and the Flight Response. *J. Child Psychol. Psychiat.,* 2.

Freud, A. (1936), *The Ego and the Mechanisms of Defense.* New York: International Universities Press, 1946.

———— (1946), The Psychoanalytic Study of Infantile Feeding Disturbances. *The Psychoanalytic Study of the Child,* 2.

———— (1950), The Significance of the Evolution of Psycho-analytic Child Psychology. *Congrès International de Psychiatrie,* 5:29-36. Paris: Hermann.

———— (1951), The Contribution of Psychoanalysis to Genetic Psychology. *Amer. J. Orthopsychiat.,* 21.

———— (1952), The Mutual Influences in the Development of Ego and Id: Introduction to the Discussion. *The Psychoanalytic Study of the Child,* 7.

———— (1954a), Psychoanalysis and Education. *The Psychoanalytic Study of the Child,* 9.

———— (1954b), In: Problems of Infantile Neurosis: A Discussion. *The Psychoanalytic Study of the Child,* 9.

———— (1958), Child Observation and Prediction of Development: A Memorial Lecture in Honor of Ernst Kris. *The Psychoanalytic Study of the Child,* 13.

———— (1963a), Regression as a Principle in Mental Development. *Bull. Menninger Clin.,* 27.

———— (1963b), The Concept of Developmental Lines. *The Psychoanalytic Study of the Child,* 18.

———— & Burlingham, D. (1943), *War and Children.* New York: International Universities Press.

———— ———— (1945), *Infants without Families.* New York: International Universities Press.

———— & Dann, S. (1951), An Experiment in Group Upbringing. *The Psychoanalytic Study of the Child,* 6.

Freud, S. (1895), Project for a Scientific Psychology. In: *The Origins of Psychoanalysis.* New York: Basic Books, 1954.

—— (1900), The Interpretation of Dreams. *Standard Edition*, 4 & 5.*
—— (1905a), Fragment of an Analysis of a Case of Hysteria. *Standard Edition*, 7.
—— (1905b), Three Essays on the Theory of Sexuality. *Standard Edition*, 7.
—— (1905c), Jokes and Their Relation to the Unconscious. *Standard Edition*, 8.
—— (1909), Notes upon a Case of Obsessional Neurosis. *Standard Edition*, 10.
—— (1910), The Antithetical Meaning of Primal Words. *Standard Edition*, 11.
—— (1911), Formulations on the Two Principles of Mental Functioning. *Standard Edition*, 12.
—— (1912), A Note on the Unconscious in Psychoanalysis. *Standard Edition*, 12.
—— (1914a), Fausse Reconnaissance (*Déjà Raconté*) in Psycho-Analytic Treatment. *Standard Edition*, 13.
—— (1914b), On Narcissism: An Introduction. *Standard Edition*, 14.
—— (1915a), The Unconscious. *Standard Edition*, 14.
—— (1915b), Instincts and Their Vicissitudes. *Standard Edition*, 14.
—— (1916-1917), Introductory Lectures on Psycho-Analysis. *Standard Edition*, 15 & 16.
—— (1917a), Mourning and Melancholia. *Standard Edition*, 14.
—— (1917b), A Metapsychological Supplement to the Theory of Dreams. *Standard Edition*, 14.
—— (1919), The 'Uncanny.' *Standard Edition*, 17.
—— (1920), Beyond the Pleasure Principle. *Standard Edition*, 18.
—— (1921), Group Psychology and the Analysis of the Ego. *Standard Edition*, 18.
—— (1922), Dreams and Telepathy. *Standard Edition*, 18.
—— (1923), The Ego and the Id. *Standard Edition*, 19.
—— (1924a), The Loss of Reality in Neurosis and Psychosis. *Standard Edition*, 19.
—— (1924b), A Short Account of Psycho-Analysis. *Standard Edition*, 19.
—— (1924c), The Economic Problem of Masochism. *Standard Edition*, 19.
—— (1925a), Negation, *Standard Edition*, 19.
—— (1925b), An Autobiographical Study. *Standard Edition*, 20.
—— (1926a), Inhibitions, Symptoms and Anxiety. *Standard Edition*, 20.
—— (1926b), The Question of Lay Analysis. *Standard Edition*, 20.
—— (1926c), Psycho-Analysis. *Standard Edition*, 20.
—— (1927), The Future of an Illusion. *Standard Edition*, 21.
—— (1930), Civilization and Its Discontents. *Standard Edition*, 21.
—— (1931), Female Sexuality. *Standard Edition*, 21.
—— (1932), Dreams and the Occult. *New Introductory Lectures on Psychoanalysis*. New York: Norton, 1933.
—— (1938), Splitting of the Ego in the Defensive Process. *Collected Papers*, 5. London: Hogarth Press, 1950.
—— (1940), *An Outline of Psychoanalysis*. New York: Norton, 1949.

* See footnote on p. 359.

Furfey, P. & Muehlenblein, J. (1929), The Validity of Infant Intelligence Tests. *J. Genet. Psychol.*, 40.

Gamper, E. (1926), Bau und Leistung eines menschlichen Mittelhirnwesens, II. *Z. ges. Neurol. Psychiat.*, 104.

Gardner, R., Holzman, P. S., Klein, G. S., Linton, H., & Spence, D. P. (1959). *Cognitive Control: A Study of Individual Consistencies in Cognitive Behavior* [*Psychological Issues*, Monogr. 4]. New York: International Universities Press.

―――& Long, R. I. (1962a), Control, Defence and Centration Effect: A Study of Scanning Behaviour. *Brit. J. Psychol.*, 53.

――― ―――(1962b), Cognitive Controls of Attention and Inhibition. *Brit. J. Psychol.*, 53.

Gastaut, H. (1958), Données Actuelles sur les Mécanismes Physiologiques Centraux de l'Emotion. *Psychol. Franç.*, 3.

Gentry, E. F. & Aldrich, C. A. (1948), Rooting Reflex in Newborn Infants. Incidence and Effect on It of Sleep. *Amer. Dis. Child.*, 75.

Gesell, A. L. (1940), *The First Five Years of Life*. New York: Harper.

―――(1952), *Infant Development. The Embryology of Early Human Behavior*. New York: Harper.

―――(1954), The Ontogenesis of Infant Behavior. In: *Manual of Child Psychology*, ed. L. Carmichael, 2nd ed. New York: Wiley.

―――& Amatruda, C. S. (1947), *Developmental Diagnosis: Normal and Abnormal Child Development*, 2nd ed. New York: Hoeber.

―――& Ilg, F. L. (1937), *Feeding Behavior in Infants*. Philadelphia, London, Montreal: Lippincott.

――― ―――(1949), *Child Development: An Introduction to the Study of Human Growth*. New York: Harper.

Gibson, E. R. & Walk, R. D. (1960), The "Visual Cliff." *Sci. American*, 202.

Gibson, J. (1963), The Useful Dimensions of Sensitivity. *Amer. Psychologist*, 18.

Gifford, S. (1960), Sleep, Time and the Early Ego: Comments on the Development of the 24-Hour Sleep-Wakefulness Pattern as a Precursor of Ego Functioning. *J. Amer. Psychoanal. Assn.*, 8.

Glover, E. (1930), Grades of Ego-Differentiation. In: *On the Early Development of Mind*. New York: International Universities Press, 1956.

―――(1932), A Psycho-Analytical Approach to the Classification of Mental Disorders. In: *On the Early Development of Mind*. New York: International Universities Press, 1956.

―――(1933), The Relation of Perversion-Formation to the Development of Reality-Sense. *Int. J. Psycho-Anal.*, 14.

―――(1935), The Developmental Study of Obsessional Neuroses. *Int. J. Psycho-Anal.*, 16.

―――(1943), The Concept of Dissociation. In: *On the Early Development of Mind*. New York: International Universities Press, 1956.

―――(1945), Examination of the Klein System of Child Psychology. *The Psychoanalytic Study of the Child*, 1.

―――(1947), *Basic Mental Concepts: Their Clinical and Theoretical Value*. London: Imago.

―――(1953), *Psycho-Analysis and Child Psychiatry*. London: Imago.

——— (1961), Some Recent Trends in Psychoanalytic Theory. *Psychoanal. Quart.*, 30.

Goldfarb, W. (1943), Effects of Early Institutional Care on Adolescent Personality. *J. Exp. Educ.*, 12.

——— (1945), Effects of Psychological Deprivation in Infancy and Subsequent Stimulation. *Amer. J. Psychiat.*, 102.

——— (1955), Emotional and Intellectual Consequences of Psychologic Deprivation in Infancy: A Re-evaluation. In: *Psychopathology of Childhood*, ed. P. H. Hoch & J. Zubin. New York: Grune & Stratton.

——— (1958), Reactions to Delayed Auditory Feedback in Schizophrenic Children. In: *Psychopathology of Communication*, ed. P. H. Hoch & J. Zubin. New York: Grune & Stratton.

Gouin Décarie, T. (1962), *Intelligence et Affectivité chez le Jeune Enfant.* Neuchâtel: Delachaux & Niestlé. English translation: *Intelligence and Affectivity in Early Childhood.* New York: International Universities Press (in press).

Greenacre, P. (1941), The Predisposition to Anxiety. *Psychoanal. Quart.*, 10.

——— (1954), In: Problems of Infantile Neurosis: A Discussion. *The Psychoanalytic Study of the Child*, 9.

Greenson, R. R. (1949), The Psychology of Apathy. *Psychoanal. Quart.*, 18.

Grunebaum, H. (1960), Sensory Deprivation and Personality. *Amer. J. Psychiat.*, 116.

Guex, G. (1948), Aggressivité Réactionelle dans l'Angoisse d'Abandon. *Rev. Franç. Psychanal.*, 12.

Gunther, M. (1955), Instinct and the Nursing Couple. *Lancet*, 1.

Haldane, J. B. S. (1955), Animal Communication and the Origin of Human Language. *Sci. Prog.*, 43.

Hammett, F. S. (1922), Studies of the Thyroid Apparatus. *Endocrin.*, 6.

Harlow, H. F. (1958), The Nature of Love. *Amer. Psychologist*, 13.

——— (1959), Love in Infant Monkeys. *Sci. American*, 200.

——— (1960a), Primary Affectional Patterns in Primates. *Amer. J. Orthopsychiat.*, 30.

——— (1960b), Affectional Behavior in the Infant Monkey. In: *Central Nervous System and Behavior*, ed. M. A. B. Brazier. New York: Josiah Macy, Jr., Foundation.

——— (1960c), Development of the Second and Third Affectional Systems in Macaque Monkeys (in press).

——— (1960d), The Maternal and Infantile Affectional Patterns (in press).

——— (1960e), Nature and Development of the Affectional Systems (in press).

——— (1962), The Heterosexual Affectional System in Monkeys. *Amer. Psychologist*, 17.

——— & Zimmerman, R. (1959), Affectional Responses in the Infant Monkey. *Science*, 130.

Hartmann, H. (1939), *Ego Psychology and the Problem of Adaptation.* New York: International Universities Press, 1958.

——— (1950), Comments on the Psychoanalytic Theory of the Ego. *The Psychoanalytic Study of the Child*, 5.

——— (1952), The Mutual Influences in the Development of Ego and Id. *The Psychoanalytic Study of the Child*, 7.

—— (1953), Contribution to the Metapsychology of Schizophrenia. *The Psychoanalytic Study of the Child*, 8.

—— (1955), Notes on the Theory of Sublimation. *The Psychoanalytic Study of the Child*, 10.

—— Kris, E., & Loewenstein, R. M. (1946), Comments on the Formation of Psychic Structure. *The Psychoanalytic Study of the Child*, 2.

—— —— —— (1949), Notes on the Theory of Aggression. *The Psychoanalytic Study of the Child*, 3/4.

Hebb, D. (1946), On the Nature of Fear. *Psychol. Rev.*, 31.

—— (1949), *The Organization of Behavior*. New York: Wiley.

Hécaen, H. & Ajuriaguerra, J. (1952), *Méconnaissances et Hallucinations Corporelles. Intégration et Désintégration de la Somatognosie*. Paris: Masson.

Hermann, I. (1936), Sich-Anklammern—Auf-Suche-Gehen. *Int. Z. Psychoanal.*, 22.

Heron, W., Bexton, W. H., & Hebb, D. O. (1956), Visual Disturbances after Prolonged Perceptual Isolation. *Canad. J. Psychol.*, 10.

Herring, A. (1937), An Experimental Study of the Reliability of the Buehler Baby Tests. *J. Exp. Educ.*, 6.

Hess, E. H. (1959), Imprinting: An Effect of Early Experience; Imprinting Determines Later Social Behavior in Animals. *Science*, 130.

Hetzer, H. & Jenschke, M. T. (1930) Nachprüfung von Testgutachten im 2. Lebensjahr. *Z. Kinderforsch.*, 37.

—— & Reindorf, B. (1928), Sprachentwicklung und soziales Milieu. *Z. angew. Psychol.*, 29.

—— & Wislitzky, S. (1930) Experimente über Erwartung und Erinnerung beim Kleinkind. *Z. Psychol.*, 118.

—— & Wolf, K. (1928), Baby Tests. *Z. Psychol.*, 107.

Hill, A. et al. (1958), Virus Disease in Pregnancy and Congenital Defects. *Brit. J. Prevent. Soc. Med.*, 12.

Hoffer, W. (1949), Mouth, Hand and Ego-Integration. *The Psychoanalytic Study of the Child*, 3/4.

—— (1950), Development of the Body Ego. *The Psychoanalytic Study of the Child*, 5.

Hooker, D. (1939), Fetal Behavior. *Res. Publ., Assn. Nerv. & Ment. Dis.*, 19.

—— (1942), Fetal Reflexes and Instinctual Processes. *Psychosom. Med.*, 4.

—— (1943), Reflex Activities in the Human Fetus. In: *Child Behavior and Development*, ed. R. G. Barker et al. New York: McGraw-Hill.

—— (1952), *The Prenatal Origin of Behavior*. Lawrence: University of Kansas Press.

Hubbard, R. M. (1931), A Study of the Reliability and Validity of the Buehler Infant Scale. *J. Genet. Psychol.*, 47.

Hug-Hellmuth, H. (1913), *A Study of the Mental Life of the Child*. Washington: Nervous and Mental Disease Monographs, 1919.

Inhelder, B. (1956), Die affektive und kognitive Entwicklung des Kindes. *Schweiz. Z. Psychol.*, 15.

—— (1962), Some Aspects of Piaget's Genetic Approach to Cognition. In: *Thought in the Young Child*. Monograph of the Society for Research in Child Development.

Isakower, O. (1938), A Contribution to the Pathopsychology of Phenomena Associated with Falling Asleep. *Int. J. Psycho-Anal.*, 29.
———— (1954), Spoken Words in Dreams. *Psychoanal. Quart.*, 23.

Jacobson, E. (1953), The Affects and Their Pleasure-Unpleasure Qualities in Relation to Psychic Discharge Processes. In: *Drives, Affects, Behavior*, ed. R. M. Loewenstein. New York: International Universities Press.
———— (1954), The Self and the Object World. *The Psychoanalytic Study of the Child*, 9.
———— (1964), *The Self and the Object World*. New York: International Universities Press.
James, W. T. (1952), Observations on the Behavior of Newborn Puppies. II: Summary of Movements Involved in Group Orientation. *J. Comp. Physiol. Psychol.*, 45.
Jensen, K. (1932), Differential Reactions to Taste and Temperature Stimuli in Newborn Infants. *Genet. Psychol. Monogr.*, 12.

Kaila, E. (1932), Die Reaktionen des Säuglings auf das menschliche Gesicht. *Ann. Univ. Aboensis*, 17, and *Z. Psychol.*, 135.
Kanner, L. (1957), *Child Psychiatry*, 3rd rev. ed. Springfield: Thomas.
Kardiner, A. (1939), *The Individual and His Society*. New York: Columbia University Press.
———— (1945), The Alorese: Analysis of Alorese Culture. In: *The Psychological Frontiers of Society*. New York: Columbia University Press.
———— (1954), The Emotional Effects of Social Stress and Deprivation. II. The Road to Suspicion, Rage, Apathy and Societal Disintegration. In: *Beyond the Germ Theory*, 1, ed. I. Galdston. New York: Health Education Council.
Kennard, M. A. (1948), Myelinization of the CNS in Relation to Function. In: *Problems of Early Infancy*, ed. M. J. E. Senn. New York: Josiah Macy, Jr., Foundation.
Kestenberg, J. S. (1956), On the Development of Maternal Feelings in Early Childhood: Observations and Reflections. *The Psychoanalytic Study of the Child*, 11.
Kinsey, A. et al. (1953), *Sexual Behavior in the Human Female*. Philadelphia: Saunders.
Kirman, B. H. (1955), Rubella as Cause of Mental Deficiency. *Lancet*, 26.
Klein, G. S. (1959), On Subliminal Activation. *J. Nerv. Ment. Dis.*, 128.
Köhler, O. (1954), Das Lächeln als angeborene Ausdrucksbewegung. *Z. menschl. Vererb.- & Konstitutionslehre*, 32.
Köhler, W. (1925), *The Mentality of Apes*. New York: Harcourt, Brace.
Kris, E. (1934), The Psychology of Caricature. In: *Psychoanalytic Explorations in Art*. New York: International Universities Press, 1952.
———— (1951), Some Comments and Observations on Early Autoerotic Activities. *The Psychoanalytic Study of the Child*, 6.
———— (1953), Discussion Remarks on L. S. Kubie's Paper, Modern Concepts of the Organization of the Brain. *Psychoanal. Quart.*, 22.
———— (1955), Neutralization and Sublimation. *The Psychoanalytic Study of the Child*, 10.

Kubie, L. S. (1953), The Distortion of the Symbolic Process in Neurosis and Psychosis. *J. Amer. Psychoanal. Assn.*, 1.

LaBarre, W. (1947), The Cultural Basis of Emotions and Gestures. *J. Pers.*, 16.

Laforgue, R. (1930), On the Eroticization of Anxiety. *Int. J. Psycho-Anal.*, 11.

Lebovici, S. (1960), La Relation objectale chez l'Enfant In: *Psychiatrie de l'Enfant*. Paris: Presses Universitaires de France.

———— (1962), The Concept of Maternal Deprivation: A Review of Research. In: *Deprivation of Maternal Care: A Reassessment of Its Effects*. Geneva: World Health Organization, Publ. Health Papers, 14.

———— & et al. (1956), La Psychanalyse des Enfants. In: *Psychanalyse d'aujourd-hui*. Paris: Presses Universitaires de France.

———— & McDougall, J. (1960), *Un Cas de Psychose Infantile:. Étude.Psychana-lytique*. Paris: Presses Universitaires de France.

Leitch, M. A. (1948), A Commentary on the Oral Phase of Psychosexual Development. *Bull. Menninger Clin.*, 12.

Levine, M. L. & Bell, A. (1950), The Treatment of Colic in Infancy by Use of the Pacifier. *J. Ped.*, 37.

Levine, R., Chein, I., & Murphy, G. (1942), The Relation of the Intensity of a Need to the Amount of Perceptual Distortion. *J. Psychol.*, 13.

Levy, D. M. (1934), Experiments on the Sucking Reflex and Social Behavior of Dogs. *Amer. J. Orthopsychiat.*, 4.

———— (1943), *Maternal Overprotection*. New York: Columbia University Press.

Lewin, B. D. (1946), Sleep, the Mouth and the Dream Screen. *Psychoanal. Quart.*, 15.

———— (1948), Inferences from the Dream Screen. *Int. J. Psycho-Anal.*, 29.

———— (1950), *The Psychoanalysis of Elation*. New York: Norton.

———— (1953a), Reconsideration of the Dream Screen. *Psychoanal. Quart.*, 22.

———— (1953b), The Forgetting of Dreams. In: *Drives, Affects, Behavior*, ed. R. M. Loewenstein. New York: International Universities Press.

Lewis, H. (1954), *Deprived Children*. London: Oxford University Press.

Lezine, I. (1956), Recherches sur la Psychologie du Premier Age. *Schweiz. Z. Psychol. & ihre Anwendungen*, 15.

Lilly, J. C. (1956), Mental Effects of Reduction of Ordinary Levels of Physical Stimuli in Intact, Healthy Persons. *Psychiat. Res. Rep.*, 5.

Lipton, E. L., Steinschneider, A., & Richard, J. B. (1960), Autonomic Function in the Neonate. II. Physiologic Effects of Motor Restraint. *Psychosom. Med.*, 22.

Lorenz, K. (1935), Companionship in Bird Life. In: *Instinctive Behavior*, ed. & tr. C. Schiller. New York: International Universities Press, 1957.

———— (1950), The Comparative Method in Studying Innate Behaviour Patterns. *Sympos. Soc. Exp. Biol.*, 4. London: Cambridge University Press.

Lourie, R. (1949), The Role of Rhythmic Patterns in Childhood. *Amer. J. Psychiat.*, 105.

MacFarlane, J. W. (1953), The Uses and Predictive Limitations of Intelligence Tests in Infants and Young Children. *Bull. World Health Organ.*, 9.

Mahler, M. S. (1952), On Child Psychosis and Schizophrenia: Autistic and Symbiotic Child Psychoses. *The Psychoanalytic Study of the Child*, 7.

───── (1957), On Two Crucial Phases of Integration Concerning Problems of Identity: Separation-Individuation and Bisexual Identity. Abstracted in Panel, Problems of Identity, rep. D. Rubinfine. *J. Amer. Psychoanal. Assn.*, 6, 1958.

───── (1960), Symposium on Psychotic Object Relationships. III. Perceptual De-differentiation and Psychotic "Object Relationship." *Int. J. Psycho-Anal.*, 41.

Margolin, S. G. (1953), Genetic and Dynamic Psychophysiological Studies of Pathophysiological Processes. In: *The Psychosomatic Concept in Psychoanalysis*, ed. F. Deutsch. New York: International Universities Press.

───── (1954), Psychotherapeutic Principles in Psychosomatic Practice. In: *Recent Developments in Psychosomatic Medicine*, ed. E. D. Wittkower & R. A. Cleghorn. Philadelphia: Lippincott.

Mead, G. H. (1934), *Mind, Self and Society*. Chicago: University of Chicago Press.

Mead, M. (1928), *Coming of Age in Samoa*. New York: Morrow.

───── (1935), *Sex and Temperament*. New York: Morrow.

───── & McGregor, F. C. (1951), *Growth and Culture*. New York: Putnam.

Meili, R. (1953), Beobachtungen über charakterologisch relevante Verhaltensweisen im dritten und vierten Lebensmonat. *Schweiz. Z. Psychol. & ihre Anwendungen*, 13.

───── (1957), *Anfänge der Charakterentwicklung*. Bern: Hans Huber.

Minkowski, M. (1922), Über frühzeitige Bewegungen. Reflex und muskuläre Reaktionen beim menschlichen Fötus und ihre Beziehungen zum fötalen Nerven- und Muskelsystem. *Schweiz. med. Wschr.*, 52.

───── (1924-1925), Zum gegenwärtigen Stand der Lehre von den Reflexen in entwicklungsgeschichtlicher und anatomisch-physiologischer Beziehung. *Schweiz. Arch. Neurol. Psychiat.*, 15/16.

───── (1928), Neurobiologische Studien am menschlichen Fötus. In: *Abderhaldens Handbuch d. biol. Arbeitsmethoden*, 5. Berlin: Urban.

Moltz, H. (1960), Imprinting: Empirical Basis and Theoretical Significance. *Psychol. Bull.*, 57.

Montagu, M. F. A. (1950), Constitutional and Prenatal Factors in Infant and Child Health. In: *Problems of Infancy and Childhood*, ed. M. J. E. Senn. New York: Josiah Macy, Jr., Foundation.

───── (1953), The Sensory Influences of the Skin. *Texas Rep. on Biol. & Med.*, 11.

───── (1963), *Prenatal Influence*. Springfield: Thomas.

Morris, G. (1946), *Signs, Language and Behavior*. New York: Prentice-Hall.

Müller, F. (1864), *Facts and Arguments for Darwin*, tr. W. S. Dallas. London: Murray, 1869.

Murphy, L. B. (1957), Psychoanalysis and Child Development. *Bull. Menninger Clin.*, 21.

Needham, J. (1931), *Chemical Embryology*. London: Macmillan.

Novikoff, A. B. (1945), The Concept of Integrative Levels and Biology. *Science*, 101.

Nunberg, H. (1930) The Synthetic Function of the Ego. In: *Practice and Theory of Psychoanalysis*. New York: International Universities Press, 1955.

Orsten, Per-Ake & Mattson, A. (1955), Hospitalization Symptoms in Children. *Acta Paediatrica*, 44.

Peiper, A. (1951), Instinkt und angeborenes Schema beim Säugling. *Tierpsychol.*, 8.
———— & Thomas, H. (1953), Leerlaufendes Brustsuchen. *Mschr. Kinderheilk.*, 101.
Piaget, J. (1919), La Psychanalyse dans ses Rapports avec la Psychologie de l'Enfant. *Bull. Société Alfred Binet de Paris*, 20.
———— (1923), *The Language and Thought of the Child*. New York: Meridian Books, 1955.
———— (1933), La Psychanalyse et le Développement Intellectuel. *Rev. Franç. Psychanal.*, 6.
———— (1936), *The Origins of Intelligence in Children*. New York: International Universities Press, 1952.
———— (1937), *The Construction of Reality in the Child*. New York: Basic Books, 1954.
———— (1942), Les Trois Structures Fondamentales de la Vie Psychique: Rythme, Régulation et Groupement. *Rev. Suisse Psychol. Pure Appliquée*, 1.
———— (1945), *Play, Dreams and Imitation in Childhood*. New York: Norton, 1951.
———— (1947), *The Psychology of Intelligence*. Paterson, N.J.: Littlefield, Adams, 1960.
———— (1954), *Les Relations entre l'Affectivité et l'Intelligence dans le Développement Mental de l'Enfant*. Paris: Centre de Documentation Universitaire.
———— (1955), Les Stades du Développement Intellectuel de l'Enfant et de l'Adolescent. In: *Le Probléme des Stades ou Psychologie de l'Enfant*. Paris: Presses Universitaires de France.
———— (1956), The General Problems of the Psychobiological Development of the Child [and Discussion Remarks]. In: *Discussions on Child Development*, 4, ed. J. M. Tanner & B. Inhelder. New York: International Universities Press, 1960.
———— (1957), Logique et Equilibre dans le Comportement du Sujet. In: *Études d'Epistemologie Génétique*, 2: *Logique et Equilibre*, ed. L. Apostel. Paris: Presses Universitaires de France.
———— & Inhelder, B. (1951), Die Psychologie der frühen Kindheit. In: *Handbuch der Psychologie*, ed. D. Katz. Basel: Schwabe.
Pichon, E. (1953), *Le Développement Psychique de l'Enfant et de l'Adolescent. Évolution Normale, Pathologique, Traitement*. Paris: Masson.
Polak, P., Emde, R., & Spitz, R. A. (1964a), The Smiling Response to the Human Face: I. Methodology, Quantification and Natural History. *J. Nerv. Ment. Dis.*, 139, No. 2.
———— ———— ———— (1964b), The Smiling Response: II. Visual Discrimination and the Onset of Depth Perception. *J. Nerv. Ment. Dis.*, 139, No. 5.
Portmann, A. (1951), *Biologische Fragmente zu einer Lehre vom Menschen*. Basel: Schwabe.
———— (1953), *Das Tier als soziales Wesen*. Zurich: Rhein Verlag.

Prechtl, H. F. R. (1952), Angeborene Bewegungsweisen junger Katzen. *Experientia*, 8.
—— (1956), Die Eigenart und Entwicklung der frühkindlichen Motorik. *Klin. Wschr.*, 34.
—— & Klimpfinger, S. (1955), *Entwicklung der frühkindlichen Motorik* [Film]. Max Planck Institut f. Verhaltensforschung.
—— & Schleidt, W. M. (1950), Auslösende und steuernde Mechanismen des Saugaktes. *Z. vergl. Physiol.*, 32.
Putnam, M. C., Rank, B., Pavenstedt, E., Anderson, A. N., & Rawson, I. (1948), Case Study of an Atypical Two-and-a-Half-Year-Old. *Amer. J. Orthopsychiat.*, 18.

Rangell, L. (1954), The Psychology of Poise, with a Special Elaboration on the Psychic Significance of the Snout or Perioral Region. *Int. J. Psycho-Anal.*, 35.
Rank, O. (1924), *The Trauma of Birth*. New York: Harcourt Brace, 1929.
Rapaport, D. (1958), *The Structure of Psychoanalytic Theory: A Systematizing Attempt* [*Psychological Issues*, Monogr. 6]. New York: International Universities Press, 1960.
—— (1960a), Psychoanalysis as a Developmental Psychology. In: *Perspectives in Psychological Theory*, ed. B. Kaplan & S. Wapner. New York: International Universities Press.
—— (1960b), On the Psychoanalytic Theory of Motivation. In: *Nebraska Symposium on Motivation*, ed. M. R. Jones. Lincoln: University of Nebraska Press.
—— & Gill, M. (1959), The Points of View and Assumptions of Metapsychology. *Int. J. Psycho-Anal.*, 40.
Redfield, R. (1930), *Tepoztlan: A Mexican Village*. Chicago: University of Chicago Press.
Reichenberg, W. (1937), The Buehler Test as an Index of Environmental Influence on Child Development. *Bull. Menninger Clin.*, 1.
Rench, B. (1960), *Evolution above the Species Level*. New York: Columbia University Press.
Reyniers, J. A. (1946, 1949), Germ-Free Life Studies. *Lobund Reports*, 1 & 2.
Ribble, M. A. (1938), Clinical Studies of Instinctive Reactions in Newborn Babies. *Amer. J. Psychiat.*, 95.
Richards, T. W. & Nelson, V. L. (1939), Abilities of Infants during the First Eighteen Months. *J. Genet. Psychol.*, 55.
Riesen, A. H. (1947), The Development of Visual Perception in Man and Chimpanzee. *Science*, 106.
—— (1950), Arrested Vision. *Sci. American*, 183.
Ripin, R. & Hetzer, H. (1930), A Study of the Infant's Feeding Reaction during the First Six Months of Life. *Arch. Psychol.*, 18.
Ritvo, S. & Solnit, A. J. (1958), Influences of Early Mother-Child Interaction on Identification Processes. *The Psychoanalytic Study of the Child*, 13.
Robertson, J. (1953), *A Two-Year-Old Goes to Hospital* [Film]. Tavistock Child Development Research Unit, London.
—— (1958), *Young Children in Hospital*. London: Tavistock Publication.
Robertson, W. O. (1961), Breast Feeding Practices. Some Implications of Regional Variations. *Ann. Publ. Health*, 51.

Rosenblith, W. A. (1961), *Sensory Communication*. New York: Wiley.

Rosenthal, M. J. (1952), A Psychosomatic Study of Infantile Eczema. I. The Mother-Child Relationship. *Pediatrics*, 10.

—— (1953), Neuropsychiatric Aspects of Infantile Eczema (Special References to the Role of Cutaneous Pain Receptors). *Arch. Neurol. Psychiat.*, 70.

Rosner, A. (1959), Psychoanalysis and Modern Learning Theory. *Psychoanal. Quart.*, 28.

Rubinow, O. & Frankl, L. (1934), Die erste Dingauffassung beim Säugling: Reaktionen auf Wahrnehmung der Flasche. *Z. Psychol.*, 133.

Ruegamer, W. R., Bernstein, L., & Benjamin, J. D. (1954), Growth, Food Utilization and Thyroid Activity in the Albino Rat as a Function of Extra Handling. *Science*, 120.

Sand, E. A. (1962), Le Régime Alimentaire du Nourrisson, son Sévérage: Étude d'un Echantillon de Population Urbane Belge. *Courrier*, 11.

Sander, L. W. (1962), Issues in Early Mother-Child Interaction. *J. Amer. Acad. Child Psychiat.*, 1.

Sandler, J. (1961), The Hampstead Index as an Instrument of Psycho-Analytic Research. *Int. J. Psycho-Anal.*, 42.

Sanford, R. N. (1936), The Effects of Abstinence from Food upon Imaginal Processes: A Preliminary Experiment. *J. Psychol.*, 2.

—— (1937), The Effects of Abstinence from Food upon Imaginal Processes: A Further Experiment. *J. Psychol.*, 3.

Schleidt, W. M. (1960), Über angeborene Verhaltensweisen des Menschen. *Therap. Berichte*, 32.

Schur, M. (1955), Comments on the Metapsychology of Somatization. *The Psychoanalytic Study of the Child*, 10.

—— (1958), The Ego and the Id in Anxiety. *The Psychoanalytic Study of the Child*, 13.

Scott, J. P., Fredricson, E., & Fuller, J. L. (1951), Experimental Exploration of the Critical Period Hypothesis. *Personality*, 1.

—— & Marston, M. V. (1950), Critical Periods Affecting the Development of Normal and Maladjustive Social Behavior of Puppies. *J. Genet. Psychol.*, 77.

Seitz, A. (1940), Die Paarbildung bei einigen Cichliden. *Z. Tierpsychol.*, 4.

Selye, H. (1950), *The Physiology and Pathology of Exposure to Stress*. Montreal: Acta, Inc.

—— & Fortier, C. (1950), Adaptive Reaction to Stress. *Psychosom. Med.*, 12.

Shannon, C. E. & Weaver, W. (1949), *Mathematical Theory of Communication*. Urbana: University of Illinois Press.

Shirley, M. (1931), The Sequential Method for the Study of Maturing Behavior Patterns. *Psychol. Rev.*, 38.

Silberer, H. (1911), Symbolik des Erwachens und Schwellensymbolik überhaupt. *Jb. psychoanal. & psychopath. Forsch.*, 2.

Simmel, G. (1908), *Soziologie: Untersuchungen über die Formen der Vergesellschaftung*. München-Leipzig: Duncker & Humbolt.

Simmel, M. L. (1961), The Absence of Phantoms for Congenitally Missing Limbs. *Amer. J. Psychol.*, 74.

Simonsen, K. M. (1947), *Examination of Children from Children's Homes and*

Day Nurseries by the Buehler-Hetzer Developmental Tests. Copenhagen: Arnold Busk.

Soddy, K. (1956), *Mental Health and Infant Development,* 2 Vols. New York: Basic Books.

Solomon, P., ed. (1961), *Sensory Deprivation.* Cambridge: Harvard University Press.

Soto, R. (1937), Porque en la casa de cuna no hay dispepsia transitoria? *Rev. Mex. de Puericultura,* 8.

Spelt, D. K. (1948), The Conditioning of the Human Foetus in Utero. *J. Exp. Psychol.,* 38.

Spitz, R. A. (1935), Frühkindliches Erleben und Erwachsenenkultur bei den Primitiven. *Imago,* 21.

——— (1936a), Integrierung und Differenzierung. Paper presented in the Vienna Psychoanalytic Society.

——— (1936b), Vom Einschlafen und Aufwachen. Paper presented in the Vienna Psychoanalytic Society.

——— (1937), Wiederholung, Rhythmus, Langeweile. *Imago,* 23.

——— (1945a), Hospitalism: An Inquiry into the Genesis of Psychiatric Conditions in Early Childhood. *The Psychoanalytic Study of the Child,* 1.

——— (1945b), Diacritic and Coenesthetic Organizations. *Psychoanal. Rev.,* 32.

——— (1946a), Hospitalism: A Follow-Up Report. *The Psychoanalytic Study of the Child,* 2.

——— (1946b), Anaclitic Depression: An Inquiry into the Genesis of Psychiatric Conditions in Early Childhood, II. *The Psychoanalytic Study of the Child,* 2.

——— (1947a), *Birth and the First Fifteen Minutes of Life* [Film]. New York University Film Library.

——— (1947b), *Grief, a Peril in Infancy* [Film]. New York University Film Library.

——— (1948a), *The Smiling Response* [Film]. New York University Film Library.

——— (1948b), *Autoerotism in Infancy* [Film]. New York University Film Library.

——— (1950a), Psychiatric Therapy in Infancy. *Amer. J. Orthopsychiat.,* 20.

——— (1950b), Anxiety in Infancy: A Study of Its Manifestations in the First Year of Life. *Int. J. Psycho-Anal.,* 31.

——— (1950c), Digital Extension Reflex. *Arch. Neurol. Psychiat.,* 63.

——— (1951), The Psychogenic Diseases in Infancy: An Attempt at Their Etiologic Classification. *The Psychoanalytic Study of the Child,* 6.

——— (1952), Authority and Masturbation: Some Remarks on a Bibliographical Investigation. *Psychoanal. Quart.,* 21.

——— (1953a), Aggression: Its Role in the Establishment of Object Relations. In: *Drives, Affects, Behavior,* ed. R. M. Loewenstein. New York: International Universities Press.

——— (1953b), *Anxiety* [Film]. New York University Film Library.

——— (1953c), *Shaping the Personality* [Film]. New York University Film Library.

——— (1954), Genèse des Premières Relations Objectales. *Rev. Franç. Psychanal.,* 28.

—— (1955a), Childhood Development Phenomena: 1. The Influence of the Mother and Child Relationship and Its Disturbances. 2. The Case of Felicia. In: *Mental Health and Infant Development,* ed. K. Soddy. London: Routledge & Kegan Paul.

—— (1955b), The Primal Cavity: A Contribution to the Genesis of Perception and Its Role for Psychoanalytic Theory. *The Psychoanalytic Study of the Child,* 10.

—— (1955c), A Note on the Extrapolation of Ethological Findings. *Int. J. Psycho-Anal.,* 36.

—— (1956a), Countertransference: Comments on Its Varying Role in the Analytic Situation. *J. Amer. Psychoanal. Assn.,* 4.

—— (1956b), Some Observations on Psychiatric Stress in Infancy. In: *Fifth Annual Report on Stress,* ed. H. Selye & G. Heuser. New York: M. D. Publications.

—— (1957), *No and Yes: On the Genesis of Human Communication.* New York: International Universities Press.

—— (1958), On the Genesis of Superego Components. *The Psychoanalytic Study of the Child,* 13.

—— (1959), *A Genetic Field Theory of Ego Formation (With Implications for Pathology).* New York: International Universities Press.

—— (1960a), Discussion of Dr. Bowlby's Paper, Grief and Mourning in Infancy and Early Childhood. *The Psychoanalytic Study of the Child,* 15.

—— (1960b), Dawn of the Mind: On the Genesis of Ideation. Unpublished.

—— (1961), Early Prototypes of Ego Defenses. *J. Amer. Psychoanal. Assn.,* 9.

—— (1962), Autoerotism Re-examined: The Role of Early Sexual Behavior Patterns in Personality Formation. *The Psychoanalytic Study of the Child,* 17.

—— (1963a), Ontogenesis: The Proleptic Function of Emotion. In: *The Expression of Emotions,* ed. P. H. Knapp. New York: International Universities Press.

—— (1963b), Life and the Dialogue. In: *Counterpoint,* ed. H. Gaskill. New York: International Universities Press.

—— (1963c), The Evolution of the Dialogue. In: *Drives, Affects, Behavior,* Vol. 2, ed. M. Schur. New York: International Universities Press (in press).

—— (1964), The Derailment of Dialogue: Stimulus Overload, Action Cycles, and the Completion Gradient. *J. Amer. Psychoanal. Assn.,* 12.

—— & Wolf, K. M. (1946), The Smiling Response. *Genet. Psychol. Monogr.,* 34.

—————— (1949), Autoerotism: Some Empirical Findings and Hypotheses on Three of Its Manifestations in the First Year of Life. *The Psychoanalytic Study of the Child,* 3/4.

St. Augustine. *Confessions,* Book XI, Chapter 26. Inquiry into the Nature of Consciousness.

Stendler, C. B. (1950), Sixty Years of Child Training Practices. *J. Ped.,* 36.

Stern, M. M. (1961), Blank Hallucinations: Remarks about Trauma and Perceptual Disturbances. *Int. J. Psycho-Anal.,* 42.

Stone, L. J. (1952), Some Problems of Filming Children's Behavior: A Discussion Based on Experience in the Production of Studies of Normal Personality Development. *Child Development,* 23.

—— (1954), A Critique of Studies of Infant Isolation. *Child Development,* 25.

Swan, C. (1949), Rubella in Pregnancy as Aetiological Factor in Congenital Malformation, Stillbirth, Miscarriage and Abortion. *J. Obstet & Gyn. Brit. Emp.*, 56.

Szekely, L. (1954), Biological Remarks on Fears Originating in Early Childhood. *Int. J. Psycho-Anal.*, 35.

Thorpe, W. H. & Zangwill, O. L. (1961), *Current Problems in Animal Behavior.* London: Cambridge University Press.

Tilney, F. & Casamajor, L. (1924), Myelinogeny as Applied to the Study of Behavior. *Arch. Neurol. Psychiat.*, 12.

—— & Kubie, L. S. (1931), Behavior and Its Relation to the Development of the Brain. *Bull. Neurol. Inst. N.Y.*, 1.

Tinbergen, N. (1951), *The Study of Instinct.* Oxford: Clarendon Press.

U.S. Children's Bureau (1938), *Infant Care.* Washington: U.S. Government Printing Office.

—— (1942), *Infant Care.* Washington: U.S. Government Printing Office.

Volkelt, H. (1929), Neue Untersuchungen über die kindliche Auffassung und Wiedergabe von Formen. *Berichte über den 4. Kongress für Heilpädagogik.* Berlin: Springer.

von Frisch, K. (1931), *Aus dem Leben der Bienen.* Berlin: Springer.

von Holst, E. & Mittelstaedt, H. (1950). Das Reafferenzprinzip (Wechselwirkungen zwischen Zentralnervensystem und Peripherie). *Naturwissenschaften*, 37.

von Senden, M. (1932), *Space and Sight. The Perception of Space and Shape in the Congenitally Blind before and after Operation.* London: Methuen, 1960.

Vosburg, R. (1960), Imagery Sequence in Sensory Deprivation. *Arch. Gen. Psychiat.*, 2.

Waelder, R. (1936), The Problems of the Genesis of Psychical Conflict in Earliest Infancy. *Int. J. Psycho-Anal.*, 18, 1937.

—— (1960), *Basic Theory of Psychoanalysis.* New York: International Universities Press.

Wallach, H. (1959), The Perception of Motion. *Sci. American*, 201.

Warren, H. C. (1935), *Dictionary of Psychology.* London: Allen & Unwin.

Watson, I. B. (1928), *Psychological Care of Infant and Child.* New York: Norton.

Weidemann, F. (1959), I. Das Kind im Heim: Untersuchungen über die Entwicklung des Heimkindes. II. Heimkind und Heimmilieu: Untersuchungen über die Ursachen der heimkindlichen Entwicklungsverzögerung. *Z. Kinderpsychiat.*, 26.

Weil, E. & Pehu, M. (1900), Un Syndrome Gastrique Particulier chez le Nourrisson. *Lyon Méd. Gazette*, 95.

Whiting, J. W. M. (1953), *Child Training and Personality: A Cross-Cultural Study.* New Haven: Yale University Press.

Wieser, S. & Domanowsky, K. (1959), I. Zur Ontogenese und Pathologie des Schreckverhaltens. II. Schreckverhalten des Säuglings: Schreck und Moro-Reflex. *Arch. Psychiat. & Z. ges. Neurol.*, 198.

Williams, D. H. (1951), Management of Atopic Dermatitis in Children. Control of the Maternal Rejection Factor. *Arch. Dermatol. & Syphilology*, 63.

Windle, W. F. (1950), *Asphyxia Neonatorum*. Springfield: Thomas.

Winnicott, D. W. (1953), Transitional Objects and Transitional Phenomena. *Int. J. Psycho-Anal.*, 34.

Wohl, W. (1960), Developmental Studies of Perception. *Psychol. Bull.*, 57.

Wolf, M. (1935), Erprobung der Bühlerschen Entwicklungsteste an Kindern aus gehobenem sozialen Milieu. *Arch. ges. Psychol.*, 94.

Wolff, P. H. (1959), Observations on Newborn Infants. *Psychosom. Med.*, 21.

—— (1960), *The Developmental Psychologies of Jean Piaget and Psychoanalysis* [*Psychological Issues*, Monogr. 5]. New York: International Universities Press.

—— (1963), Developmental and Motivational Concepts in Piaget's Sensorimotor Theory of Intelligence. *J. Amer. Acad. Child Psychiat.*, 2.

Yerkes, R. M. & Yerkes, A. W. (1936), Nature and Conditions of Avoidance (Fear) Response in Chimpanzees. *J. Comp. Psychol.*, 21.

Zeigarnik, B. (1927), Über das Behalten von erledigten und unerledigten Handlungen. *Psychol. Forsch.*, 9.

Zulliger, H. (1932), Zur Psychologie des Kinderspieles. *Z. psychoanal. Päd.*, 6.

Indices

Name Index

379

Subject Index